Introduction to Fashion Merchandising

Introduction to
Fashion Merchandising

Evelyn Grace

Tarrant County Junior College

Prentice-Hall, Inc., Englewood Cliffs, New Jersey 07632

Library of Congress Cataloging in Publication Data

GRACE, EVELYN, 1913–
   Introduction to fashion merchandising.

   Bibliography: p.
   Includes index.
   1. Clothing trade.   2. Merchandising.   3. Fashion.   I. Title.
HD9940.A2G7   658.8′687   78-1318
ISBN 0-13-483206-X

Printed in the United States of America

10 9 8 7 6 5 4 3 2 1

PRENTICE-HALL INTERNATIONAL, INC., *London*
PRENTICE-HALL OF AUSTRALIA PTY. LIMITED, *Sydney*
PRENTICE-HALL OF CANADA, LTD., *Toronto*
PRENTICE-HALL OF INDIA PRIVATE LIMITED, *New Delhi*
PRENTICE-HALL OF JAPAN, INC., *Tokyo*
PRENTICE-HALL OF SOUTHEAST ASIA PTE. LTD., *Singapore*
WHITEHALL BOOKS LIMITED, *Wellington, New Zealand*

Acknowledgments

Grateful appreciation is extended to these people and their business organizations for their interested help:

Jess A. Farber, Filene's Special Events Director, Boston.

Betty Franklin, Assistant Editor, FORBES, INC., New York.

Donald R. Dvorovy, J. C. Penney Company, Inc., New York.

Reeves Wetherill, Dir. of Public Relations, John Wanamaker, Philadelphia.

J. B. Brunell, Vice-President, I. Magnin, San Francisco.

Heather Summerfield, Press Officer, Harrods, London, England.
Public Relations Dept., Bloomingdale's, New York.

Keith A. Smith, Publicity Director, Younkers, Des Moines.

H. Keith Nix, Director of Public Relations, Neiman–Marcus, Dallas

Loyd L. Turner, Vice-Pres., Tandy Corporation, Fort Worth

James M. Donovan, Jr., American Textiles Manufacturers Institute, Inc., Charlotte, N.C.

Doris Covington, Burlington Industries, Inc., Greensboro, N.C.

Le Ann L. Nelson, Asst. Dir., Wool Education Center, American Wool Council, Denver, Colo.

Emmett E. Robinson, National Cotton Council of America, Memphis

Grace Beller, Executive Dir., International Silk Association (U.S.A.) New York

Sherry Kelner, Celanese Fibers Marketing Company, New York.

Clyde Utt, Apparel Mart, Dallas

Ernest L. Arms, National News Director, Sears, Roebuck and Co., Chicago

Kenneth R. Darre, Corporate News Director, Montgomery Ward & Co., Chicago

Pat L. Harris, Vice President, Public Relations, Gerald D. Hines Interests, Houston

Lyn Sohlen, Public Relations, Rich's, Atlanta.

Harold S. Stevenes, Secretary, Garfinckel's, Washington, D.C.

Don K. Harris, Vice President, Harris' Department Stores, San Bernardino, Ca.

B. L. Trippett, Manager Product Publicity, NCR, Dayton, Ohio

Herb Doherty, Otis Elevator Company, New York.

Mignonne Cleneay, Foley's, Houston

Martha G. Payne, Director Public Relations and Special Events, Woodward & Lothrop, Washington, D.C.

About the author

Dr. Evelyn Grace is a professor of Mid-Management and Coordinator of Fashion Merchandising at Tarrant County Junior College in Hurst, Texas. She received a B.S. and an M.A. from Drake University and an Ed. D from North Texas State University.

Dr. Grace is a member of The Fashion Group, Inc., Dallas chapter, a charter member and past president of Texas Junior College Management Educator's Association, a member of the Advisory Board of Texas Distributive Education Clubs of America, Junior Collegiate Division and a past member of the Sears Roebuck Foundation Board of Directors. She is also on the Fashion Advisory Board of Dillard's Department Stores and a member of the Texas Vocational Association, the American Vocational Association, the Texas Junior College Teachers' Association, and the Texas Association of Distributive Education Teachers. She has also served as a training director at Montgomery Ward.

Contents

Preface

This is an introductory fashion merchandising book written to meet the needs so often experienced by young men and women who want to advance in careers of fashion. To select the contents of this book, the author questioned several fashion merchandising graduates who are now in full-time fashion positions. These people indicated what they considered to be most essential to them in their current positions. Their responses guided the selection of what is included here for you.

Basically, these people felt that to succeed in fashion merchandising, a person has to know how to get the right fashion job to begin, how to do well on the right fashion job, and what to learn in order to advance in fashion merchandising positions. The book is organized into these three parts. It introduces you to several areas of fashion knowledge. All of these warrant much more in-depth study, and should not be overlooked in your preparation and education.

Most people in beginning jobs in fashion merchandising experience the same needs, and these requirements are similar to the needs of the fashion veterans. For this reason, it is hoped that this book will help you not only enter the world of fashion merchandising but also to advance as rapidly as knowledge, experience, and opportunity allow. Several important features will facilitate your understanding of merchandising concepts:

1. *Chapter Objectives.* These objectives should help you understand the most important parts of the chapters and what you should know after you have finished reading them. You can review your reading to see if you fully understand the essential concepts, and if you can

apply them to your job. Try to think of yourself as a fashion manager, and ask yourself how to use the information to your best advantage.

2. *Use of Specific Fashion Merchandising Terminology.* The ability to know and use technical fashion language shows that you are familiar with the fashion business. It will enhance communication with your associates, enabling you to understand what is discussed at store policy meetings and to converse in one-to-one conversations with supervisors and customers. Specific terms that you should know are printed in the margins of the book. They are explained in the accompanying text as well as in the glossary at the end of the book. Learn them, understand them, and use them!

3. *Marginal Questions.* Short questions also appear in the margins of the textbook to give you an overview of the adjoining text. They will show you why the text material was written, and should aid your understanding of the material. Some questions about fashion merchandising may be controversial in nature; authorities in the fashion business sometimes have differing viewpoints. In such cases, the text shows you both sides of the question, so you can decide which you think is more logical. You may find it interesting to discuss the questions with your job associates to get their opinions. The questions will stimulate an interesting discussion, making a worthwhile learning experience for you.

4. *Illustrations, Charts,* and *Tables.* The various photographs, tables, and charts are provided as easy references to help you visualize and remember important subject matter. Do not skip over this informative material. It will help you remember important facts about fashion.

5. *Conclusions.* At the end of each chapter there is a brief conclusion. It is not the purpose of the conclusion to repeat all the information in the chapter but to emphasize the high points in the chapter discussion.

6. *Review Questions.* Questions are posed at the end of chapters for class discussion purposes. They should help you make a concrete application of what you have learned from your reading. They should assist in crystallizing your fashion knowledge.

7. *Suggested Student Activities.* Although what you *see* in this book will tell you about fashion merchandising, what you *do* after you have read each chapter will be even more valuable in your learning. The activities suggested at the end of each chapter are geared to help you see how fashion operates in your own area. Activities are almost limitless wherever you live because fashion activity is all around you.

8. *Some of the "Greats" in Fashion Merchandising.* Each chapter features a famous fashion store and its founder that will provide you with background information about what is happening in the world of fashion.

While retailing, or some form of trading, has existed about as long as civilization itself, it has not always enjoyed the honorable and respected place in business that it has today. Many of today's great merchandising companies are responsible for changing the undesirable practices that existed in early retailing and trading.

When you realize that there are almost two million merchandising businesses in existence today in the U.S. alone, you will appreciate how difficult it was to select our "greats." Many of those that are included began in a very small way, and their famous founders experienced years of hard work and even initial failures. It is important for you to understand the principles that helped them succeed. All had a similar dedicated determination and a purposeful philosophy, all set out to accomplish their goals in different ways in totally different geographical locations.

Some of the "greats" are large mail-order chains, some are independently owned department or specialty stores, and some have become public corporations of tremendous size. All are known and respected throughout the world. You will think of many others that may also have been included. Study them on your own—they are equally important. See the list of "Other fashion books that will interest you" at the end of the book.

9. *Case Problems.* At the end of each chapter there are a few short fashion merchandising case problems for you to solve.

Not only is problem solving on a personal basis important to us all, but the solution of various kinds of merchandising problems will often mean the difference between success or failure for a fashion merchandising business.

Since there is rarely a single solution to any problem that will work in 100 percent of the cases, these problems are posed to give you an opportunity to discuss and apply what you have learned in the chapter. Other students may have a different solution than yours. The questions should stimulate interesting discussion outside class as well as in the classroom.

The purpose of this book is to present a meaningful and realistic body of information about the complex and dynamic field of fashion merchandising. It is as contemporary as possible, thanks to the contributions of many current merchandisers in successful businesses.

The numerous merchandisers who have willingly given of their time to help in the preparation of this book have shown a strong interest in training those who seek careers in fashion merchandising. Their efforts will be amply repaid if you become as successful as opportunity allows in your projected fashion career.

The list of individuals who have influenced my thinking about fashion merchandising and to whom recognition is due is almost limitless. I do offer my sincere gratitude to the reviewers of the manuscript, my editors Stephen Cline, Marian Hartstein, and Maureen Wilson.

To my students, also, I owe more than words. They studied and reviewed the manuscript and made significant contributions regarding the classroom effectiveness of the book.

And finally, to my husband and sons, I owe sincere thanks. It was their encouragement and enthusiasm over my "new project" that enabled the book finally to come alive.

E. G.

Objectives

1. To prepare students for beginning fashion positions leading to advanced leadership in the fashion industry

2. To develop personal skills, behaviors, and knowledge for the advancement of men and women into the growing American world of fashion

3. To provide a basic knowledge of consumer characteristics and their relationship to buying, selling, and merchandising in the fashion business

4. To identify and develop the student's leadership and supervisory skills

5. To provide a fundamental knowledge of human relations in order to improve the student's ability to think analytically and increase his/her general knowledge of how to succeed in the world of fashion

6. To help develop initiative and competence so the student will be able to make adjustments to future changing conditions

7. To acquaint students with opportunities, demands, and rewards of careers in fashion, particularly those in the areas of merchandising

8. To develop within the student a desire for continuous growth both professionally and individually

9. To develop ideals, habits, and attitudes that will be useful on the job and in everyday living

10. To encourage students to make a contribution to the business economy of our country by ethical participation in an area of endeavor that is meaningful and personally rewarding

Part One

The World of Fashion Merchandising

Chapter 1

What is fashion merchandising?

Objectives

When you have read this chapter, you should be able to

1. Define fashion as it is understood by authorities in the field
2. Explain how fashion touches almost all parts of our lives
3. Show why some people think that fashion has some bad aspects—and state your reasons for agreeing or disagreeing with them
4. Define fashion merchandising
5. Identify the many kinds of fashion merchandising businesses and classify them
6. Explain the economic importance of the fashion industry
7. Tell others why a famous fashion specialty store—Filene's of Boston—became so authoritative in the field of fashion

FILENE'S

Boston, Massachusetts

William Filene, a tailor who emigrated from Germany, opened his first tiny store in Boston in 1849. He was honest, diligent, and warm-hearted, but success did not come easily to him. It was not until his sons Edward and Lincoln became active that the firm he founded entered its period of rapid and successful growth.

The first little store didn't last very long. Stores were opened in Salem and Lynn, Massachusetts, as well as in Bath, Maine, with an intervening unsuccessful attempt at manufacturing, before William Filene again opened in Boston in 1881. This store was 24 feet square and described as "one of the most modern of the day with its genuine white marble floor and most artistic windows." Filene respectfully called the attention of the public to the fact that "purchasers can save a large percentage on esmerelda and embroidered sleeves from 25 cents to $3 a pair . . . dress trimmings, consisting of braids, cords, gimps, and tufted trimmings in the latest patterns . . . French, chantilly, barege and tissue veils . . . lisle thread and silk gloves and mitts . . . and cotton stockings."

By 1890, the business had expanded and a five-story and basement building was leased. The space was believed to be the greatest in Boston devoted exclusively to women's ready-to-wear and accessories.

Who were the "famous brother partners" in retailing?

After the opening of the new store, W. Filene retired and his sons Edward and Lincoln became one of the most famous brother partnerships in retailing. Edward became president, and Lincoln was in charge of personnel. Together they did all the store buying.

The store's business continued growing, and the firm again transferred to larger quarters, trebling their selling space. The old building became a "Baby-to-Miss" annex, the first definite appeal to youth.

How does the famous Filene's Basement operate?

In 1909, Filene's Automatic Bargain Basement, one of the store's most famous innovations, was inaugurated. Under this system, basement goods are automatically reduced 25 percent after twelve selling days, another 25 percent if still unsold at the end of eighteen selling days, and a third 25 percent if they remain after twenty-four selling days. If they are still on hand after thirty days, items are given to Boston charities. Many businesspeople thought that Filene's would surely go bankrupt with such a system, but the basement began showing a profit after a few years. It is still in existence today, and remains unique. Though often imitated, it has never been copied successfully. It is a clearinghouse for stocks of distress merchandise, and a guaran-

[1] Stacy Holmes, *A Brief History of Filene's*, rev. ed. (Boston, Mass.: Filene's, 1972), pp. 1–31.

teed marketplace to help a manufacturer liquidate unsold stock. Filene's pays cash so the manufacturer can get into production for the next season. It is a beehive of activity not only because Bostonians have become such regular patrons but because travelers make a beeline for it when they reach Boston. End-of-season merchandise in over fifty fine stores is sent here and there's hardly a great and glamorous store whose label has not been found in Filene's Basement at one time or another. Sir Noel Coward, the British actor, playwright, and wit, summed up the feeling of Filene's Basement enthusiasts this way: "For my musical comedy *Sail Away* I wrote a song with the title, 'The Customer's Always Right.' You know, I never really believed it until I saw Filene's Basement."

By 1912, the annual sales volume of the store had grown to $4,500,000, and it moved to its present site at the corner of Washington and Sumner streets. Decorated with American Beauty roses, the new store opened at 8:30 A.M. and by 5 P.M. 235,000 persons had visited it. This same year marked Filene's expansion into the men's clothing field.

Who started the
Federated Department
Stores?

In 1929, Filene's joined with the Lazarus family, which operated stores in Columbus and Cincinnati, and the principals of Abraham & Straus in Brooklyn, and Bloomingdale's in New York City, to form *Federated Department Stores*, which went on to become the country's largest and most profitable department store operation. Lincoln Filene was chairman of the Federated board for many years after the merger.

In 1935, Filene's became the first store in New England to be air-conditioned. Subsequently, the first branch store opened, marking Filene's as a pioneer in what has developed into the still-expanding area of suburban branch stores and regional shopping centers. The Northampton store reached a peak during World War II when it became official outfitter for all the United States Navy Wave officers. After the war, Filene's was among the first stores in the country to pioneer in large regional shopping centers with ample parking, as compared to the small stores in the center of suburban towns, which had been the prewar pattern.

Who pioneered in
developing shopping
centers?

Filene's has often been called "The World's Largest Specialty Store." If it has any claim to this article, it would be because of its appreciation of the importance of fashion and the expertise developed in presenting fashion merchandise to the residents of its great New England market area. It specializes in ready-to-wear fashion clothing and accessories for men, women, and children and has developed this specialty into a business well in excess of $100 million a year.

Is fashion big
business?

One evidence of Filene's early recognition of the importance of fashion was the establishment in 1910 of a Paris office. From its Paris address Filene's mailed its customers handsome brochures on fashion, printed in Europe and illustrated with hand-tinted steel engravings. Filene's fashion buyers continue to make regular trips not only to Paris but to all the other fashion capitals of the world.

In the years following World War I, Filene's published a maga-

What helped Filene's develop its fashion image?

zine called *Clothes,* profusely illustrated in color, comparable in quality to the national fashion magazines of its day. This did much to solidify the store's reputation with customers as a fashion authority. Filene's also set up a clothes institute which produced fashion shows and good grooming lectures; provided information on fabrics, colors, and styles; and answered personal requests for fashion information to solve the individual problems of customers.

Do designers come to the U.S. from abroad? Why?

At the end of World War II, Filene's was the first American department store to visit the old and new couturiers that sprang up in Paris at the conclusion of hostilities. As a result, many of the top designers visited the store in Boston: Christian Dior, Jacques Fath, Pierre Balmain, Roberto Capucci, Pierre Cardin, Emilio Pucci, and many, many others. Practically every great name in the American fashion industry has also been intimately associated with Filene's. Nettie Rosenstein, Pauline Trigère, James Galanos, and Norman Norell, for example, have all traveled to Boston to receive Filene's coveted Design Talent Award.

FRENCH CHAMBRE SYNDICALE DE LA HAUTE COUTURE

As evidence of the stature achieved by Filene's in the world of fashion, the French government sent the great steamship *Ile de France* to Boston, and a government-sponsored fashion show was staged by members of the *French Chambre Syndicale de la Haute Couture* on board. The show was a climax of a storewide promotion of French fashion merchandise of such magnitude that other stores and museums in the city joined in saluting France for the period. While the French promotion was perhaps the most elaborate and far-reaching, it was by no means the last of Filene's storewide international events; other international promotions have included Ireland, Mexico, Hawaii, and Great Britain, to name a few. The technique proved so effective that British, French, Swiss, Scandinavian and similar "fortnights" have become a feature of department store sales promotion all over the country.

How does Filene's promote fashion?

The various and imaginative forms taken by Filene's fashion presentations have become world-famous. The store has shown fashion on trains, planes, and ocean liners; at race meets; on baseball diamonds; and even in the concourse of Grand Central Station in New York City.

How did Filene's get a copy of a famous wedding dress so soon?

One fashion miracle accomplished by Filene's was the reproduction of Princess Margaret's wedding dress, which was shown in a prominent window six hours after she said "I do." It was achieved by wire photos, a live description over international telephone wires, and the rapid and skillful work of a group of Filene's dressmakers on this side of the Atlantic. Significant of the prophetic nature of Filene's fashion instincts was the fact that Nettie Rosenstein's evening gown exhibited in a preelection fashion show by a model representing a First Lady was the identical gown later chosen by Mrs. Eisenhower for her first Inaugural Ball. (Unfortunately, Filene's did not sell this dress to Mrs. Eisenhower. Her husband had promised a store in Texas that she would get her dress there.)

FIG. 1-1. Recently opened suburban branch store, located in Chestnut Hill, Massachusetts. (Courtesy of Filene's, Boston)

How about men's fashions at Filene's?

It is not just in the field of women's fashions that Filene's has been a trail-blazer—Filene's Men's Store sponsored the first men's fashion show in Boston, featuring a personal visit from the leading Roman menswear creator, Savini of Brioni. The Mayor of Boston was an eager participant. The picture of him as he was being fitted for the show received national attention when it was published in *Life* magazine. Filene's Men's Store was the first American business firm to persuade four great custom houses from the West End of London to participate in a joint presentation of British menswear with an American store. They included Prince Philip's tailor, Queen Elizabeth's bootmaker, Sir Winston Churchill's shirtmaker, and the same custom firm that made hats for Charles Dickens, who lived over that hat shop on Bond Street.

Today, Filene's provides authoritative fashion information not only for its customers but also for fashion editors of newspapers and magazines, students, and perhaps equally important, manufacturers, whose faith in Filene's fashion judgment is reflected throughout the fashion world.

7

This chapter invites you to learn about fashion merchandising, which is variously described as glamorous, exciting, dynamic, fascinating, powerful, symbolic, and mysterious. It could be all of these things, but is a great deal more, too. Certainly the fashion business has many glamorous aspects, and it can be truly exciting almost all the time. For a career choice, it is without doubt one of the most dynamic areas of endeavor because of its constant challenge. To really understand the fashion business, to really develop a "flair" for it, you must not only understand fashion itself, but you must also develop a thorough knowledge of merchandising as well. The purpose of this chapter is to introduce you to the importance of the world of fashion merchandising.

What Is Fashion?

FASHION

Fashion authorities define fashion in individual ways, but all generally agree that *it is the currently accepted, widespread style or group of styles in dress and personal accessories that is generally established and adopted during a particular time or season by men, women, and children.*

Is fashion of recent origin?

Fashion historians see an important relationship between fashion and the cultural and economic development of countries worldwide. Clothing styles can actually be traced back some fifty centuries— through about the past 5,000 years. In early Greece, Rome, Egypt, and Babylonia, a fashion in dress definitely distinguished the wearer for his or her position or rank in the society. For the most part, the costuming was a type of tunic draped about the body and fastened with some form of decorative jewelry, if the wearer could afford such a luxury.

The ancient Greeks probably achieved the most graceful costumes known in those days, and some of their clothing was not strikingly different from that worn much later. On celebration days, in honor of a great military conquest, the royalty often wore clothing elaborate with gold embroidery and purple in color to distinguish their nobility.

The history of costuming is exceedingly interesting, and several sources of such history are cited at the end of the book. Another important reason for understanding fashion history is that there are many recurring styles found in fashion history.

What Are Fashion Cycles?

FASHION CYCLES

The recurring styles in fashions that seem to repeat themselves down through the centuries are referred to as fashion cycles. There is a clear sequence of fashion phenomena in which evidences of returns to earlier modes can be seen. But, even though fashions may repeat themselves, sometimes hundreds of years later, sometimes less than ten years later, they never return to exactly the same type of garment originally worn. The reason for this is that during the space of ten years or longer the technical development of fabrics usually has changed, as have the manufacturing processes for the garments.

Do fashions ever return exactly?

The evolution of fashion cycles is also closely related to the social behavior of people at the time. Actually, fashions change very gradually, because the people wearing them change very slowly also. Although there may be great extremes in overdressing or underdressing at some particular time, when people recognize the extremes there is usually a gradual return to a more conservative way of dressing.

Today, with the rapidity of travel between continents, fashion is universally similar. Western dress is generally accepted as the clothing style in most countries, although some countries exhibit their native costumes on special holidays. To travel in a foreign country would be indeed disappointing to tourists if some of the traditional costuming were not seen. But for the most part, people in Hong Kong, London, San Francisco, Paris, Rome, or New York will be dressed similarly.

How do people dress in other countries?

Actually, fashion today touches almost all parts of our lives. It affects our behavior and activities in almost all the things we do. And careers in fashion are by no means limited to the apparel business alone, even though many people believe fashion concerns clothing exclusively. Fashion trends actually affect us directly and indirectly, consciously and unconsciously, in almost all of our consuming wants and needs. For example, fashion probably affected your choice of a car to drive, its color, and the interior you selected, although you may not have been aware that you were following a fashion trend when you made your choice. Fashion may have affected the kind of home or apartment that you chose, and the type of furniture and the color of the appliances you selected for it. Fashion tastes are involved in the recreation you enjoy, and the sports equipment and clothing that you use. Indirectly, fashion affects the kinds of food we eat, and the kinds of china, glassware, silverware, and cookware we use. So fashion is a part of our entire lifestyle, and in turn it reflects the times, the environment, and the conditions in which we live. Just as art forms in the past have been a reflection of the times in which they were created, fashions are likewise a reflection of life as it exists at the time the fashion is current.

Is fashion limited to clothing?

Probably you will find that fashion's constant but gradual change is responsible for much of its charm, glamor, and interest. This change comes about through advanced techniques in the development of exciting new textiles with their increased comfort and wearability, all kinds of advances in the production of fashion goods, and the enlarged buying and selling methods of our multi-unit fashion enterprises—all

Why does fashion change?

contributing to fashion as a very *big* business. In fact, this constant change in fashion is often criticized by some economists who feel that fashion is really not a good thing for society.

Fashion—Good or Bad?

Those who view fashion in a negative way argue that fashion forces people to discard good clothing before it wears out, and thus encourages wastefulness. These people believe that consumers blindly follow a fashion trend like a flock of sheep following their leader. Perhaps this is true of some individuals, but no one is ever obligated in any way to make fashion changes from one season to another. We are completely free to make our own choices about the styles of clothing we will wear.

Some health specialists complain that new fashions are often injurious to our well-being. Some have been. The recent height of platform soles on shoes did cause many serious injuries and broken bones. Not too long ago, women wore very pointed, high-heeled shoes, which resulted in many of them needing foot specialists in later years. Business attire for men still emphasizes the importance of the coat and tie, even though wearing them in hot weather may be quite uncomfortable. Currently, new fabrics and textures are being developed in men's fashions to make them more comfortable and acceptable. When women first began to enter the business world, their clothing was tightly cinched in at the waist, and the skirts were long and cumbersome. Fashion brought about a change in this type of clothing, allowing more freedom of movement and greater comfort.

It is ironic that probably those who speak most vehemently against fashion trends may be unconsciously following a fashion trend at the very time they are attacking it. Probably they are dressed in a conventional manner that is considered appropriate according to the current fashion trend.

Those of us who believe that fashion is good think that there is a great deal to be said in its favor. When we consider fashion as it really exists and discard the extreme—short-lived fads—we find that some basic fashion designs have actually been around for thousands of years. Fashion changes are never as rapid and as radical as the critics would have us believe. The fashion silhouette for women, for example, consists of three basic "shapes" that have existed throughout history. They are the bell, tubular, and back fullness, or bustle, and all recur from time to time in women's fashion.

Probably one of fashion's greatest benefits is in the degree of psychological reinforcement it gives an individual. Not too long ago, a television commercial said, "When you look *good*, you feel *good*, and when you feel *good*, you do *good*." This sentiment illustrates the psychological reinforcement that fashion gives us—in spite of its poor

FIG. 1-2.

grammar usage! It has long been observed that fashion gives a psychological "lift" to patients who are suffering from deep depression. When an ill person begins to show a new interest in personal appearance (or current fashions), it is usually a sign of recovery.

Fashion is certainly associated with progress in many spheres of human activity, as we have already discussed. We have one of the highest standards of living in the world in our country, and fashion has certainly had a role in its development.

So, despite the critics, it is not likely that fashion will be abolished. American families spend in excess of $30 billion a year on their clothing needs, most of which are influenced to a large extent by fashion. As a result, fashion is responsible for one of the largest industries in the world—the clothing industry—and gives employment to millions of people in our country, as well as stimulating international trade.

*Will fashion ever be
abolished?*

To what extent the values of fashion outweigh their evils is best illustrated by the fact that fashion has defeated its critics for centuries, and it is probable that it will continue to do so.

What Is Merchandising?

Like fashion, merchandising has been given many different meanings by people in business. The American Marketing Association says that merchandising is "the planning and supervision involved in marketing particular merchandise at places, times, prices, and in quantities that will best serve to realize the marketing objectives of a business."

*Just what is
merchandising?*

Therefore, we would define merchandising as involving *all the activities necessary to determine and satisfy the wants and needs of consumers.* Merchandisers must secure and distribute goods effectively to the ultimate consumer. They must offer the goods at the time and in a place where they can be conveniently purchased. They must carry the quantities and qualities that consumers want. Above all, the prices must be fair. This credo is sometimes referred to as the five "rights" in retailing—the right goods, at the right time and place, in the right quantities and assortments, in the right qualities, at the right prices.

Retailers are probably more involved in merchandising activities because they sell goods directly to the ultimate consumer. We will discuss the characteristics of the retailing field in this respect. However, we should not overlook the vast importance of the merchandising functions performed by manufacturers.

How do apparel manufacturers help retail store buyers?

Apparel manufacturers provide retailers with the fashion merchandise they will be able to offer to their customers, and assist them in presenting the quality of fashion apparel at the right times. Manufacturers of ready-to-wear apparel and accessories present their new lines about four or five times a year, inviting retail buyers to visit their showrooms to make their selections. At these shows, retail buyers select the assortments of apparel they will offer their customers in the coming season—spring, summer, fall, or winter. Jet travel has added a fifth season to the fashion buying calendar—midwinter resort time, formerly referred to as the *cruise* season. It is an exciting new fashion dimension and rivals the conventional seasonal collections for the designer and vacationer alike.

The challenge in merchandising is to serve consumers well in their rapidly changing world environment by correctly determining the kinds of apparel that will fit their lifestyles best. Evaluating available information and developing a profitable business operation is the motivation for good merchandising practices.

The increasingly rapid changes in merchandising and retailing methods mean that successful fashion businesspeople must be able to anticipate the customers' needs, evaluate them, and predict in what way their store can best meet the changes flexibly and efficiently.

The objectives of the merchandising activities in all types of retail organizations revolve around a sales plan that reaches the best possible sales potential and profit goals. To achieve this plan, fashion merchandisers must study the general business outlook, the local economic conditions, the competition, and many other factors. This is where the real excitement and challenge lies in merchandising. Correct and intelligent planning is a must.

FASHION
MERCHANDISING

Fashion merchandising, therefore, is the performance of all the activities necessary for supplying all the apparel needs and wants of your potential customers at the time and place they need them, in the right qualities and quantities, and at prices that are satisfactory to them. Distributing these fashion apparel items in the most efficient way is the goal of a fashion business operation so that profit potential can be realized.

IS FASHION MERCHANDISING NEW?

Just as some form of clothing preferences or fashions have existed for thousands of years, so also has a form of fashion merchandising. Although the kind of merchandising of fashion with which we are familiar today hasn't always existed, some form of trading and retail selling has been around as long as civilization itself. As mentioned in the preface to this book, fashion merchandising hasn't always enjoyed the respected place in business that it has today. Many of the earliest traders and retailers were unscrupulous and dishonest with their customers. Their merchandise carried no guarantees, prices of goods were "what the public would bear," and there was no "money-back-if-you-are-not-satisfied" policy.

What factors encouraged unscrupulous store policies?

Country stores that were scattered throughout the Middle West in the 1850s had friendly pot-bellied stoves and cracker barrels. But while they provided a snug place for farmers to sit and swap stories, they were not necessarily good places for farmers to buy goods. Prices were high and the choice of goods very limited. If the farmer complained, the storekeeper reminded him that the "wholesalers set the prices," and he could take his business elsewhere if he desired. Since the storekeeper was often the only merchant for miles around, the farmer had little choice. If the farmer had eggs, butter, goosefeathers, or something else to trade for merchandise, there was a lot of haggling over prices, with both sides trying to get the best of the deal. The farmer usually lost out. Moreover, he usually bought a year's supply of goods on credit, relying on his next crop for payment. This system put him completely at the mercy of the country store.

Patent medicines were a good example of the unscrupulous merchandising that existed in young America. They were advertised as being able to cure anything and everything, including diseases you didn't know you had. Their sales depended largely on the appeal to fear. It wasn't until 1907 that the U.S. government put a stop to such misrepresentation in advertising.

Whatever became of patent medicines?

It came as a startling surprise when some merchants during this period began to offer the money-back guarantee on their goods, because up to this time *caveat emptor* (let the buyer beware) had been the general rule of business—or the less elegant "Never give a sucker an even break."

CAVEAT EMPTOR

Many of our great retailing companies of today were responsible for changing the earlier unsavory practices with their one-price-to-all systems, their guarantees of merchandise, and their multiple services to customers. You can read about several of them in the special feature sections at the beginnings of each chapter in this book. This was a very important period of development in the U.S., but you can readily see that going into business of any kind was a frustrating and difficult experience. Some businesses did succeed, and the merchandising principles they established are the same basic ones that exist today. These were the companies who pioneered the ethical climate in fashion retailing that we enjoy now.

Filene's of Boston has been the special feature in this chapter. This company's fashion judgment is reflected throughout the fashion world today and is closely followed by customers, fashion editors, and fashion designers. Its many fashion "firsts" are not only interesting, but are enlightening to the understanding of fashion as it exists today.

Fashions U.S.A.—A Brief History[1]

Just as our lifestyles are vastly different from those that existed when our country declared its independence over 200 years ago, so are our fashions of today enormously different for men, women, and children.

Almost totally influenced by foreign fashion in 1776, today we are the proud trend-setter of world fashion. The way this came about is an intriguing story. We will review fashions in the U.S.A. briefly from 1776 to the present.

1776–1850

During the revolutionary years as our nation tried to shake off all the influences of England, it became a patriotic duty for men and women to develop their own fashions made from what was available in America.

In the Eastern cities particularly, men and women of wealth had followed European fashions from England and France as closely as they could from the textiles and publications brought over from London. But this changed rapidly as the colonies began discouraging the purchase of any British goods by levying fines against those who bought them.

So the fashion of America during its early years was homespun and buckskins. This was particularly true in the wilderness areas where there was little choice except to rely on what nature produced.

Textile mills began to develop in New England during this period, and they were soon producing cloth of fairly good quality. Credited with the early mill development are Samuel Slater and Francis Cabot Lowell. Both were English textile technologists who immigrated to America, bringing their vast knowledge of textile manufacture with them.

[1] *The Changing American Woman—200 Years of American Fashion,* Women's Wear Daily (New York: Fairchild Publications, 1976), pp. 8–142.

1776-1850

FIG. 1-3. (Top right: Courtesy of Harry T. Peters Collection, Museum of the City of New York. Center and bottom right: Courtesy, Sears, Roebuck & Co.)

Working conditions in the early textile mills were very poor compared to today's standards, and toward the end of this period, factory girls began to rebel against 72-hour workweeks and unsatisfactory conditions. They preferred instead white-collar jobs as clerks, secretaries, and sales help, although these kinds of jobs were chiefly held by men at this time.

In 1841, Amelia Bloomer introduced her divided skirt for women —nicknamed "bloomers" by the snickering public. They never became popular during her lifetime, but came into fashion later for cycling and swimming. Around 1850, Levi Straus introduced his tough, almost indestructible fabric for miners' work pants. Little did he realize that a century later denim blue jeans would be recognized worldwide as the American uniform.

Throughout this book, you will read again and again about the early developments of some of our present great fashion companies. All were influenced by the times—all showed typically American ingenuity in their early years as necessity demanded.

1850–1900

Central and Western United States began to develop during this period. The great city of Chicago, which had about 30,000 residents in 1850, was known as a "mudhole." Streets were indeed covered with seemingly bottomless mud much of the time, and the devastating fire that started in Mrs. O'Leary's cow barn in 1871 completely destroyed the heart of the city.

The Civil War occurred during this period, also. Starting in 1861, it lasted four long, hard years, and was followed by one of the worst business depressions the United States had ever experienced. However, there were some developments during the Civil War which eventually moved fashion ahead. Eli Whitney (known especially for his development of the cotton gin, which solved a great problem for cotton producers in the South) developed interchangeable parts for use in his musket factory, which supplied great amounts of war supplies. This innovation eventually moved industry into our great mass production system.

Another "spinoff" of the war was ready-made clothing. The sewing machine Elias Howe had developed in 1845 had greatly increased clothing production before the war, but people still thought that "store-bought" clothing could not possibly fit well because no two persons had the same measurements, and the only way to get a good fit in a suit or dress was to have it made at home or by a tailor. The makers of the Civil War uniforms found that if they made many different sizes, they could provide almost everybody with a fairly good fit.

FIG. 1-4. (Courtesy, Mrs. Laura Hogsett Portwood Collection and Amon Carter Museum, Fort Worth, Texas.)

They kept track of the sizes of uniforms they made and noted that certain combinations of measurements were more common than others. For example, they found that many men with a 36-inch waist also had a 30-inch trouser length. Thus began standardization in sizes of ready-made clothing; this development ultimately affected the entire clothing industry.

Of considerable importance to merchandising was Edison's invention of the first practical "electric" lamp in 1880. Telephones were developed during this time also, but there were few lines to use them. Communications also improved when the continental railroad system was finished between New York and San Francisco in 1885, and the cities were linked by a seven-day time interval. (See the I. Magnin story in Chapter Four.)

Lifestyles changed for both men and women and so did their fashions. Sports, particularly bicycling, became the national fad for both men and women. But no longer could women wear bustles and yards of fabric trailing after them as they played tennis and rode bicycles. Therefore, the shirtwaist costume—a high-necked, long-sleeved bodice worn with a flowing skirt—became the uniform of the day. It was glorified by the drawings of Charles Dana Gibson and proclaimed as the "wholly American" look. The Gibson Girl silhouette soon appeared on both sides of the Atlantic.

By 1890, there were almost 4,000,000 women in the work force, thanks to the invention of the typewriter. And, although men's apparel manufacturers had been first with ready-made clothes, women's apparel was becoming more important. The first graded paper pattern in 1863 helped the development of manufacture of ready-made women's apparel.

Of special interest at this point are the "Instructions to Employees" that Carson, Pirie, Scott and Co. of Chicago used in the 1850s. They were typical of the requirements of the time in merchandising:

> Store must be open from 6:00 A.M. to 9:00 P.M. the year 'round.
> Store must be swept; counters, base shelves and show cases dusted; lamps trimmed, filled, and chimneys cleaned; pens made; doors and windows opened; a pail of water, also a bucket of coal brought in before breakfast (if there is time to do so) and attend customers who call.
> Store must not be opened on the Sabbath unless necessary, and then only for a few minutes.
> The employee who is in the habit of smoking Spanish cigars, being shaved at the barber's, going to dances and other places of amusement will surely give his employer reasons to be suspicious of his integrity and honesty.
> Each employee must not pay less than $5.00 per year to the church and must attend Sunday School regularly.
> Men employees are given one evening a week for courting, and two if they go to prayer meeting.
> After 14 hours of work in the store, the leisure hours should be spent mostly in reading.

1900–1920

The twentieth century saw ready-to-wear manufacturing rise for men, women, and children. With its growth came more workers and increased demand for better working conditions. The ILGWU (International Ladies' Garment Workers' Union) formed in 1900 did better the working conditions. Seventh Avenue in New York began during this period and was to become the world's greatest garment center.

FIG. 1-5. (Top left and top right: Courtesy, Dolly Ware. Bottom right: Courtesy, Mrs. Ben F. Thompson.)

It was still a man's world, but that was changing, too. The American woman finally won the right to vote in 1920, and she no longer was the sit-at-home, seen-but-seldom-heard person of years past. World War I sent many women to work for the first time. The result was fashion liberation for them. Their breath-taking corsets were eliminated in favor of narrower skirts, lower necklines, and shorter lengths.

19

The motion picture (although silent) became the new Saturday-night recreation and Mary Pickford, Dorothy and Lillian Gish, and the heroic Pearl White were watched anxiously by the entire country. The Ziegfeld Follies in New York and on the travel circuit set new examples of what was considered American beauty.

Men were beginning to be more fashion-conscious also, and some of the transitory appeal of their fashions began to appear, as had been apparent in women's ready-to-wear for some time. The great Phillips–Van Heusen shirt industry was rising and the attached shirt collar dominated 90 percent of the market. This did away forever with the stiff, uncomfortable, detachable celluloid collar popular just before this period.

THE '20s

American fashions took a radical turn in the early '20s. Men and women were dancing the Charleston. This craze eliminated the long dresses so popular just a few years before. Skirts were shortened to just below the knees, silk stockings came into vogue, expensive as they were, and women bobbed their hair and wore rouge and long strands of costume jewelry around their necks.

Hollywood was influencing the thinking of youth, and sex appeal became the new interest. Gloria Swanson, Joan Crawford, and Clara Bow were the flappers of the period and great influencers of fashion for women.

It was the jazz age, and clothing matched the period. For men, zoot suits went with the jazz business—they were crazy models with no linings—but they sold.

Production and consumer spending was at an all-time high just three years after the postwar recession. Chain stores spread throughout the states. Installment buying became the way to buy and reached a peak of $6 billion a year. Many-threaded sewing machines were whizzing along at the rate of several thousand stitches a minute. More product advertising appeared, turning luxury items into necessities.

Until the stockmarket crashed, no one believed that the glittering life could ever end.

THE '30s

The '30s started with the memory of the stockmarket crash and the reality of the Depression—and ended with the impending World War II. But the years between were filled with dreams and fantasies.

Radio became the home center of entertainment, as Amos 'n Andy, Edgar Bergen and Charlie McCarthy, Fred Allen and Jack Benny brought their programs to people everywhere. These were the years of the Lucky Strike Hit Parade, and the top ten tunes were on everyone's lips.

THE '20s

FIG. 1-6. (Top left: Courtesy, Mrs. P.D. Henry. Top right: Courtesy, Mrs. Ben F. Thompson. Bottom: Courtesy, Mrs. P.D. Henry.)

The movies were the big escape, and were also the greatest influencers of fashion. Marlene Dietrich, Greta Garbo, Janet Gaynor, Bette Davis, Jean Harlow, Jeanette MacDonald, and Ginger Rogers were some of Hollywood's leading stars. Fred Astaire, Nelson Eddy, Clark Gable, and Spencer Tracy were their leading men. Shirley Temple was the little child star that captivated hearts and had every little girl longing for curly locks and short, fluffy dresses.

Gilbert Adrian designed for the Hollywood stars and when he designed a puffed-sleeve ruffled dress for Joan Crawford in 1932, her loyal subjects couldn't wait to buy a simplified version at an affordable price. The development of the new man-made fiber, rayon, made it possible.

Jitterbug was the dance craze, and Benny Goodman, Artie Shaw, and Glenn Miller had the "big bands" of the era.

Sportswear was popular during this period, and for women, swimsuits became one-piece and figure-revealing. Men's clothes became more structured because of the silver screen. Men on the screen played golf in the mornings in knickers and argyles, lunched and lounged in suits in the afternoon, went to their clubs and changed into evening clothes for dinner at eight.

Because it was difficult to get French fashions, retail stores started promoting ready-made clothes by American designers.

THE '40s

The 1940s brought World War II, and for the women of America, it brought a fashion fallout that changed the way they would dress forever.

Uniforms for men and women were the order of the early decade. Sequined eagles and flags showed up on evening dresses and soon women were wearing spiffy, cropped coverups known as Eisenhower jackets.

With the war, too, came government regulations controlling the amount of fabric civilians could use. Skirts were limited to 72 inches around, ruffles disappeared, cuffs were banished from coats and suits for both men and women, hems stifled at two inches, and pockets were limited to one of a patch-type. Fabric shortages brought a burst of skimpy playclothes, and lack of zippers brought wraparounds. Making an impact, too, was the convertible costume, which could take its wearer from daytime to evening with just a slip of its jacket or skirt, and a change to evening jewelry.

For the younger crowd, uniforms were in order, too, as the teenagers firmly established themselves. They made a mad attempt to look just like everyone else, and the sloppy men's shirt over rolled-up jeans and bobby sox was their favorite garb.

On the California beaches, something strange was making waves:

THE '30s

FIG. 1-7. (Top left: Courtesy, Sears, Roebuck & Co. Bottom right: Courtesy, Mrs. P.D. Henry.)

THE '40s

FIG. 1-8. (Bottom: Courtesy, Wide World Photos. Left: Courtesy, Sears, Roebuck & Co.)

sportswear. Men and women were getting caught up in a carefree, easy lifestyle.

The '40s were, for America, the beginning for standing on its own ready-to-wear. Cut off from Paris fashion leadership by the war, Americans began to make their own fashion decisions. Much of their inspiration came from their neighbors to the north and south. Patchworks were borrowed from the pioneers, fringed leathers from the Indians, overalls from workmen, frilled cottons from the south—Mexico —and lumberjack plaids from the north—Canada.

Claire McCardle, Norman Norell, and Claire Potter made early marks as fashion names, followed by Charles James, Hattie Carnegie, and Bonnie Cashin.

By 1945, technology was making its impact. High-speed cutters helped turn out millions of suits and dresses in weeks. Home permanents were introduced for women. DuPont's miracle new fiber nylon was introduced, causing women to mob the hosiery counters. After the war, nylon opened a whole vista of travel-use, wash-and-wear clothes for men, women, and children.

The Americans, caught up in mass production, excelled in sizing and construction, and by the late '40s the French were arriving to study American techniques.

But with all its practicalities, war-imposed basics, uniforms, and dresses as simple as the shirtwaist, the '40s had plenty of room for fads. Hats for women were extravagant creations piled high with flowers and feathers. Matching handbags, gloves, and ankle-strapped shoes focused attention on legs that were covered by longer and fuller skirts (the aftermath of fabric shortages and the Dior New Look).

THE '50s

Television, the miraculous medium of the 1950s, mirrored the heart and soul of America in this decade. It became the major link to the nation's consciousness in the '50s just as the movies were in the '30s. Not only did it influence fashions for men, women, and children, but it molded opinion on everything else from national security to national morality, Elvis Presley, and ponytails.

Everyone yearned for security in the '50s, on both the political and home fronts. The postwar baby boom was on, and so was the race for the last frontier—Suburbia. Housing developments sprang up across the country as everyone wanted a part of the good life—a home of their own with two cars in the driveway and a barbecue grill in the yard.

This move to a more casual lifestyle was reflected in the fashions. Pants sprouted two new abbreviated lengths—pedal-pushers and Bermuda shorts—to kick around in, while full-skirted sundresses were worn by those who preferred bare shoulders instead of legs. Sleeveless

THE '50's

FIG. 1-9. (Top left: Courtesy, Neiman-Marcus. Others: Courtesy, Women's Wear Daily, "The Changing American Woman—200 Years of American Fashion" (New York, N.Y.: Fairchild Publications, 1976).

blouses and dresses became popular. Feet were tucked into sandals and sneakers. To accommodate the newly mobile, far-flung suburbanites, shopping centers sprang up miles away from center cities—here parking was easy and casual dress accepted.

The fads of the '50s took off as never before—hula hoops, full skirts with poodle appliqués, saddle shoes, and pop-it beads. Almost every girl wore a circle pin on her Peter Pan collar with her cardigan sweater. For the boys, hair went from pompadours and ducktails to flat-tops. In the image of James Dean, they sported leather jackets and blue jeans.

For most women, the shirtwaist was the dress of the decade. Available in almost every price range, it came with either a round Peter Pan or tailored shirt collar, long or short sleeves, and a fitted bodice. Two or more crinoline petticoats were worn with all the full-skirted day or evening dresses. White gloves were worn with everything.

Despite the re-emergence of Paris couture after the war, American ready-to-wear, easily wearable and highly affordable, was coming into its own. American designers were achieving prominence—Anne Fogarty, Pauline Trigère, Anne Klein, Mollie Parnis. Many of the volume ready-to-wear firms were becoming large, successful operations.

THE '60s

Some called the '60s savage. This was a decade that saw the assassination of John F. Kennedy, Martin Luther King, and several other prominent people. It was also a period when youth took issue with the Establishment and questioned contradictory values that previous generations had lived by.

Hippies with their long, flowing hair, addiction to jeans, and put-down of pretentious dressing influenced every other segment of society. Suddenly it became all right to wear jeans to a party, or a long dress to classes. Miniskirts, a symbol of freedom, became micro-mini as the decade progressed.

At the same time, women adopted pants and pantsuits for their city day and evening uniform. They were becoming more aware of themselves as people who did not necessarily have to live out a predetermined role, and used the fresh look of pantsuits to make a sociological statement to this effect.

Status symbols—the signature scarf, Gucci shoes, Vuitton bags—came into being for those who couldn't cope with the newfound freedom in dressing and needed the reassurance of something safe.

In the midst of all this, the American people found a new type of star—Jacqueline Bouvier Kennedy. What she wore and the way she wore it became an instant fad: the bouffant hairstyle, pillbox hats, chain-handled bags carried by a gloved hand, the simple, sleeveless dress with pearls inside the neckline, low-heeled shoes, glamorous but simple evening gowns. Her whispery voice, perfect posture, and eternal smile clinched the mystique.

THE '70s

The crazy yeah-yeah days of the '60s were on the wane by 1970. Students now turned to the cold reality of job hunting, and the women who had clung to their crayon-colored Courrèges miniskirts and vinyl boots searched for a less flamboyant uniform. In the '60s American affluence had been taken for granted, even flaunted. In the '70s, recession made it chic to be discreet.

Ultrasuede, a synthetic suedelike fabric from Japan, became the status fabric of the '70s. It began with Halston's shirt-dress in the fall of '72 and symbolized the emphasis on fashion geared to easy maintenance and practicality. Washable, elegant, and expensive, it soon found its way into both men's and women's suits, jackets, coats, and luggage.

With the "longuette" and the "bigskirt," hemlines dropped. The popularity of pants increased for women. More important than hemlines or shapes, however, was the switch to "unconstructed" clothes— softer fabrics, sweater dressing, coats and dresses that wrapped, and the layered look.

With emphasis on exercise and activity, American sports gained momentum. American men and women turned to designers for clothes as easy and uncostumey as tennis and jogging garb. Soon much active sportswear began to take on designer labels.

Many designers became celebrities as recognizable as the stars they dressed: Calvin Klein, Diane von Furstenberg, Halston, Albert Capraro, Bill Blass, Oscar de la Renta. Their names turned everything from sheets to furs to sunglasses into instant status symbols. Fashion was no longer limited to clothes and the rise and fall of hemlines: it became an attitude and lifestyle reflected in the all-encompassing areas of designer products.

The Women's Movement, no longer the explosive issue it had been in the '60s, settled into a quieter, stride-making time. Many women—Chris Evert, Kay Graham, Sarah Caldwell, Barbara Walters —were at the top of their fields.

The rediscovery of fashion by men in the peacock revolution of the late '60s surged ahead in the '70s, exploding into wider ties, colored shirts, leisure suits, velveteen or Ultrasuede blazers, three-piece vested suits, and the well-coordinated look. The ever-versatile doubleknits began to give way to the natural fibers—silk, wool, linen, cotton denim, or blends of these.

FIG. 1-10. (Top left: Courtesy, the Fort Worth Star Telegram. Bottom: Courtesy, Women's Wear Daily, "The Changing American Woman—200 Years of American Fashion" (New York, N.Y.: Fairchild Publications, 1976).

THE '70s

FIG. 1-11. (Courtesy: Women's Wear Daily, "The Changing American Woman—200 Years of American Fashion" (New York, N.Y.: Fairchild Publications, 1976).

What Are the Fashion Businesses Today?

You are already aware that there are many kinds of retailing businesses today and that they range in size from the very large *multiple-unit businesses* to the *individualized smaller stores*. No doubt you have selected wearing apparel in many kinds of retail stores.

MULTIPLE-UNIT
BUSINESSES
INDIVIDUALIZED
SMALLER STORES
*How can fashion
businesses
be classified?*

Retailing businesses may be classified according to the type of ownership, the kinds of apparel they handle, the size of the stores, the type of services offered to their customers, or even by the type of customer they desire to serve. Some are located in large shopping centers, some in smaller shopping areas, and some may even be free-standing in your community. Some are grouped in the downtown areas, while others are situated closer to the customers in one particular section of a city.

Probably one of the most popular forms of ownership for many years has been the independently owned and individualized type of single store. In these establishments—sole proprietorships—the owners manage and operate the store perhaps with the help of their family. Sometimes such independently owned stores are small operations, often referred to as mom-and-pop stores, but frequently they grow in size and carry many lines of apparel for the entire family. Sometimes they open additional stores in other sections of a city, or they may even expand operations into other parts of the country. Many individualized stores in New York, for example, are currently opening branch stores in other thriving business centers throughout the country, to the delight of customers who have long read their advertising in national magazines. When an individualized ownership store begins to expand, the ownership may also change. Additional management personnel is employed, and the type of store financing changes to meet the needs of the expansion. As you read the histories of some of the great companies in this book, you will notice how many started as individualized ownerships.

*What is the most
common form of
ownership?*

Another common type of retail apparel store is the chain-store operation. The management and control of such stores is usually in a centralized headquarters, although there is considerable evidence that decentralized management is developing. More of the responsibilities for the merchandising functions are being carried out in division or territorial offices, and these territorial executives have considerable autonomy within their geographic areas. As you may be aware, chain operations are very large in some instances and some have stores in all parts of the country. Some have fewer stores in their organization and may operate in one state or area only. Beginning fashion merchandising students are often unaware that many of these chain-store operations are limited in the amount of expansion that they can make because of the short supply of educated, experienced management personnel to operate new branch stores. So your opportunities may be

CHAIN STORES

almost unlimited when you become qualified to assume the responsibilities of apparel management in these chain-store businesses.

You may also be aware of another type of store operation—the manufacturer-owned store. Such stores may specialize in one kind of apparel—men's clothing, shoes for children, or for the whole family, or ladies' ready-to-wear and accessories, or clothing for children and infants alone. The manufacturers have opened these kinds of stores believing that such operations are more profitable to them in presenting their merchandise, especially in areas where the traffic volume of sales warrants great expectations. They may carry only their own manufactured lines of apparel exclusively, or they may fill out their own lines by selecting additional lines from outside resources.

If a store handles only one principal line of apparel merchandise, it is called a single-line store. Such stores may enlarge and become departmentalized, handling clothing for the whole family. Then they are called "departmentalized stores."

Specialty stores usually handle a limited variety of goods, but their assortment in each variety may be extensive. In a specialty men's shoe store, for example, you would expect to find a wide range of styles, colors, sizes, and prices from which to choose.

The table on p. 33 will help you understand the many kinds of classifications of the major kinds of fashion merchandising stores. It may also help you determine what direction you may wish to take in the fashion business.

The Importance of Fashion Merchandising in Our Economy

There are almost 2 million retail stores in our country. Not all of them can be classified as fashion stores, but the largest majority of them are fashion-influenced, directly or indirectly.

Fashion merchandising began to come alive in our country in the 1900s. This was the time when a shift in the economy changed scarcity to abundance. At this time, consumers began to be more selective in their buying habits and the types of merchandise they desired as well as in the types of businesses they selected for their buying.

Our Gross National Product (GNP)—*the total dollar value of the goods and services produced in our country*—grew to over a trillion dollars in 1970. As a result, personal income had grown in 1974 to an annual rate of almost $1.2 trillion. Personal income growth is significant in fashion merchandising because it is an indication of the amount of money people have to spend for goods and services. In 1970, America's retailers received about $365 billion in their wages, salaries, or commissions. These figures do not actually include over a million active proprietors of unincorporated individually owned businesses, who devote most of their time to their own businesses. We observed

TABLE 1-1. How to Recognize and Classify Major Fashion Merchandising Stores

BY OWNERSHIP

1. Single-unit independently owned stores
2. Multi-unit independently owned stores
3. Chain-owned stores
4. Manufacturer-owned stores

BY KIND OF BUSINESS

1. Departmentalized stores
2. Specialty stores

BY SIZE OF BUSINESS

1. Number of employees
2. Annual sales volume

BY RELATIONSHIP WITH OTHER
BUSINESS ORGANIZATIONS

1. Unaffiliated
2. Voluntarily affiliated
3. Affiliated with manufacturer
4. Franchised

BY CONSUMER CONTACT

1. Regular store
2. Direct mail order

BY TYPE OF LOCATION

1. Central business district
2. Shopping center
3. Free-standing

BY TYPE OF SERVICE

1. Full customer service
2. Limited customer service (cash and carry)
3. Self-service

BY LEGAL ORGANIZATION

1. Proprietorship
2. Partnership
3. Corporation

earlier in this chapter that these unincorporated businesses comprise a very dominant and important area of the fashion business.

The total persons employed in retailing today is well over 13 percent of the civilian labor force. There are, for example, over 33 million women in business, and 70 percent of these are in fashion-related areas.

It should be obvious to the student that fashion merchandising activities hold an important place in the economy of our country and of other countries as well. International trade in fashion goods is extensive. You have only to visit a retail store to be aware of how much of the fashion merchandise has been produced in other countries.

You will be interested in looking at Table 1-2 which lists the largest retailing businesses in the United States. The size and scope of operation almost defies description, but bears out how huge the fashion industry has become, primarily because the businesses are predominantly fashion-oriented.

Conclusion

While fashion merchandising is not limited to the retailing of clothing alone, we are concentrating on this particular aspect of merchandising because this is where the beginning person often starts a fashion career.

TABLE 1-2. The Largest Retailing Companies (Emphasis on Apparel)* (Ranked by Sales) (U.S.'s Biggest Corporations)

company	1976 sales ($000,000)	% change over 1975	rank	assets ($000,000)	rank	% change over 1975	profits ($000)	rank	% change over 1975	number of employees	chief executive	salary	rank among 798 biggest corps.
1. Sears, Roebuck** (Chicago)	18,832	11.0	8	18,857	16	12.4	686,513	13	34.4	433.0	Arthur M. Wood	423,760	106
2. S. S. Kresge (K mart Corp.) (Troy, Mich.)	8,484	23.2	18	2,866	153	20.5	266,574	43	32.7	191.0	Robert E. Dewar	350,000	204
3. J. C. Penney (N.Y.)	8,354	8.8	21	3,484	128	8.0	228,100	51	20.3	183.0	Donald V. Seibert	398,705	125
4. F. W. Woolworth (N.Y.)	5,152	10.8	46	2,093	231	-3.7	108,200	148	8.7	204.1	Lester A. Burcham	402,843	118
5. Federated Dept. Stores (Cincinnati, Ohio)	4,447	19.8	54	2,269	207	23.3	168,124	73	6.8	108.0	Ralph Lazarus	450,000	80
6. Montgomery Ward*** (Mobil Corp.) (Chicago)	4,049	7.1	—	2,492	—	—	190,507	—	—	123.0	Leo H. Schoenhofen	—	—
7. May Dept. Stores (St. Louis, Mo.)	2,133	5.7	144	1,456	361	4.5	69,432	259	4.1	59.0	David E. Babcock	285,000	296
8. Dayton-Hudson (Minneapolis, Minn.)	1,899	12.2	165	1,058	480	12.0	65,663	274	28.0	30.0	William A. Andres	357,294	190
9. Allied Stores (N.Y.)	1,814	2.4	182	1,172	439	6.5	61,395	289	12.5	55.0	Thomas M. Macioce	500,000	52
10. Associated Dry Goods (N.Y.)	1,539	10.6	218	753	—	—	40,637	432	5.7	57.5	Richard R. Pivirotto	235,000	406
11. R. H. Macy (N.Y.)	1,469	13.2	231	848	—	—	42,973	408	58.4	39.0	Donald B. Smiley	261,939	339
12. Melville (Shoes) (Harrison, N.Y.)	1,228	35.2	276	472	—	—	61,004	295	37.6	32.9	Francis C. Rooney, Jr.	236,100	403
13. Colonial Stores (Atlanta, Ga.)	975	-0.7	359	177	—	—	11,612	—	—	11.6	Ernest F. Boyce	227,980	421
14. First National Stores (Somerville, Mass.)	974	4.2	359	117	—	—	-1,502	—	—	17.2	Allen H. Haberman	120,833	701
15. Mercantile Stores (N.Y.)	701	11.2	455	385	—	—	29,200	—	—	16.5	Leon F. Winbigler	314,821	250

* "Dimensions of American Business: A Roster of the U.S.'s Biggest Corporations," *Forbes, Inc.*, Annual Directory Issue, May 15, 1977, pp. 202–43.
** Figures include unconsolidated subsidiaries
*** "Our Best Year," Montgomery Ward, Report for Employees, 1977, pp. 29–33

The exciting challenge in fashion merchandising lies in the changes that occur gradually and frequently in apparel. The techniques of textile development and clothing construction, as well as the increasingly different methods employed by fashion businesses, evidence the tremendous growth in fashion in our country since the early 1900s.

Fashion merchandising is important to the development of the economy and standard of living in our country not only because of the vast number of people serving in this endeavor but also because of the great capital investment required to operate the merchandising enterprises.

Review Questions

1. Define or identify the following familiar fashion merchandising terminologies:
   a. Federated Department Stores
   b. French Chambre Syndicale de la Haute Couture
   c. Fashion
   d. Fashion cycles
   e. Fashion merchandising
   f. Ready-to-wear
   g. Caveat emptor
   h. Multiple-unit businesses
   i. Individualized smaller stores
   j. Chain stores
   k. Manufacturer-owned stores
   l. Specialty stores
   m. Departmentalized stores
   n. GNP—Gross National Product
2. How can you determine what fashion is at a given time?
3. Is fashion a characteristic of how we live today? Why or why not?
4. Why do people throughout the world dress similarly today?
5. Is fashion limited exclusively to apparel?
6. Do you feel that apparel manufacturers play an important role in fashion merchandising?
7. How can fashion retailing businesses be classified? Can you suggest other classifications that might be used?
8. How important is fashion in our economy? The world?
9. Which company is the largest retailing business in the world? Why does it hold this rank?
10. Who were the "famous brother partners" in retailing? Why do you think their fashion business became so highly respected among fashion authorities?

Suggested Student Activities

1. Prepare a research paper on the history of men's and women's fashions, using for reference "Other Fashion Books That Will Interest You" at the end of this text.

2. Identify the fashion-related businesses in your community. Then classify them as shown in the chart on page 33.
3. Select one or more departmentalized stores in your community and analyze the fashion departments for men, women, and children. Use some of the following criteria:
   a. Location of the department in the store. Is it adjacent to another fashion department? Is it near the accessories areas? How prominent is the department from the standpoint of traffic into and through the store?
   b. Approximate size of the departments in comparison with other departments in the store.
   c. Sales staff in the departments.
   d. Special customer services offered in the stores.
4. While visiting fashion stores in your community, identify merchandise that originated in another country. Compare qualities and prices with similar U.S.–produced merchandise. Identify the differences and give your reasons why you think the differences exist.

Case Problems

Case 1-1. Jim was forced to become a high school dropout because of family finances. He got a job with a local department store in the stockroom and from there advanced to a selling position in menswear. As the company grows, Jim senses that he is not getting promotions like some of his friends are, and feels that his lack of education is holding him back. He passes his high school equivalency test and then does well on his college entrance exam. Now he wonders what he should take in college.

1. Would you suggest that he take fashion merchandising? Why or why not?
2. Will his chances of advancing be better in his present company if he understands merchandising better?
3. What are the opportunities for Jim in the future if he takes fashion merchandising courses?

Case 1-2. Mary Ann didn't have time to hold a part-time job while she was in high school, as many of her friends did. She was busy being a cheerleader, a member of the debating club, and a participant in school plays. She really doesn't know what she would like to do in the future, but she thinks she might enjoy fashion merchandising. She asks you what it is all about.

1. What would you tell her about fashion merchandising?
2. Do you think her chances of becoming successful in a fashion career are promising? Why?

Case 1-3. George is a quiet fellow—he likes courses in science and math and makes better-than-average grades in these subjects. He hopes to go to college after high school, but he really needs to get a job to become self-supporting as soon as possible. He is wondering about entering merchandising in college, but he has never taken a business course and feels he knows very little about it.

1. Would you recommend the fashion merchandising college curriculum to him?
2. If not, what suggestions would you make to him about a career in business?

Case 1-4. Mrs. Brown has just sent her last child to college. She realizes that for the first time in many years she is now free to pursue some of her own interests. What she would really like to do is enter the business of fashion, but she fears that she may be too old (she's a vivacious, attractive 40-year-old) to enter business and that probably no one will want to hire her. She would really like to go back to college and finish her degree, but she wonders if she can really do it.

1. Do you think Mrs. Brown would feel uncomfortable in college today?
2. Should she pursue her desire to enter the world of fashion? Why or why not?
3. Do you think she could get a job in fashion?

Case 1-5. Neal Johnson has just reached retirement age with the U.S. Air Force. He feels that he has many productive years left and is planning a new career for himself in business. He has talked to some personnel directors in large department stores and has had offers for sales-floor jobs. His main interest is really management responsibility, and he is willing to train for such a position, but none of the companies he has interviewed with have been overly enthusiastic about starting him at that level. He wonders what he should do, and if it would be wise to go back to college for awhile.

1. Do you think he should go back to college and try to get a degree?
2. Should he accept a sales position even though he wants management responsibilities?
3. What courses would you recommend that he take in college if he decides to go?

Chapter 2

Career opportunities in fashion merchandising

Objectives

When you have read this chapter, you should be able to

1. Explain the beginning job area in which a student of fashion merchandising may begin to get basic fashion experience, and the importance of doing so
2. Name three important criteria for reaching successful goals, and how to acquire them
3. Identify the good fashion jobs available to both men and women, depending on their commitment to fashion responsibilities
4. State how young people have great opportunity for advancement in all kinds of fashion businesses
5. List with detail the requirements, functions, salaries, and advantages or disadvantages of many kinds of fashion opportunity at the manufacturing level, the retailing level, and in related fashion areas
6. Describe how the many retailing practices developed by J. C. Penney through his Golden Rule Stores changed retailing in the United States

The lengthy career of James Cash Penney spanned the growth of American retailing from the local drygoods stores to the national department store chains, a change he was instrumental in developing.

JCPenney

Where did Penney's begin? How?

While the great retailing institutions were growing in the large cities, the Penney stores were having their beginning in Wyoming in the Rocky Mountain mining towns. Mr. Penney's career is particularly noted for the introduction of the profit-sharing principle to national retailing, and his further development of the code of business ethics considered commonplace today but an innovation in the rugged western communities in which the Penney chain had its start more than seventy years ago.

James Cash Penney's (his middle name was real) insistence on a "reasonable" profit, and only first-quality merchandise at a single price for all, established him as one of the top merchants of the century. The chain of nearly 1,700 stores that bears his name today is an outgrowth of the standards of fair play and honest dealing instilled into Penney early in his life by his Baptist minister–farmer father. His life is an inspirational example to any person in fashion retailing today, as well.

Young Penney's first department store job was "clerking" for $2.27 a month in his hometown of Hamilton, Missouri. From there he

FIG. 2-1. James Cash Penney (1875–1971) was one of America's greatest merchants. His first Golden Rule store in Kemmerer, Wyoming, opened in 1902, marked the beginning of the growth of the multi-billion dollar merchandising company.

(Courtesy, J. C. Penney Company, Inc.)

[1] *History of J. C. Penney* (New York: J. C. Penney Company, Inc.).

went to Colorado for reasons of health, and later to work for Callahan & Johnson in their small Evanston, Wyoming store. The partners were impressed by the industry and sagacity of their young employee, and gave him an opportunity to buy for $2,000 a one-third interest in their new store to be opened in Kemmerer, Wyoming. Although married and a father, Mr. Penney had managed to save $500. He borrowed the rest and within one year paid off the debt and acquired one-third interest in still another Callahan & Johnson store.

It was this Kemmerer store, called the "Golden Rule Store" that marked the beginning of the Penney Company. The store proved an immediate success, thanks in part to the preparatory advertising build-up Penney secured by going from door to door in the small mining town, handing out advertising broadsides.

The Golden Rule Store proved something of a novelty for the frontier community, whose residents had previously done most of their shopping at the company stores run by mining interests. Under Mr. Penney, the Golden Rule operated strictly on a cash-and-carry basis, a policy that remained unchanged in the Penney Company until the introduction of credit in 1958. Opening-day receipts totaled nearly $500, and predicted the fine financial record other Penney stores were to show in following years.

By 1907, Callahan & Johnson decided to dissolve their partnership and sold Mr. Penney their interest in the four small drygoods stores in the Rocky Mountain region. As sole owner of the flourishing small chain, Mr. Penney decided to perpetuate the profit-sharing incentive system that proved so successful in Kemmerer. He set about looking for ambitious young people whom he carefully trained for the responsibilities and rewards of partnership while allowing them a fairly free hand in the actual operation of their stores. Each new manager was given the opportunity to buy one-third interest in the store. Because of his practice of sharing profits, Penney became known as "the man with a thousand partners." Today, though not partners in the stores they operate, managers still rely on profit as a basis for compensation. Penney executives and other members of the company's management group are also compensated on the basis of yearly profits of the company.

In 1912 the name "Golden Rule Store," a reflection of Mr. Penney's belief in applying Christian principles to business, was changed to J. C. Penney Stores, and the chain was incorporated a year later. In 1917, carrying out a firmly held belief in placing responsibility on the people he worked with, Penney turned over the presidency of the company to Earl Sams, and became chairman of the board, a post he held until 1958. He served as a member of the board of directors until his death in 1971 at the age of 95.

In the early twenties the regional character of the chain altered as Penney stores opened in all sections of the country. By 1927 there

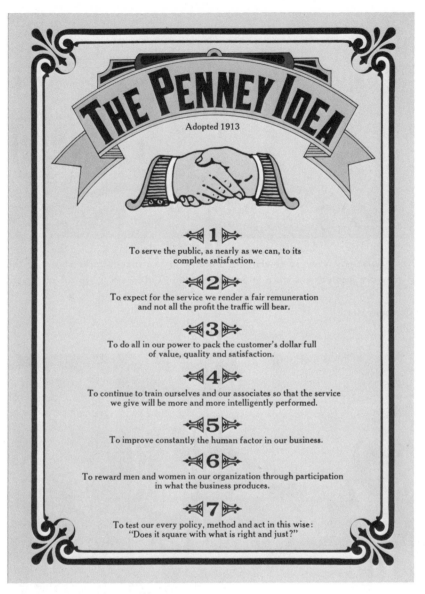

THE PENNEY IDEA

Adopted 1913

1
To serve the public, as nearly as we can, to its complete satisfaction.

2
To expect for the service we render a fair remuneration and not all the profit the traffic will bear.

3
To do all in our power to pack the customer's dollar full of value, quality and satisfaction.

4
To continue to train ourselves and our associates so that the service we give will be more and more intelligently performed.

5
To improve constantly the human factor in our business.

6
To reward men and women in our organization through participation in what the business produces.

7
To test our every policy, method and act in this wise: "Does it square with what is right and just?"

FIG. 2-2. In 1913 there were forty-eight Golden Rule stores when "The Penney Idea" was adopted. This set of principles was to guide management operations of the Golden Rule stores, and it is just as powerful today as it was when it was first developed.
(Courtesy J. C. Penney Company, Inc.)

were more than 800 stores doing an annual business of more than $150 million.

FIG. 2-3. While store exteriors may vary somewhat to conform to the architectural styles of the shopping malls in which they are located, this store in San Bernardino, California is typical of current exteriors.

(Courtesy, J. C. Penney Company, Inc.)

FIG. 2-4. An atmosphere of informality is maintained throughout the junior shop display and merchandise areas of Penney stores nationwide.

(Courtesy, J. C. Penney Company, Inc.)

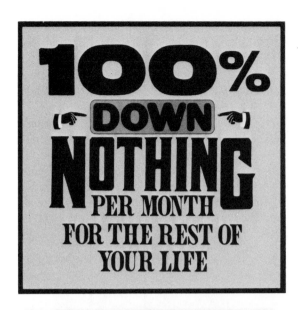

FIG. 2-5(a). J. C. Penney's cash-only policy sign
on his original store.
FIG. 2-5(b). In 1958 the Penney Company began
to issue credit cards for use in their stores.
(Courtesy, J. C. Penney Company, Inc.)

Although the Penney Company continued to grow far beyond the original concept of a chain of regional drygoods stores, Mr. Penney maintained his early practice of attending new-store openings and frequently visiting those already established. Even late in life, he was not above waiting on a customer, and his warm personal dealings with thousands of shoppers earned him a legion of friends everywhere.

It was not uncommon for a customer to approach Mr. Penney at an opening and recall how his father or even his grandfather had been waited upon by the founder years before. This genuine respect and interest in customers was matched by an equally firm loyalty toward Penney "associates," as Mr. Penney always called those who worked with him in the company. This first-name friendliness and respect for the individual talents of his managers became one of the distinctive assets of the chain.

Speaking to a reporter in 1960, a year when the Penney chain reported sales of nearly $1½ billion, Penney remarked: "I can tell you without reservation that the success of this company is due to the application of the Golden Rule to every individual, the public, and all of our activities." Many times in later years he stated: "It doesn't take genius to succeed."

He is also credited with these valuable words: "There are people who, when the principles of business success are explained to them, do not find the answer sufficiently intellectual to be satisfying. In retailing, the formula happens to be a basic liking for human beings, plus integrity, plus industry, plus . . . the ability to see the other fellow's point of view." America lost one of its last great merchant princes when J. C. Penney died. He left behind a $2.7 billion empire of retail stores across the nation.

If a man does not keep pace with his companions, perhaps it is because he hears a different drummer. Let him step to the music he hears.

HENRY DAVID THOREAU

The purpose of discussing career opportunities in fashion merchandising is to help you hear your "drummer" in one of the diversified and rewarding careers that are available to men and women in fashion businesses. When you upgrade your education and increase your fashion experience, then your career goal becomes more distinct. You not only have a better understanding of the progression into advanced positions of fashion responsibility, but should have a more definite perception of what these positions require. Then you will know how to prepare for them and how to proceed toward your advancement.

Fashion Careers

Men and women find fundamentally satisfying and rewarding careers in fashion merchandising. While a fashion merchandising career need not be limited to the apparel business alone, this is where we focus our attention because it is where a college student often begins a merchandising career. It is generally agreed that if you understand the merchandising functions they may be applied similarly to many different types of consumer goods.

Is fashion for women only?

There is a longstanding belief among the majority of the consuming public that fashion is a woman's sphere, and that the only jobs in fashion merchandising are held exclusively by women. Nothing could be further from the truth. Men and children are interested in fashion in their apparel and are becoming increasingly more fashion-conscious all the time. And men have long held exciting jobs in fashion businesses.

There are actually many excellent and promising jobs for men and women as executives in fashion merchandising. For women, especially, there are probably more executive-level opportunities in fashion than in any other field of business endeavor. Many women have distinguished themselves and proven to be very successful in the management of large fashion enterprises all over the world. In our own country Elizabeth Fairall climbed from the level of salesperson to vice-president of the Julius Garfinckel Company of Washington, D.C. Geraldine Stutz, a truly dynamic woman in retailing, is president of Henri Bendel. Mrs. Carrie Neiman, the creator of the Neiman-Marcus style, helped found the well-known specialty store, Neiman-Marcus. Another famous woman, often considered America's "Number One" career woman, was Dorothy Shaver. In 1945 she was elected president of Lord & Taylor, a large New York City department store, by an all-male board of directors. Under her management the business grossed in excess of $40 million some years. At a time when Paris fashion designs were worshipped by most American stores and magazines, she set up the Lord & Taylor American Design Awards to encourage the "American Look." You will also read about Mary Ann Magnin in Chapter Four. The great San Francisco–based I. Magnin began as her idea and dream and the underlying principles she established for style, fine quality, and good taste have been faithfully followed.

But for the most part, the large fashion enterprises are still headed by men at the executive levels. For whatever reasons this may be, it is reasonable to expect that more and more women will be progressing into higher positions of responsibility in the fashion businesses of the future. Many women in the past have not had a lifetime commitment to their jobs, considering them only a stopgap between school and family. As a result, fashion businesses have been somewhat reluctant to give women as much responsibility and training as they give to men in the same positions. There is much evidence that this is now changing because women are beginning to qualify themselves to hold responsible fashion jobs. They are proving capable of advancing on these jobs right on through their family years, just as men have always done. The old concept that woman's place is in the home is finally disappearing from the scene. Women of today are finding out that if they choose, they can be something exciting in addition to being a wife and mother, and they are showing the business world that they mean it. Some men even concede that women who have outside business interests are more interesting companions in their homes. The point to be made here is that women, as well as men, *can* develop into

Can a woman become an executive in a fashion business?

If women can be fashion executives, why are there so few?

Is a woman's place in the home?

executive leaders, depending upon their career goals and their determination to reach them.

Fashion Career Requirements

I want to succeed in the fashion business—so what must I do?

A good career in fashion merchandising, just as with any worthwhile career, requires a good education, good experience, and some opportunities for success. If you get the best fashion merchandising education you can and secure the best possible experience in a fashion business, you will learn just how the fashion business operates, and the opportunities and successes will follow. You, yourself, are responsible for the first two elements—education and experience—they will enable opportunity and success to fall into place, and you will progress in a career that is intriguing, financially rewarding, and personally gratifying.

Where you hope to be in fashion a few years from now will be pretty much up to you individually. But, within realistic boundaries, you can become almost anything you want to be if you're willing to "pay the price." It will not happen overnight. It takes several years of education and experience, great enthusiasm for what you are seeking, unfailing eagerness to learn and continue to learn, and a considerable

Does it really pay to get good experience?

willingness on your part to be flexible and broadminded. It's a fact that we always prize what we pay dearly for. When the conditions are stiff and the specifications rigid, we have greater respect and appreciation for our accomplishments. So do our peers. The price you pay in your fashion apprenticeship training will be eminently worthwhile to you in every possible way.

Since we are emphasizing good fashion experience as one of the important criteria for successful advancement in a fashion career, we emphasize beginning a fashion-related job in the real business world just as soon as possible. Don't just look at the salary on your first job, because it will probably be minimum. Actually, it may even be more than you're really worth in your early learning years. Look for the kind of job that you can't wait to begin every day because you've found something that really challenges you—something that you love to do so much that you can't wait to get started on it every day. Working days should always be happy days. Look also for a job where you know you will receive thorough training. A beginning job can give you great insight into the world of fashion and help you discover many reasons why it will be fun and exciting to spend your working days in this kind of a career. Perhaps there will be some things that you prefer doing over others—you might not like all of your entry-level responsibilities. You might not like to work in the stockroom, for example, but a well-organized fashion department needs excellent backup stock that can be located quickly when your department is rushed. To work in stock is one of your best opportunities to become thoroughly familiar with all the merchandise features of the lines carried. To accomplish any job quickly and enthusiastically is the mark of the successful person.

The advisability and importance of "learning by doing" is receiving widespread acceptance educationally by colleges all across the country. Many colleges today emphasize the importance of fashion internships, fashion practicums, or on-the-job training, and reward the student for a well-planned, carefully coordinated work-study program by giving college credits for it. The length of time spent on "learning by doing" varies somewhat among colleges, but it is generally agreed that students should be employed part-time in the fashion world the whole time they are studying in the fashion curriculum. Then, at graduation they have not only their degree but some excellent experience as well, and advancement will come more quickly. On-the-job fashion training works very much like the science laboratory works for the student of science, for example. In the classroom you discuss the theories and concepts—then in your laboratory you practice what you are learning, applying your knowledge in the most effective way. Whether you are in a college that emphasizes fashion training or not, you can still benefit by entering the fashion world just as soon as possible.

A beginning job in fashion that provides excellent training and usually fits in well with a college curriculum is on the sales floor of a large department store, a chain organization, a specialty store, or a smaller fashion boutique. Actually, fashion sales-floor experience is a basic training area for any career in fashion. This is where you can learn a great deal about the most influential factor in the fashion business—the consumers.

Where do you begin?

Understanding the wants and needs of the *all-important consumer* is basic in all the areas of production, distribution, and sales promotion of fashion goods. The consumer completes the manufacturing and retailing efforts of many people, because until something gets sold no one really profits. And making a profit is certainly one of the most important objectives of any business endeavor.

Today, there is almost an insatiable demand for qualified and ambitious young people in the continuing dynamic expansion of retail store facilities and the ever-increasing merchandise assortments and services they present to America's shoppers. Retailing is the front line of our American system of mass distribution and is of vital importance in distributing the fashion merchandise of our enormously capable mass production system. It is actually a career wonderland of opportunities for the qualified, serious student of fashion merchandising.

*Can young people
succeed in a
fashion job?*

Another important reason for understanding the interesting and diversified occupations in fashion is that it can give direction to your efforts. When you understand the functions and requirements of each type of job, it is easier to choose your role and the direction you wish to take. It could eliminate your wandering aimlessly from one job to another.

How does advancement on a fashion job happen?

The direction you take in your working life can be compared to climbing a big tree. As a child, you may have indulged in some tree climbing or wanted to do so. It was hard, slow work at first because you were young and inexperienced in tree climbing, but you were nevertheless motivated to get as high into that tree as you could safely climb. As you climbed up the trunk of the tree, you began to find many interesting branches you could climb and explore, but you probably chose a particular one. Circumstances, situations, localities, and opportunities all influence and determine the particular branch you choose to climb in your fashion business life. Knowing the approximate destination of your branch will help you make a wiser selection of what alternative to choose in the early part of your climbing. By all means choose a branch that is leading somewhere you would like to be some day in fashion merchandising. A look at Figure 2-6 will help you see the possible directions you can go in if you climb any particular branch in fashion.

What about fashion salaries?

You can depend on one thing for sure—good salaries always follow the prepared individuals who know where they are going. You will always be properly and equitably rewarded for your services if you have the appropriate knowledge and experience for a job, and then work at it enthusiastically. Experience is something you can never buy—the only way to get it is to work for it. Only through good experience can you develop the skills and competencies to operate in fashion businesses profitably and successfully.

Are there any job openings?

Well-educated, motivated people are in demand as employees and their opportunities to move ahead are excellent in the fashion area. Young people will be especially encouraged by the remarks of Arthur M. Wood, president of Sears, Roebuck and Company, who recently said in a speech in Chicago, "One-fifth of all Sears' executive employees who prove to be promotable are moving into executive positions at a rapid rate. For individuals with college degrees, executive status, on the average, is reached within four years." There can be a great fashion future for you in the ever-growing American world of fashion, but your future will be what *you* want to make it.

Kinds of Fashion Jobs

Fashion jobs exist not only at the retailing level, but in the production areas as well. We will discuss some of these jobs—their titles, possible salary ranges, functions performed, abilities required, and some of the advantages and disadvantages of each. Many jobs exist that are directly related to your fashion merchandising training and experience,

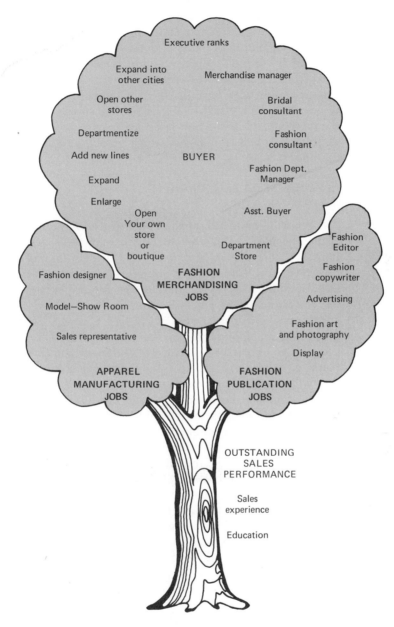

FIG. 2-6.   Fashion Advancement

and you should be qualified to get started toward advancement in them soon after your graduation. Numerous other auxiliary fashion jobs are available, also, and might be of interest to you if you are willing to secure a little more specialized training.

It is difficult to describe in detail all the available jobs which can be filled by fashion-trained individuals because the jobs vary somewhat from one business to another. Salaries, also, are variable. But we can give you a good basis of information about the general opportunities in the fashion world. The jobs actually spread all the way through the retailing and production areas, and into many auxiliary areas, such as publishing and advertising, which usually require more specialized training.

APPAREL MANUFACTURING

FASHION MARKETS

What are fashion marketplaces?

We will begin with apparel manufacturing because this is where fashion begins. Clothing manufacturers offer their new fashion collections at "market" four and sometimes five times a year. For a long time New York City was the primary marketplace for fashions in the U.S., but others are rapidly developing. Buyers for retail stores attend the market showings regularly. Among the other prominent markets are those found in the cities of Dallas, Chicago, St. Louis, Miami, Atlanta, and California. Buyers are more mobile than they once were and they go to markets in many cities oftener than they did just a few years ago. At the marketplaces, the store buyers select the assortments they will offer their own customers.

DESIGNER

Can I become a fashion designer with a merchandising study background?

New apparel lines actually begin on the designing boards at the manufacturing areas several months in advance of the new season. The *designer* presents original designs, and they are carefully analyzed in terms of the cost of producing the garments before the manufacturing executives decide to put them into their line for their next showing.

The fashion merchandising curriculum will not teach you all that you need to know if you wish to become a designer. This calls for specialized education in art elements, textiles, and pattern making. Nevertheless, your basic merchandising courses will help you understand the wants and needs of the consumer for whom you will be designing. The better designers take a conservative approach to their techniques and their designs are usually an outgrowth of current fashion apparel that is being accepted and worn. There are excellent job opportunities in fashion design, but they are probably more limited than other fashion areas, such as retailing.

What do manufacturer sales representatives do?

At the manufacturing level of activity, your fashion merchandising preparation will best help you if you have an opportunity to become a *manufacturer's sales representative*. This job is very important, not only in the showrooms during market showings but also out in the territory. Whether a manufacturer is a large publicly owned firm or a smaller operation, the need for good sales representation is a must in the organization. This type of job is likely to require considerable travel because it is necessary to contact retail buyers between markets in their assigned territory. Sales reps carry their sample lines with them and take orders or reorders for the apparel.

Since a territory may cover several states, sales representatives must be efficient organizers of time in order to see as many potential buyers as possible during their working hours. Sometimes travel time from place to place is most efficiently arranged at night, when the buyers are not available to look at the resource sales representative's lines in the stores.

In order to find opportunities in sales representation, it helps if you are located in or near the geographical areas where apparel manufacturing is a major business. Actually, fashion apparel is produced in many parts of our country, and you will become more aware of it when you begin to think in terms of fashion apparel manufacturing as a possible career employment area. The production area in fashion is important—without it probably no other fashion job could exist. The manufacturers work many months in advance of the fashion seasons and are of considerable importance in interpreting *fashion trends*.

FASHION TRENDS

Women sometimes become sales representatives after a period of time as *showroom models*. The showroom model must be of sample size and have a well-proportioned figure for showing the new collection each market season to its best advantage. Such modeling jobs usually exist only during the market showing weeks unless a manufacturing business keeps its showroom open year-round. The important thing about the experience of the showroom model is that this is an excellent training ground for becoming a showroom salesperson and then going on to become a sales representative for the company. Models may become acquainted with buyers and recognize them when they return to market season after season. Also, they can observe the showroom salespeople and learn the best methods of presenting the line and answering buyers' questions. For many years, modeling was almost exclusively for women. But today, while it is still a small part of a large industry, the need for photogenic men to help sell men's fashions is increasing. If you are interested in showroom modeling, a short course in modeling techniques will be helpful.

*What do showroom
models do?*

Manufacturing sales representatives who are selling on a yearly commission basis sometimes receive peak salaries, ranging all the way from $10,000 to $100,000 and upwards. The best sales representatives sell very wisely and have a thorough understanding of the buyers' needs. They must act as fashion consultants, and frequently write up apparel orders for buyers, planning the correct assortments, colors, and sizes on the basis of how much the buyer is *open to buy*. This can be quite complicated when dealing with the *coordinates* in apparel.

OPEN TO BUY

The sales representative must be able to present the customer

COORDINATES

selling benefits of their merchandise to the buyers and show their lines of clothing quickly, efficiently, and pleasantly. Market weeks are physically exhausting but it's a "happy" kind of exhaustion because the results of the sales during market set the wheels of production rolling at the manufacturing plant, and the rush begins to get the apparel produced and into the stores on time.

While this is not necessarily an occupation that is adaptable as a training position while you are in college, it is certainly one that you should not overlook after you have completed your education. If you live in or near a market area, you might be able to get a few days' release from your regular part-time fashion job in order to work in the market either as a model or showroom salesperson. Employers are usually pleased to see that students get this kind of experience, and are quite cooperative. Table 2–1 shows the jobs in the manufacturing area and some of the specifications of each. The table should help you understand these jobs.

Could I begin to get experience in the market right away?

FASHION RETAILING JOBS

There are many more fashion opportunities available in the fashion retailing field than at the manufacturing level. Good jobs exist in the many large department stores, the multiple chain-store organizations, the specialty stores for men, women, and children, or in the smaller, more exclusive fashion boutiques. Your beginning here will probably be as a floor salesperson. The yearly salary ranges from $4,000 to $12,000 and up. Compensation for the experienced and capable floor salesperson is sometimes paid as a straight salary, a salary plus commission on sales, or as a straight commission. One of the more satisfactory plans for an experienced salesperson who has a good-sized customer clientele is the base salary plus commission. For example, you might be paid $20 per day for a sales quota of $500. For every sale you make beyond your quota you are paid a commission of perhaps 5 percent. On the sales floor of a store that enjoys considerable fashion traffic and where high-fashion ready-to-wear is carried, you could easily earn upwards of $1,000 a month if you were an especially good fashion salesperson with a loyal customer following. Some salespeople of this caliber enjoy their customer relationships so much that they would rather do this kind of work than any other in the field of fashion merchandising.

BOUTIQUE

Do fashion salespeople always earn minimum wages?

FASHION MERCHANDISING ADVANCEMENT

With an outstanding sales performance experience record and your college education, you may advance to the position of *assistant department buyer* in a larger departmentalized store. Both men and

ASSISTANT BUYER

women do well in such positions. Salaries at this level range from $7,000 to $12,000 a year, or more.

The assistant department buyer assists the department buyer in all buying responsibilities, and follows up on the purchases of all merchandise for the department to make sure that items are in the store on time, properly priced and marked, and placed in stock. This person may be responsible for ordering some assigned lines of merchandise and may handle most of the reorders. A great deal of the assistant department buyer's time is spent on bookwork, so he/she is on the sales floor only occasionally.

Do I always have to sell to be successful in merchandising?

From the position of assistant department buyer, you can advance to *department buyer.* Those with education, training, and an excellent floor selling record can advance quite rapidly. In this position your salary and responsibilities increase because you are now fully responsible for the purchasing of all the apparel that will be carried in your department. You accomplish this by attending the markets regularly and by consulting with the manufacturing sales representatives who call on you in the store. You also work with your own store merchandising manager and some of the other store executives in planning sessions related to sales promotion, advertising, and general operation of your department.

DEPARTMENT BUYER

Excellent customer sense is necessary as well as a thorough understanding of fashion trend information, because as a buyer you must secure the right merchandise and have it in your store for your customers at the right time and price. You will be evaluated by your store executives on the basis of the number of markdowns you may have to take to clear a slow-selling line of merchandise which you may not have purchased wisely. While it is normal to clear your inventory through markdowns at the end of a season, too many markdowns are not acceptable and can be disastrous to your career. You can't afford to have such markdowns occur too often.

Temperamentally, a buyer must have great poise and emotional control because the pace of activity is rapid, often requiring quick decisions. Travel can be one of the more exciting parts of this job, but don't count on doing a great deal of sightseeing during the market showings. In New York, for example, you would spend most of your days in the area of Seventh Avenue—the market showroom area—and in the evenings you would be busy finalizing your planning of assortments to buy and making out orders. Seventh Avenue is an exciting area to be during the showings.

SEVENTH AVENUE

If you carry exclusive import apparel in your department, you will probably travel to foreign markets in France, Italy, Germany, Spain, or to the Orient, particularly Hong Kong. This is an interesting job and offers much challenge.

Table 2-2 will provide you with a glimpse of the various types of fashion retailing jobs. Salaries of buyers vary so much that it is difficult

TABLE 2-1.   Fashion Positions in the Manufacture of Apparel

title of job	yearly salary	job description	abilities required	advantages
SHOWROOM MODEL (Men or women)	$6,000–$12,000+	Models sample lines of apparel in manufacturer's showroom, principally during markets.	Must make clothes look terrific. Must be able to wear sample size perfectly.	Exciting work–thought of as very glamorous. May be allowed to buy samples when showing ends, and about the time needed in the wardrobe. May become showroom salesperson.
SHOWROOM SALESPERSON (Men or women)	$7,800–$100,000+	Sells apparel in the showroom to retail buyers who represent stores in other parts of the country.	Must be able to sell wisely. Must get well-acquainted with store buyers, their stores, locations, and type of customer clientele they serve. Must have a good memory for detail. Must be able to show lines of clothing quickly, efficiently, and pleasantly.	Possibly very big money, if working on commission. Actually no ceiling on this plan of compensation. Could earn more than owner of firm.
MANUFACTURER'S REPRESENTATIVE (Men or women)	$12,000–$150,000+	Sells apparel in the showroom during market weeks. Sells the manufacturer's lines of apparel in the territory, traveling from city to city, to buyers by contacting them in their own stores. Checks their stocks, suggests reorders, assists in all ways possible.	Should be able to be of assistance to buyers in display and rack arrangements. Must be able to advise buyers about what to stock and when to get other types of clothing assortments.	Opportunity to travel and observe clientele of each store visited; meet store executives. Gain better knowledge of buyers' needs.

TABLE 2-1. Fashion Positions in the Manufacture of Apparel (cont.)

title of job	yearly salary	possible drawbacks	background	comments
SHOWROOM MODEL (Men or women)	$6,000–$12,000+	May work only during market shows, four to five times a year for about a week at a time. Must maintain sample-size figure—can neither gain nor lose weight.	Probably requires a modeling course, and experience in modeling.	Should be outgoing, tireless. Must have considerable poise and emotional control.
SHOWROOM SALESPERSON (Men or women)	$7,800–$100,000+	May work only during weeks of market showings, four to five times yearly. Could be employed all year if market remains open.	High school and college (merchandising major) preferred. Retail selling experience.	
MANUFACTURER'S REPRESENTATIVE (Men or women)	$12,000–$150,000+	Could be in territory long periods of time, away from home location.	High school and college.	

TABLE 2-2. Fashion Positions In the Retailing of Apparel

title of job	yearly salary	job description	abilities required	advantages
FASHION SALESPERSON (Men or women)	Minimum hourly wage at entry level, to $12,000 and upward at experienced level. May be straight salary, salary plus commission, or commission only.	May sell all types of apparel, such as women's clothing—coats, suits, formal gowns, dresses, shoes, furs; men's clothing—suits, accessories, shoes; boy's clothing, girl's clothing, or infants, on the sales floor of retail businesses. Calls customer clientele about special sales or new merchandise. Makes special orders.	Describes, and sells to individual fashion customers utilizing knowledge of the characteristics, quality, and merit benefits. Suggests matching colors, styles, and accessories. Advises customer on how to wear. Must know fashion trends.	Usually pleasant surroundings in which to work, and interesting people to work with. May lead to advanced positions. A basic training area for almost all of the advanced fashion positions. Excellent sales record is possible. May be selected for junior executive management training.
DEPARTMENT STORE ASSISTANT BUYER (Men or women)	$7,000–$12,000 and upward.	Makes sure merchandise purchased in market or on reorder is in the store, in place, and on time. Assists buyer in all responsibilities, and may place orders for assigned lines or reorders.	Ability to handle bookwork. Great organization ability important.	This position is regarded as the first level of fashion executive status.
DEPARTMENT STORE BUYER (Men or women)	Varied depending on expertise. $8,000–$35,000 and upward.	Selects and orders merchandise from showings of manufacturing representatives, basing selection on nature of clientele, demand for specific merchandise, and experience as a buyer. Authorizes payment of invoices or return of merchandise. Conducts staff meetings with selling personnel to introduce new apparel. Prices items for resale. May buy in foreign countries.	Excellent customer "sense," knowing how to buy the right apparel, reorder appropriately, and not have to take too many markdowns. Calm, poise, and emotional control important at all times. Ability to make fashion decisions quickly. Know about sales promotion, advertising, and store operation. In-store executive training usually required.	Buying trips to many markets in the U.S., plus possible foreign buying. Good chance of promotion to executive ranks in upper echelons of store.

MANY OTHER TYPES OF JOBS THAT MIGHT BE AVAILABLE IN RETAILING: fashion coordinator, traveling stylist, fashion illustrator, fashion display, fashion director, merchandising manager, etc.

TABLE 2-2. Fashion Positions In the Retailing of Apparel (cont.)

title of job	yearly salary	possible drawbacks	background	comments
FASHION SALESPERSON (Men or women)	Minimum hourly wage at entry level, to $12,000 and upward at experienced level. May be straight salary, salary plus commission, or commission only.	Hours of work can extend from early openings in stores to late closings. Must be on feet a great deal of the time; could be tiring work depending on person's enthusiasm.	High school and or college. College fashion merchandising desirable if advancement is hoped for in fashion.	Good opportunity to learn a great deal about the operation of a fashion business. Should attain an ability level to be a fashion consultant to customers—*not* a "sales clerk."
DEPARTMENT STORE ASSISTANT BUYER (Men or women)	$7,000–$12,000 and upward.	Days are full of activity, sometimes very rushed. Usually works on Saturdays.	College merchandising education essential. Outstanding record on sales floor often a prerequisite.	Must work well with people and have excellent human relations ability. Cannot be overassertive at this level.
DEPARTMENT STORE BUYER (Men or women)	Varied depending on expertise. $8,000–$35,000 and upward.	Job involves considerable responsibility. Selecting proper assortments of apparel to carry in the department at the qualities and prices customers need is sometimes very difficult and time-consuming.	College merchandising education again essential.	Offers great potential for success in merchandising. Feeling of being a part of the main operation of the store, and having some opportunity to influence the direction the store takes.

MANY OTHER TYPES OF JOBS THAT MIGHT BE AVAILABLE IN RETAILING: fashion coordinator, traveling stylist, fashion illustrator, fashion display, fashion director, **merchandising manager**, etc.

to state even an approximate figure. Store executives are rather reluctant to quote salaries because there is much variance in them. Salaries in fashion, just as in other types of employment, depend on ability, experience, education, and the expertise involved in getting the job done well. They are generally very good salaries because of the amount of responsibility that is required. The encouraging part about these salaries and jobs for a student is to know that advancement is possible to this position and that the salaries will be equal to ability level.

OTHER FASHION-RELATED JOBS

There are many other fashion-related jobs that might be of interest to you and that might become available to you. For some of them you may need additional specialized training.

Fashion magazines have many interesting jobs in advertising, copywriting, and reporting of fashion news. While a knowledge of fashion merchandising and good marketing techniques is highly desirable in such jobs, you should have additional education in journalism methods. Fashion writers for magazines and newspapers are very important in fashion, and are sometimes quite influential in setting fashion trends.

Can I do anything else in fashion?

It is impossible in this chapter to explain all the possible jobs you may enter, and it would be helpful if you read some of the books suggested in "Other Fashion Books That Will Interest You," at the end of this book. For example, there are some imaginative and creative jobs that you can actually create yourself. Recently, a young woman developed an outstanding business for herself by becoming a fashion consultant in a large city. She directed her efforts to the total development of a new image for a small group of selected clients. She advises them on all the aspects of their appearance, helping them select well-coordinated wardrobes that will fit all the important occasions they need during a season. She creates a total new look for her clients who need and appreciate her expert assistance. Such a job appears to be fun and exciting, and surely exceedingly different. It is a good example of what imagination and creativeness can do.

To say that the "sky is the limit" in creative possibilities in fashion may be an exaggeration, but there are many opportunities open to the educated and experienced person. Remember that one of the most important criteria for doing creative work in fashion begins with a good understanding of the basics in fashion merchandising technique.

Conclusion

Fashion is all around us. So are fashion-related jobs. After reading this chapter, you should be aware of the great importance of the fashion merchandising job beginning on the sales floor of a store that you like.

If you are wondering where large department stores find their junior executive candidates, then the words of Frank L. Perry, president of Dillard's Department Stores, Inc., will be of interest to you.

> Dillard's is a forward-looking, rapidly expanding company, and we are searching for bright and capable people to prepare for executive positions. We believe the best place to find these people is right in our own stores.

If you work as a fashion salesperson, it isn't enough to be just a "sales clerk." You must become a fashion consultant to your customers. You must build a customer clientele that looks to you for advice on all of their fashion needs. This is where the fun and excitement is—it is also where you can best show your ability, initiative, and potential to the store manager. There truly is a demand for bright and capable people for junior executive positions in most companies. The greatest thing about your fashion merchandising education lies in the vast field of opportunity that is ahead of you.

1. Define or identify the following. (Use the glossary if necessary.)
   a. Designer
   b. Manufacturer's sales representative
   c. Showroom model
   d. Boutique
   e. Department store buyer
   f. Seventh Avenue
   g. Assistant buyer
   h. "Open to buy"
   i. "Golden Rule Store"
   j. Fashion markets
   k. Fashion trend
   l. Coordinates

2. Why are there so few women executives in the field of fashion? Is this changing? How?

3. What are the requirements for advancement in a fashion career?

4. Why is fashion experience required for advancement? How do you get it?

5. Some business careers have a tendency to "ceiling out" in regard to salaries. What are some of these? Do you feel that fashion jobs "ceiling out"?

6. Explain the career opportunities in fashion apparel manufacturing for men and women.

7. Do all fashion buyers have to go to New York City to make their seasonal apparel purchases?

8. Describe the fashion retailing job you would like to have two

Review Questions

years from now. What are the requirements for it? Advantages or disadvantages?

9. Select a branch on the "fashion tree" and chart your progress to your goal.

10. How did James Cash Penney influence the direction in merchandising for American businesses?

Suggested Student Activities

1. Select a committee of two or three of your classmates to visit with a personnel interviewer in a large department store in your area. Ask the personnel interviewer what is expected of the new fashion employee. Report to the class.

2. List as many fashion executives in your area as you can. Note if there are more men or women in these positions. Why do you think this is the case?

3. Talk to fashion buyers and ask them how often and where they go to market. How long before the new seasons open do they buy merchandise? Do they try to visit the showrooms of new resources on their market trips? Why?

4. If you have a fashion apparel manufacturer in your area, arrange for your class to visit the business. Observe how its merchandise lines are designed, constructed, finished, and shipped. What is this company's method of introducing its lines to prospective buyers—by sales representatives in the territory, and/or through showings at regular area markets?

5. Ask a few fashion merchandising executives how they advanced to their positions of responsibility. What training and experience did they have? How long have they been in the fashion business?

Case Problems

Case 2-1. Marie has been on the selling floor in the women's sportswear department of a large store since she graduated from high school two years ago. Her sales are usually above "quota," and she enjoys her work with customers. She feels, however, that she would like to move into a position of more responsibility with her company, and wonders how she might make the store executives more aware of her ambitions.

1. What would you recommend that she do?
2. To whom should she talk in regard to advancement?
3. Do you think it is possible that her own department manager may not be aware of her desires?

Case 2-2. At the time George received his degree in fashion merchandising, he had been with an individually owned specialty men's store for three years. His bosses appear to like him very much because he has developed a good customer following and his sales are above average. However, he sees that there is little further advancement with his present store and wonders how to proceed to locate another position where he could advance into management.

1. Would you advise that he talk to his manager about it?
2. Would you advise talking to personnel people in other companies?
3. What should he say to them?

Case 2-3.   Debra is a starry-eyed senior in high school. She has just discovered that women become buyers for fashion departments in large stores, and thinks that she wants to become one just as soon as possible. She visualizes the glamorous life that fashion buyers lead going to markets in all the big, exciting cities and sometimes to Europe or the Orient. She knows you are a fashion merchandising student, so she asks your opinion about it.

1. What would you tell Debra to consider carefully if she wants to become a buyer of fashion?
2. Is her information correct about the glamor aspects of buying?

Case 2-4.   Cathy is about 5 feet tall, wears size 14 dresses and tends to be a little plump. She has a pretty face but has a slight complexion problem which she is trying to overcome. She especially likes new fashion items and thinks she would like to become a fashion model for them.

1. What would you explain to her about fashion modeling that would help her make a decision?
2. Would you recommend that she become a model, or would you recommend another direction that she might take in the world of fashion?

Case 2-5.   John is excited. When he accompanied the buyer in his department store to market recently, he met a sales representative who told him of a new men's suit manufacturer who wanted to hire field representatives. The salary would be on the basis of commission on sales. It's exactly what John would like, but he would have to stop his fashion merchandising courses. Since he lacks only a few months of completing his degree, he wonders what he should do. It sounds like just the opportunity he has been looking for, and he hates to pass it up.

1. Do you think it would be wise for John to stop college at this time and try to become a manufacturer representative?
2. Should he talk to the suit manufacturer about the job or not?
3. Do you think if he passes up this opportunity he will be sorry later?

Chapter 3

Getting the right fashion merchandising job

Objectives

When you have finished reading this chapter, you should be able to

1. Role-play with a classmate and demonstrate a professional job application that will be impressive to a potential employer
2. Explain the many aspects of preparation for job seeking and tell how they should be done
3. Describe the ways you can show poise, confidence, and optimism during an interview
4. State and answer some of the probable questions you will need to answer during an interview
5. List some of the follow-up techniques you might use after the interview is over
6. Name the three merchandising principles which John Wanamaker inaugurated that have had a profound effect on department store ethics and procedures, throughout the country

If someone said to you, "Meet me at the eagle," would you know where they were going to be? Millions of people would know exactly where you would meet, and not all of the people would necessarily be from Philadelphia. *Wanamaker's!*

In the center of the Grand Court is the famous Wanamaker eagle —the trademark of the store. The magnificent Grand Court in Wanamaker's main store, which is located in the center of Philadelphia next to City Hall, is nine stories high and can accommodate about 10,000 people. The eagle has been the place where people have been meeting in downtown Philadelphia for many, many years.

What does the eagle do for Wanamaker's?

The Grand Court is famous for still another reason. Above its gallery stands the world's largest and most majestic organ. Organ music has been part of the John Wanamaker tradition since the old Pennsylvania freight depot became the Wanamaker Store in Philadelphia. The founder believed that music inspiration should be a part of daily lives and work.

An organ in a department store? Why?

When the new Philadelphia store was nearing completion, Wanamaker, in one of his tours of inspection, was so impressed with the possibilities of the Grand Court as a music center, that he said, "I want the finest organ in the world built up there above that gallery!"

Because it would have taken too long to design and install the kind of organ he had in mind, the Louisiana Purchase Exposition organ in St. Louis was acquired. It was loaded into thirteen freight cars and taken to Philadelphia, where it was rebuilt in the Grand Court and heard publicly for the first time on June 22, 1911.

Of such things were the dreams of John Wanamaker made. Not only was he the founder of one of America's foremost mercantile corporations, but he found time from the very beginning to be an outstanding citizen in Philadelphia and nationally, as well.

He began his merchandising career in 1856, at the age of 16, when he was employed in the retail clothing store of Barclay Lippencott at a salary of $2.50 a week. He left there for a better position with Joseph M. Bennett, proprietor of the Tower Hall Clothing Store, at that time the largest business of its kind in Philadelphia. In later years, Mr. Bennett delighted in telling his friends:

> John was the most ambitious boy I ever saw. We used to go to lunch together and he would tell me how he was going to be a great mer-

[1] *A Short History of the Life of John Wanamaker* (Philadelphia: Wanamaker's).

63

FIG. 3-1. In the center of the Grand Court of Wanamaker's main store is the famous Wanamaker Eagle. Above the gallery of the Grand Court stands the world's largest organ, installed in 1911. (Courtesy, John Wanamaker, Philadelphia.)

chant. He seemed to be a natural born organizer; always organizing something. These are the things which probably account for his great success as a merchant now.[2]

On April 8, 1861, three days before the outbreak of the Civil War, young Wanamaker opened his own small clothing store. The outlook for the new business wasn't very encouraging. The sales for the first day were only $24.67, and the total sales for the first year were less than $25,000. However, the first eight years were marked by the same spirit of close application with which John Wanamaker had ap-

[2] *A Short History of the Life of John Wanamaker* (Philadelphia: Wanamaker's).

FIG. 3-2. John Wanamaker (1838–1922), a great American citizen and a man of unbounded determination, high resolve, and vision, built the great institution that bears his name. (Courtesy, John Wanamaker, Philadelphia.)

proached everything from the time of his early youth, and his unbounded energy and unceasing devotion to all details of the business caused it to grow.

In October 1871, Wanamaker inaugurated the "one-price" system, **ONE–PRICE SYSTEM** and its subsequent success became an incentive to other merchants throughout the country to follow his leadership. Under the one–price system, the same type of goods are offered for sale at the same price to all customers. Prior to this time, a form of bargaining had existed, and prices varied among customers. A one–price system assures fairness to all customers, and today it is the law in interstate commerce.

He also conceived the "goods returned and money refunded" principle in retailing. This meant that Wanamaker's would allow their customers to return anything they had purchased if they were not completely satisfied and their money would be returned to them. From the first he stood for truth in advertising. One of his cardinal rules in business was *accuracy in word and print*. Wanamaker advertising copy and retail policies have proved to be most potent factors in the rise of department store ethics and procedures.

In 1875 he bought the old freight station of the Pennsylvania Railroad at the corner of Thirteenth and Market Streets, and opened "The New Kind of Store" by adding to his original stocks of men's and boys' clothing, women's fashions, and merchandise for the home. His new business grew enormously until the entire block was gradu-

FIG. 3-3. (right) Wanamaker's main store in the center of Philadelphia next to City Hall Square as it looks today. It was built on the site of the old grand depot and became the largest retail store in America.

FIG. 3-4. (below) The old grand depot of the Pennsylvania Railroad was the site of the first Wanamaker store, which opened in March 1877 as a "New Kind of Store" in Philadelphia.

ally absorbed; and John Wanamaker became the owner of the largest retail store of the time in America, if not in the world. The old freight depot was subsequently torn down, and upon its site now stands Wanamaker's stately twelve-story granite structure.

Not only was Wanamaker the founder and organizer of this outstanding company, but from the very beginning he devoted much of his time to personal direction and general detail. In 1921, in commemoration of his sixty years in business life, he was presented with "the freedom of the city" award in a ceremony at Independence Hall. After the ceremony, the mayor and a number of distinguished Philadelphians gave a luncheon for him. The justices of the Supreme Court of Pennsylvania adjourned to attend the ceremony in a body. Congratulatory letters and telegrams from the President and Vice–President of the United States, the governor of Pennsylvania, and many others were received, and a resolution of congratulation was adopted by the legislature. Every detail of the day's celebration showed the high place John Wanamaker held in the hearts of his fellow citizens.

Mr. Wanamaker died on December 12, 1922. Those who have followed him in the administration of the store he developed have never ceased to draw heavily on his original inspirations. His policies of fairness and honesty are always employed, and it is for this reason that the name of Wanamaker still ranks high in the business world with the customers served by its stores.

The transition from city to suburban living was reflected by Wanamaker's in the 1950s when it began to establish suburban branch stores that would better serve the rapidly increasing number of suburban dwellers. By 1974 there were twelve branch stores located in Pennsylvania, New Jersey, New York, and Delaware. The headquarters remain in Philadelphia, where the facilities of the main store are completely modernized.

Wanamaker's today continues to strive to be worthy of the great heritage left it by its founder, John Wanamaker.

If you work for a man, in heaven's name work for him! If he pays you wages that supply you your bread and butter, work for him—speak well of him, think well of him, stand by him and stand by the institution he represents.

I think if I worked for a man I would work for him. I would not work for him a part of the time, and the rest of the time work against him. I would give an undivided service or none.

If put to the pinch, an ounce of loyalty is worth a pound of cleverness.[3]

ELBERT HUBBARD

[3] Elbert Hubbard, *The Notebook of Elbert Hubbard* (Union City, N.J.: Wm. H. Wise & Co., 1927), p. 42.

JOB APPLICATIONS

Finding the fashion merchandising job you want can be one of the most exciting parts about working in fashion. Many people, however, consider it about the most difficult thing they ever do. It would seem less difficult and frightening if they were more aware of the correct techniques to use in job applications. This is the reason for this chapter.

Most authors of college textbooks assume that you already know all about job application techniques, and this may be so. We are discussing it because even though you may have already made a successful job application or two, you will most likely make several more in your lifetime. When you reach a point in your fashion career when you want to advance to more responsible positions, you will again be faced with application procedures that may be similar to your original interview with your company.

In Chapter Two we discussed many of the fashion areas in which you might work with your qualifications as a fashion merchandising college major. While we will be thinking about retailing job application techniques, the same type of technique will apply to all other jobs as well, with only slight variations.

Job application techniques will be discussed related to three areas: Preparation, the interview, and after the interview.

Preparation

Many students fail to realize that there are a number of important things they must do before they actually interview for a job. Careful preparation in these areas is vital and may determine the course of a future career. The very first step in getting ready to apply for a job is to decide *what kind of fashion job you would enjoy*—what classification of fashion business you think offers you the most potential. Having done this, you must then *locate the job opportunities.* Next comes your *development of the all-important resume.* Finally, while you are readying yourself to *appear your best* during the interview, you will want to *anticipate the questions your interviewer may ask.*

DECIDING WHAT FASHION JOB YOU WANT AND WHERE YOU WANT IT

It is important at the very beginning to think carefully about the kind of fashion job you would enjoy the most, where you want it to be, and why you think it is the right kind of job for you. In making the decision, ask yourself (1) what kind of job you are best suited to do, (2) what kind of courses in school you liked best, and (3) what kind of work is likely to make you the happiest.

In selecting the company or business that you feel would suit you best, try to look ahead two or three years and decide where you would like to be then. *Goal setting* at this point is important to your future advancement. If it is your ambition to eventually own your own store, then you would probably like working in a smaller specialty type of business to start, for example.

GOAL SETTING

Look at several kinds of stores, large and small, and select several of these to consider as possible areas of job application. Perhaps you are already familiar with several of these because you have shopped for apparel in them and have already formed an opinion about the way they do business. Analyze your preferences and decide why you like a particular type of business best.

Ask yourself if you would be proud to be associated with one of these particular places of business. Successful work experience is vital to mental well-being, and the way you feel about your work will have a great influence on your overall satisfaction with yourself and your life. Your job career will identify you in the world and provide you with the necessities and some of the luxuries you want. Therefore, it is most important that you give direction to your thought about where you want to work and why. Many people get into an area of work accidentally, and thus may spend years working in a job they don't like and of which they aren't very proud. As a consequence they lose time in getting to their work goal in life (or fail to achieve it altogether), and are really wasting the employer's money as well. You will do your very best work in something that you enjoy.

When you have reached a decision about where you would like to work and have realistically considered your qualifications to do this kind of work, you are then ready to systematically compare businesses and rate them. No doubt you will have a first and second choice.

LOCATING JOB OPENINGS

Begin your hunt for job openings by telling your friends and family, teachers and counselors, that you have certain job aspirations. Ask them who they know in fashion that might be helpful to you. Generally people are eager to help the deserving individual find employment, and their assistance can be invaluable. If your school has a placement service, register there. If you are on a cooperative work assignment in fashion merchandising, you already have an "in," because fashion businesses undoubtedly know of your college program. The more people know of your wants and needs, the greater will be the possibility that several job openings will become available to you, improving your chance of finding the best job.

COLLEGE PLACEMENT SERVICE

It is not generally recommended, but you might list with a private *employment agency*. It may charge a small percentage of your beginning salary for its services. Even though not many fashion jobs are listed with these agencies, they are occasionally helpful because of their wide acquaintance with business people.

Is it helpful to register with an employment agency?

You might read the *want ads* in the newspapers. Retail stores seldom need to advertise in this way, but sometimes they do advertise for extra holiday sales help; often these stores advertise a new store opening as well. Beginning as an extra salesperson can help you learn some part of the store operation and to work with store personnel. This is a very good way to find out if this is really the kind of business in which you would enjoy working. It is also an opportunity for you to do an outstanding sales job that could bring your abilities to the attention of a department manager who might desire your services on a more permanent basis. Unfortunately, many want ads are designed to attract the greatest number of applicants and the job description may be deceptive because of this. However, many people apparently use want ads with great success in locating job openings.

Usually, your best method of locating the job you think you want is by a process called the *cold canvass.* In this case, you simply call on personnel directors in businesses you prefer. Making an appointment is preferable and highly recommended. However, sometimes personnel officers will not make individual appointments, so you must go to see them during the hours appointed for general job interviews. Cold canvass can be very discouraging—you may hear over and over that there are no job openings. You may find yourself thinking that there just aren't any jobs available, but this is never really the case. Some business, somewhere, does need your services, and locating that business is your objective—it won't know about you until you find it.

If you hear of a job opening in a business you would like, present yourself just as quickly as you can. The old saying about the early bird catching the worm is really true. Or if you read about a new store opening in your area, go to see the personnel people. Undoubtedly they will be needing many new employees. To begin your career with a brand-new store is exciting. You have an opportunity to help arrange the store for the opening—and this provides excellent experience.

If you have prepared thoroughly for your job application, you will be confident when the right occasion arises.

KEEPING A RECORD OF YOUR APPLICATIONS

Why and how do you
keep up with the
applications you make?

Whatever method proves most satisfactory to you in locating job openings in fashion, try to be systematic about keeping a record of every employment application. Use individual cards (3 × 5 size should be adequate) and record the date you applied, the name of the business, and the title of the person to whom you talked. Note when you might return to discuss a job opening if they give you any indication of when they will be needing new people. This will make your follow-up of earlier contacts more accurate. Your second contact with this company should be easier than the first one because they will probably recognize you and may be impressed with your organization ability and persistence. Many good jobs have been secured on this second contact. Of course, it is important to make as impressive a visit as possible on each contact. Try to leave the door open for future contacts, even when you hear the sometimes-familiar remark—"No openings!" Smile when you hear this, try to appear and be optimistic and cheerful, and ask when you might apply again for possible openings. Record the information as soon as possible after leaving the personnel office. Additional information that might be added to your job-contact cards would concern size of the business, its approximate age, the number of branch stores it might have, and anything else you consider pertinent. Before you leave the store, visit several departments and study the lines of merchandise carried. The more you understand about the business to which you are applying, the more intelligent you can be in your discussion of how your qualifications can be of benefit to that business.

THE RESUME: HOW TO PREPARE IT

When you apply for a job, one of the most important things you can do is present the interviewer with a well-organized, carefully prepared personal data sheet, called a *resume.*

You prepare the resume in advance and use it in addition to the application form, which you fill out also. It should be typed, include a picture if you wish, and include several items that would not normally be asked for on a job application form.

1. PHOTOGRAPH. Although a photograph is not required, it is sometimes nice to include one, not only to help the interviewer remember you and how you look, but because a good photograph says many things about you that otherwise might not be observed. Since there is such wide variance of opinion on the use of a photograph, discuss this with your instructor before you submit one in your resume.

   If you should decide to use a photograph, be sure it is current, pleasant-appearing, and businesslike.
2. COPIES OF THE RESUME. Assuming that you will be making more than one application, prepare several *good* copies of your resume. Keep one in your personal files at all times for quick reference. The others will be left with the interviewers where you make job applications.

   Good zerox copies are essential. Resumes are basically like good advertising pieces, and must be presented and reproduced attractively.

   Sometimes job applicants have their resumes commercially printed or copied. It is not very expensive to do so and looks professional. (It may also say to an interviewer that you plan to make many applications—which may be good or possibly *bad*. This is a matter of personal judgment.)

CONTENTS OF THE RESUME

The following items are recommended for the contents of your resume. You may choose to include other information—again, personal preference is important.

1. VITAL INFORMATION: Name, address, telephone numbers where you can be reached at all times or where someone can take a message for you; age, height, weight, social security number, and condition of health should all be listed. (Health may be shown by a simple statement, such as "No absences from employment for X number of years." Use your own initiative.)
   If you are married, include the occupation of your wife or husband. If you have children, give their names and ages. If they are very young children, women should indicate satisfactory child-care arrangements for the probable working hours. An interviewer will want to be assured that adequate arrangements have been made for a young child who might be ill. In other words, would the sickness of a child cause the mother to be absent from work?

2. EDUCATION: Begin your educational qualifications by listing your last education first. College name and location as well as major study area should be shown, as well as degree earned or in progress. If in progress, give the expected date of completion.
   It may be helpful to list some of the major specialized courses you have taken. Or, if you are especially proud of your academic grades, you might include a copy of your courses and grades as a part of your resume folder. This would be definite proof of your accomplishment. Then list the high school from which you graduated, its location, and date of graduation.

3. EXPERIENCE: Just as you did for your education, list your most recent employment or current employment first. Give name of the business, location, type of work, name of your supervisor, current telephone number, and state the reason for leaving this employment if you are not currently employed. (If you have been terminated, don't be afraid to say so, and give the reason why. Most interviewers can and will check on this anyway, so complete honesty here is best.)
   Students often say that all employment interviewers ask about former experience, and wonder how they are going to get experience if it takes experience to get a job. It is not necessarily true that you can't get a good job without some experience on a former job, but you should indicate in such a case that you have shown leadership responsibility in some of your school or home activities. For example, any job experience is better than none—list volun-

teer work you may have done for a hospital, charitable organization, home for the aged, and many others. All such activities indicate to an interviewer that you have used your time wisely and that you are dependable. For example, a paper route or baby-sitting responsibilities are also evidence of dependability.

4. HOBBIES AND SPECIAL INTERESTS: Any outside-school activity or organization in which you have participated should be included. Show offices you have held and any honors or awards you may have received. While there is some disagreement on listing hobbies, the best procedure might be to list them. It has been said that "life without hobbies indicates a dull person."

5. IN-SCHOOL HONORS AND AWARDS: Recognition for an activity well performed shows your special abilities. Younger people can usually show this best in relation to school, but it could be some honor or recognition earned in another area such as civic clubs or social clubs or organizations. They should be listed specifically, with details of what the award was, when it was earned; and it might contain an additional statement about the number of participants, or anything that shows the importance of the honor or award given to you.

6. STATEMENT OF OBJECTIVES AND GOALS: Sometimes it is wise to include a short, concise statement about your goals and aspirations. You might answer the question, "Where do you expect to be in two or three years?" Or the statement might be about your reasons for seeking a certain kind of fashion job.
You must be realistic in your goal setting. It wouldn't be very realistic at the beginning of a new job to plan to be the owner-manager, or the top executive right away.

7. EXHIBITS: Pertinent publicity that you have received (e.g., about an award or honor) might be included in your resume folder. The folder isn't meant to be a scrapbook of information about you, and it should be as small as possible. But it is really a kind of autobiography, and it should contain the pertinent details. Exhibits help an interviewer know you better. They are often an interesting starting point in conversation with an interviewer.
Copies of letters could be included—from former employers stating your eligibility for reemployment in their businesses and their willingness to recommend you.
You will be able to think of several things you could include in this section. Use discretion, however.

8. REFERENCES: Last of all, include a list of people who may be contacted for reference—people who know you well and who have given you permission to use their names in this way.
List at least three or four people who are former employers, ministers in churches where you have been an active member, neighbors who are in business, or educators with whom you have studied. Sometimes it is good to include a banker or credit reference.

*Who should I list as
references?*

Merry Carol Smith   Social Security Number   246-72-4156

    1837 Pleasant Valley Street
    Anytown, U.S.A.   817-555-7651
                    Messages: 555-4511

    Age: 23   Height: 5'4"   Weight: 120
    Health: Excellent.   No absences from work for the last two years.

EDUCATION:

    My College -- 830 Campus Blvd., Anytown.   Graduating: Spring 19--.
     Major: Fashion Merchandising.
    High School South -- 500 Happy Days St., Anytown.   Graduated: 19--.
     Major: Commercial Education.

EXPERIENCE:

    5/70 -   Famous Dept. Store, Ladies Sportswear, Anytown.
    Current   Supervisor: Mr. Joe Manager.   817-555-2345.
               Part-time, 30 hours per week.   Salesperson, assist
               manager with scheduling, display, and advertising.

    9/68 -   Special Boutique, 789 Shoppers Ave., Anytown.
    5/70.   Supervisor: Mrs. Good.   817-555-3478.
               Assisted with buying, inventory records, cash-stand
               operations, markups.   Part-time sales person.

REFERENCES:

    Mr. Joe Manager, Famous Dept. Store.
    Miss Joy Toknow, Personnel Manager, Famous Dept. Store.
    Mrs. Good, Special Boutique.

IN-SCHOOL HONORS AND AWARDS:

    College: Scholarship; Dean's List for two semesters.
             State DECA Competition: Fashion Sales Promotion
               Campaign, 3rd Place Winner, 19--.
             Winner, 2nd Place, History Essay Awards Contest.

    High School: Parliamentarian, English Club; Graduated in
                 top 10 percent of class.   (Do not include high
                 school unless graduated within the past three
                 years.)

OBJECTIVES AND GOALS:

    My career goal is to become an assistant buyer or to advance
    into an area of merchandising management during the next few
    years.   I am willing to become a trainee in either of these areas.

FIG. 3-5.   Sample Resume

List all the references by name, address, telephone number, and occupation. Include information about how you have known them.

9. COVER: Place your completed resume of personal information in a businesslike folder or cover; this need not be elaborate. Be sure that all the contents are typewritten, carefully organized, accurate, complete, and neat.

REMEMBER: Your resume will set you apart from the usual job applicant and will be about the most impressive thing you can offer in applying for a job. It also adds greatly to your confidence during an interview. Occasionally, a business that has no openings and does not accept an application will accept a copy of your resume for future consideration. You might consider taking two copies of your resume to an interview, one for the interviewer and one for your reference during the conversation.

PLANNING YOUR APPEARANCE FOR THE JOB APPLICATION

Planning as appropriate and impressive an appearance as possible is another preparation area of great importance. Since the clothing you will be wearing will be judged by an interviewer during the first few seconds of your application, you should dress conservatively in business attire and be immaculate in your grooming. Do not wear dark glasses, and do not chew gum. A dress rehearsal would be worthwhile to be sure you are comfortable in your apparel, and it can be most helpful if you ask someone reliable to evaluate your appearance. Also study your personal appearance in a mirror. Ask yourself if your clothing and accessories are becoming, if they are appropriate for the business in which you hope to work, and if your hairstyle and grooming are acceptable. Some makeup is appropriate for women, but it must be classified as daytime makeup. A person should dress as maturely as possible but still conservatively. It may be helpful to you in planning your apparel for this interview to observe what the salespeople are wearing in the store where you will apply. If it is appropriate for the sales floor, it would probably be appropriate for the application interview.

How important is personal appearance in an interview?

ANTICIPATING QUESTIONS THAT WILL BE ASKED IN AN INTERVIEW

Now it is almost time for your interview, and while you are before the mirror checking your appearance you can take the opportunity to anticipate and practice answering some of the questions you think you may be asked during an interview. There are several questions that are frequently asked:

Why would you like to work for our business?
What department interests you most and why?
What are your plans for your future? Your business goals?
Have you had any retailing experience?

Nearly every interviewer will ask you why you want to work for that particular business. Since you have already considered this carefully at the beginning of your job application preparation, you should be able to be direct and specific in your answer. Don't memorize your answer because it might sound rehearsed and lacking in sincerity. Practice answering the question in different ways to experiment with a good choice of words. And practice using the YOU attitude in your answers, too. People often put too much emphasis on the pronoun "I," and what you sincerely want to express is your understanding of the *company's* needs—not your own. Practice using the name of the interviewer (if you don't know it, secure it by calling the company operator and asking for it) and say, "Miss/Mr. _____, your company needs people who will represent them well on the selling floor. You want employees who . . ."

You will probably be asked about your future plans and business goals. Before you go to the interview think about the way you can express your belief that there is a good future for you in retailing and that you are eager to begin with a business where the training opportunities will be excellent for possible advancement. Be ready to give a positive answer, not a weak one such as "Well, I guess this might be a good business in which to begin my career."

You may be asked your preference on where you would like to work. Be ready to describe the kinds of merchandise you prefer to work with, but show a willingness to work in other departments if needed. (Here is where your early preparation work will pay off.) If the interviewer should mention the stockroom, for example, and ask how you feel about beginning there, you can ask what you would be doing in that job. Some businesses start new employees in the stockroom if they foresee potential for good development in the individual and want the person to learn everything from the "bottom" of the organization. It can be a very interesting place to begin, as a matter of fact. The newest merchandise comes into the receiving area first in the store, so you have an opportunity to see it and examine it ahead of almost anyone in the store. The stockroom is also an excellent place to get acquainted with store personnel in department management because they are keenly interested in the new merchandise arrival and the proper handling of it. If they like you, they might later request that you be transferred to their departments. All of this can be discussed with the interviewer especially as related to things you might do later in the organization beginning at the stockroom level.

You can expect the question of starting salary to come up during the interview. Thus you should be prepared to answer the question, "What salary do you have in mind?" This will be a good opportunity for you to tell the interviewer that what you will be paid is less important to you than the training you will receive—if you can be sincerely honest in saying this. Experience at this point in your career *is* really the most important thing, and most businesses pay at a similar wage level anyway. You could ask what the company usually pays, or ask what the interviewer suggests. You could say, appropriately, that the salary is negotiable. Occasionally, it is a good strategy to answer a question by asking a question (but not always, of course). So in answer to the question of what you expect to be paid, you could simply ask what the company usually pays. If you are employed elsewhere at the time of this application, you could state the amount of your current salary, and hope that it might be improved.

What do I say about salary?

If the interviewer should ask you about your former experience, be prepared to state where you worked and when, without stumbling over the dates of former jobs. This is an important part of your preparation procedure. Give the names of your former employers, also. Your resume can help you keep this kind of information clear in your memory. Speak well of former employment and experience. If you can't do this, it is better not to say anything, unless specifically questioned about it. Then, be completely honest, but emphasize the best things about your former employment. Be able to state your reasons for leaving a former job, but be careful about critical remarks. The reason for leaving a former job is significant in an interview because it reflects your goals and aspirations as well as your work ethics and attitudes. Loyalty to a former employer is a signal to the interviewer that you would probably be loyal to this organization as well.

How do I discuss former employers?

The Interview Procedure

Now is the big moment for which you have been preparing so carefully. You are ready for the interview.

MAKING THE INTERVIEW APPOINTMENT

Since many retail stores do not set up application appointments, you may not be able to make an appointment. You could check with the receptionist by telephone and ask what hours the personnel director sees new applicants. But do not call and ask if there are any openings, because the answer is likely to be "No." If you have been recommended by someone in the store who will be able to help you, then you might go in on appointment.

If I can't get an appointment, when can I go?

When you find out the hours for interviews, then arrange to go to the personnel office during those hours. Do not go too near the lunch hour. Try to go during conservative working hours if you cannot find out when new applicants are received.

FILLING OUT THE APPLICATION BLANK

*Should I be careful at
this point?*

If you are in luck and the company is taking applications, you will be given an application blank to fill out. The application deserves your most careful attention and should be thoroughly answered. You might ask the receptionist if you should write or print your answers. Then write in your clearest handwriting or printing—no fancy flourishes. Be sure it can be easily read. Most jobs have considerable writing and printing to be done, and this is where no errors should occur.

Do take your time in filling out the application. It is best to look it over carefully before you start. Watch your spelling—use smaller words if you cannot remember a larger word.

*What do I do if I make
a mistake?*

If you should happen to make a serious mistake in filling out the application blank, it would be best to begin a new one. Hopefully, you won't need to start over very many times, however. Still, crossouts would give a worse impression than asking for a new blank to fill out. After you finish, read over what you have written. Be sure you have followed the instructions exactly, and answered all the questions. If you do not understand a question, you can ask the receptionist what is desired. Every question is important. If a question doesn't apply to you, write "No," "None," or use the generally understood "N/A," meaning "Not Applicable."

When you have completed the application blank, hand it to the receptionist. If she isn't too busy, you might ask her to glance at it to see if it is filled out properly. Then wait quietly until it is your turn to be interviewed. This is a good time to read a book or magazine or visit quietly with another applicant.

THE INTERVIEW ENVIRONMENT

The atmosphere of an interview, friendly or otherwise, is the responsibility of the interviewer. Good interviewers establish a warm and friendly atmosphere immediately. For example, some interviewers do not sit behind a barrier such as a desk, but prefer to visit with an applicant at a round table in their offices or in a chair near the applicant. A good interviewer should never be gruff, hurried, or condescending, but rather should do everything possible to make you feel comfortable.

*How will an interviewer
act?*

As an applicant, you will be watching the interviewer just as surely as that person will be watching you. He or she will tell you many things about the company by his or her actions and manners during the interview. Interviewers sometimes lose sight of the fact that they may be making real enemies for their stores by being unfriendly or brusque during the interview of applicants. If you lose respect for an interviewer, you may also lose respect for the entire store.

*Can I act natural and
be friendly?*

The interview should be conversational. You shouldn't have a lot of point-blank questions, but the conversation should be directed with a purpose. It is your responsibility to carry the conversation along in a friendly way, also. Applicants usually are encouraged to do over half the talking in an interview. Talk freely about your background, your interests, your experience, and why you would like to work for the store. State your good characteristics and the benefits that you can bring to the store. The interviewer will respect you for being proud of your accomplishments. Look at the interviewer, be honest and straight-forward. Smile often and use the interviewer's name frequently. Try to think of the interviewer as someone interesting to meet and talk to —a new friend, for example.

A good interviewer should show interest in what you say and in getting to know you. The interviewer will not necessarily be looking for all your faults and shortcomings and should encourage you by using phrases such as, "that sounds interesting," "tell me more about that," "yes, go on," or "I didn't know about that." An interviewer ought to try to sell you on the company as being a wonderful place to work, not with high promotional stories, but by actual examples of the friendliness of the organization and why people like to work there.

Your appearance will be appraised, your experience record will be studied, and you will be compared with other applicants. Much of the decision will rest on just how much the interviewer likes you personally. If you are warm and friendly, the interviewer will sense that others in the store will find you the same way. Your interview can and should be a positive experience.

*I lost a job once—should
I admit it and say why?*

If there is anything in your past that might prove embarrassing to you if discovered later, now is the time to discuss it and give a complete, detailed report on what happened. It is so much better to tell the interviewer about it now than to have it reported later.

This should be the atmosphere you can expect in the interviewer's office. There should be nothing really frightening about it. The interviewer will be seeking the individual who can best do the job that needs to be done, and it is your responsibility to convince that person that you're the person needed to get the job done right.

THE INTERVIEW

Soon, the moment of the interview will arrive. Take a deep breath, stand tall, and smile to boost your courage as you walk into the interviewer's office. Keep smiling, and say, "Good morning, Mr./Miss _____. I am _____ _____."

When you are in the interviewer's office (and this won't necessarily be a long time) try to keep an attitude of success and optimism. You know you have much to offer the company, and you have been practicing and getting ready for this moment for quite a while. You are there to convince the interviewer that you are the person for whom this company may be looking, that you are a mature person, and that you can be a genuine asset to the company. It wouldn't be unusual to have a little "stage-fright" at this moment, but just keep breathing deeply and smiling.

The interviewer will ask you to be seated—don't sit until you are asked. Don't plop into the chair either—sit gracefully. Try to lean a little toward the interviewer in an alert position. The interviewer may start the conversation. If not, do say something very soon—for instance, you may state your reason for being there. By now you should be prepared to talk about yourself in a convincing way—your education, experience, and the reasons why you think you could be beneficial to the company. Look at the interviewer as you talk and remember to smile occasionally. Tell your story briefly, as convincingly and naturally as you can, being careful not to oversell yourself. When you conclude your story, stop talking. If the interviewer doesn't speak up at this time, you might ask if there is anything he or she would like to know in more detail. Act as if you are enjoying yourself and are appreciative of this opportunity. Remember, this is your chance to find out whether or not you want to work for this store. There isn't anything magical about evaluating the other person. You do it all the time. If you decide you do like the store and want to work there, tell the interviewer with all the enthusiasm you can develop, how much you would enjoy working there.

You should have brought along two copies of your resume, one for yourself to refer to and one for the interviewer. Probably the best time to present it is at the very beginning, before you begin telling the interviewer about yourself. As you present it, you might mention that you have brought it along to supply more information about yourself than may have been asked for in the application. This is a good conversation opener.

You have practiced answering the conventional questions that are usually asked in an interview, but what if you get a "surprise" question? Don't let it upset your poise. Consider why the question is being asked and answer it as calmly as you can. One interviewer always makes it a practice to ask two "surprise" questions to get an applicant's reaction. The first question is, "Tell me your best qualities." When that one is answered, "Now, tell me your worst qualities." Some applicants really get uneasy about this. You won't, provided you have prepared carefully. In this case you have already been thinking of all your good qualities in relation to your belief that this company needs you.

If you have any questions to ask the interviewer, this is the time to ask. But don't ask self-centered questions about days off, coffee breaks, or vacations. Show instead a regard for what the store would be employing you to do.

You will recognize when the interview is ready to conclude. A sincere thank you for the interview—for the opportunity to talk about employment with the firm—and a final statement that will help the interviewer remember you are in order. For example, you may say, "Mr./Miss _____, I do hope you will give me an opportunity to show you what I can do for _____ (name of company). I know that I can do a good job." Or, use your own ingenuity, but do leave on an optimistic note. The job may really be yours—and then, again, it may not. At any rate, you have done your best.

How can I end the interview so I'll be remembered?

After the Interview Is Over

After the interview is over, you wait for a response. Sometimes, a follow-up letter is a good practice. Write a short, friendly, and courteous letter to the interviewer with thanks for granting you the interview. Such a letter has a double purpose—it shows courtesy, and it gives you another opportunity to draw attention to your abilities for the job. Since very few applicants take the time to do this, you might double your chances of getting the job by doing so. This should be a simple, straightforward letter, on business stationery, typed or hand-written, such as Figure 3–6:

What should I do now?

Do go back to your record keeping right after the interview and record all pertinent information. If you think you may have made a mistake in answering any of the questions, note this so you can rehearse the right replies for your next application. Even if you think you will get the job, don't stop making other applications.

It is hard to wait, of course, but you probably should not call back to see what has been decided—especially not if the interviewer has said he/she will call you. One good interview with a company will help you make the second application even better because you will have so much more confidence. Even if you feel that your employment with a company looks favorable, don't count on the job until it really is yours.

If I think I'm going to get the job, should I wait to hear before making another application?

Conclusion

The purpose of this chapter was to help you to make a decision about what kind of a fashion merchandising job you want, to provide you with information about possible questions you may be asked in an interview, and about interview preparation procedures that must not be overlooked when you are job seeking. To be professional in your

Date _____

Mr. /Miss _____
Personnel Director
_____ Store
City, State. zip code

Dear Mr. /Miss _____:

Thank you for the pleasant interview yesterday. I hope I am being
considered for a job with your company.

From your description of the duties of the assistant manager that we
discussed. I believe I would be capable of performing them effectively.
My ____ years of sales experience with _____ Company and
my college courses in fashion merchandising will help me.

If I am selected for the position. it will give me great pleasure to
work with you and for you. I hope to hear from you soon. If you
have any questions, call me at ____-_____. Thank you.

Sincerely,

(Signed)

FIG. 3-6.   Letter to Personnel Director

job application is the best indication that you are going to be professional on the job as well. If you follow these simple suggestions well, someone, somewhere, is going to want you to work for them, and don't ever forget it. Soon, you will be launched in the career of your dreams.

1. Define or identify the following terms:
   a. "Meet me at the eagle"
   b. "One-price" system
   c. Goal setting
   d. Employment agency
   e. Want ads
   f. Cold canvass
   g. Resume
   h. References
   i. Application blank
   j. Job interview
2. Why do people generally fear making a job application? How can you change fear to expectation?
3. What preparations should you make before you go to make an application for a job?
4. Explain how to locate job openings.
5. What value does a record-keeping system of job applications have for you?
6. Why is a resume of your qualifications helpful to an interviewer? How can it add to your confidence in a job application situation?
7. Write or give orally an interview ending that could be used effectively.
8. What are some questions that are likely to occur in interviews? How should they be answered? Can you think of others in addition to those listed in this chapter?
9. If you had applied for a job with John Wanamaker, what do you think he might have asked you?

1. Role-play a job application with a friend. It might be of interest in class to show the right way and the wrong way to do it.
2. Prepare a personal resume suitable for job application.
3. Read the want ads in your local newspapers. Are there advertisements for sales personnel in fashion businesses? Read the want ads in WWD (*Women's Wear Daily*)—notice all the companies that are looking for "Sales Pros." Report your findings in class.
4. Secure an application blank from a local store and fill it out for practice. Ask your teacher to check it for accuracy, neatness, and clarity.

5. Write short answers to the following questions that might be asked in a job interview:
   a. Why would you like to work for our company?
   b. What would you most like to do in our company? Why?
   c. Would you be willing to accept a job temporarily in our receiving department?
   d. We only have one opening at present—in the _____ department. Would you be interested in that?
   e. What salary do you expect to earn?
   f. Are you willing to work some evenings until 9 or 10?
   g. Why did you leave your last employer?
   h. Tell me about yourself.

Case Problems

Case 3-1. Bill just can't seem to be successful at getting any job that he wants and applies for. No one seems to need anyone. He thinks he might have been hired at the last department store if he had just had some experience in retailing, but how is he going to get experience if no one will hire him? In reviewing the applications he has made, he wonders if he might have done anything wrong. Should he have shown disgust when the interviewer mentioned the starting salary? Wouldn't the interviewer respect him more if he asked for the maximum? Should he have answered all those foolish questions on the application blank that he chose to ignore? Maybe he should have worn his suit instead of his jeans and tennis shoes.

1. Can you suggest why Bill hasn't had a favorable interview?
2. What should he do in the future?
3. Suggest how Bill might have answered the questions about former experience in retailing.

Case 3-2. Jean wants to start working in a retail store. She loves clothes, but seldom buys ready-to-wear, because she likes to sew and usually makes her own clothes. She often shops in several local fabric stores for new fabrics and watches the new arrivals closely. She has never had any experience in a retail store and knows that the interviewer is going to ask her about her retail experience.

1. If you were Jean, how would you answer the question about retail experience?
2. Would you apply for a job in ready-to-wear or in fabrics? Why?
3. What might Jean wear for an interview in a fabric store, for example?

Case 3-3. Mrs. Jennings is over 45 and hasn't worked in over twenty years. When she worked she was a secretary but didn't especially like the job she had. She thinks she would like to work in fashion merchandising. She feels that she needs to do something but doesn't think her husband will like it very much if she goes to work. What she has always wanted to do is to open a small shop of her own, but she hardly knows where to begin.

1. What decisions must Mrs. Jennings make about her future?
2. Would you recommend that she open a small shop of her own? If so, what should she find out first? If not, what do you suggest that she do instead?
3. Do you think her age may be against her if she wants to work in fashion merchandising?

Case 3-4. James has just graduated from high school. He has worked in a supermarket for several years at night and on Saturdays, sacking, stocking, and, finally, as a cashier. He thinks he would like to leave the food industry and begin working in a large department store in the shopping center. He doesn't know which department he would like best and doesn't really know if he would like it as well as he does the supermarket work he has been doing.

1. What might James do to decide which business career to choose?
2. Would it help to talk to his supermarket manager about his problem? To what other people might he talk?
3. Can you suggest some college courses that he might take to help him make a wise decision?

Case 3-5. Betty grew up and graduated from high school in a small town. There are few job opportunities in her community and she realizes that she will have to go to a larger city if she hopes to work. She would like to go on to college, too, if she can afford it. She thinks it would be wise to do so because she wants to be as successful as possible. Occasionally, she and her mother shop in a larger city nearby, and Betty likes one department store there much better than any of the others because she usually finds what she wants. She would like to work in that store but thinks that she might have difficulty in getting a job there.

1. What should Betty do?
2. How can she find out more about going to college in the larger city? Would it be advisable?
3. If you were Betty, how would you proceed?

Part Two

Succeeding in the World of Fashion Merchandising

Chapter 4

What is fashion selling?

Objectives

When you have read this chapter, you should be able to

1. Explain the importance of the fashion selling job and the dignity and rewards attached
2. Summarize how a better understanding and ability to become involved in customer's apparel shopping problems is necessary in order to satisfy their needs
3. Describe the personality characteristics of the good fashion salesperson
4. State your own fashion selling techniques and procedures, including
   a. Customer approach
   b. Showing appropriate apparel to meet customer needs and wants
   c. Trading up
   d. Meeting objections and buyer resistance
   e. Closing the sale
5. Tell why a sale needs follow-through after its closing

I.magnin

CALIFORNIA SEATTLE PORTLAND PHOENIX CHICAGO

While many great department stores were rising in importance in the East and Midwest, there was an important fashion store beginning on the Pacific Coast, in one of the most beautiful cities in the world— San Francisco. This Golden Gate City had only been a part of the United States for fifty-five years, and the first transcontinental railroad had been completed only seven years before the store began.

Today, I. Magnin has twenty-two famous fashion stores that stretch southward from Seattle, Washington to La Jolla, California and extend eastward to Chicago, Illinois.

I. Magnin began as the idea and dream of Isaac and Mary Ann Magnin. Until her death in 1943, founder Mary Ann Magnin was the guiding inspiration to her sons, John and Grover, in running this famous store. The company has grown to great proportions, but the underlying principles she established—for style, fine quality, and good taste—have been faithfully followed for a century.

How did Mary Ann Magnin start her store?

The first little store started in San Francisco in 1876 as a typical pins, needles, thread, buttons, ribbons, and notions store. Mrs. Magnin made beautiful baby clothes for her store, and soon established a reputation for her fine needlework. Orders increased to the point that she had to hire helpers. Mrs. Magnin worked hard and untiringly, arising at dawn in order to arrive early at the wholesale houses to buy her materials. During the day she sold, and after six o'clock she supervised the cutting and making of garments to be worked on the next day. In addition, she took care of her family of seven children. In these early days, I. Magnin carried infants' wear, lingerie, and old-fashioned shirtwaists; bridal trousseaus and baby layettes were the specialties. Flawless workmanship became the trademark. The carriages of San Francisco ladies stood at the door of the little shop continuously.

Why was the I. Magnin store so favored in its earlier days?

Twelve years later the business moved from its neighborhood location to Market Street, then the main retail thoroughfare, and Mary Ann's son, John, later to become president of the company, entered the picture. The store had always had a fascination for him. Around the family dinner table the conversation was invariably about business, and John's eager questions were intelligently and patiently answered by his mother. She explained the fundamental practices of carrying on a successful store and instilled in her family a respect for the ethics of good business. Under maternal watchfulness John developed, and by 1892, at 21, he was in complete charge of the growing business.

[1] *Brief History of I. Magnin & Co.* (San Francisco: I. Magnin & Co.).

FIG. 4-1. Mary Ann Magnin (1849–1943), a founder of I. Magnin & Co., considered one of the store's greatest assets to be the loyalty of customers achieved through friendly and reliable service. That has been their sales story from the beginning.

(Courtesy of I. Magnin & Co., San Francisco)

In 1895 the company acquired a much larger store, which was equipped as the first "modern" store in San Francisco. It was this store that marked the beginning of the I. Magnin tradition for beautiful establishments. The stores have maintained such an outstanding visual appeal of warm simplicity that it is claimed to be possible to tell an I. Magnin store without having to see its name on the building.

What kind of store image does I. Magnin have?

The expanding "modern" store made it necessary to be in daily touch with the style creators of America and Europe, so the Magnins took a radical and unprecedented step and in 1905 established their own office in New York. From then, until John's death in 1944, I. Magnin became the only Pacific Coast store whose president was a permanent resident of New York.

Grover Magnin entered the business in 1905 and was given command of the business on the Pacific Coast while John directed all the buying from his New York office. He made his first European buying trip in 1904, thereby establishing the Magnin tradition of searching the markets of the world for fine products. From then on, I. Magnin & Co. has sent buyers to Europe every year.

On March 18, 1906, San Francisco was shocked by a severe earthquake, followed by a devastating fire that lasted four days. The loss was estimated to have been in excess of $250 million, burning five

FIG. 4-2. Founded in 1876 by Mary Ann Magnin, this present store of I. Magnin
& Co., opened on Union Square in San Francisco in 1948. It is the federated
corporate office headquarters.
(Courtesy of I. Magnin & Co., San Francisco)

square miles of the business buildings in the main part of the city, and
along with it the partially constructed new building for I. Magnin.
While reconstruction was going on, the Magnin home became the
site of business for the company.

Though this great business has grown to be one of the largest
distributors of exclusive merchandise in the world, its stores retain the
character and quality of small specialty shops.

In 1944, I. Magnin & Co. and Bullock's, Inc. were merged as a corporation, and twenty years later they became a division of Federated Department Stores. From a closely held family business, I. Magnin & Co. became part of one of the most progressive and successful retail corporations of our day. One of the greatest assets of I. Magnin is the confidence, loyalty, and respect of its customers, built through friendly and informed service.

The experience that is gained in fashion selling is useful in all phases of the fashion field; nearly all retail training programs include some selling. Many people just entering a fashion merchandising career begin at the retail sales level, and perhaps there is no better place to learn the realities of what fashion merchandising is all about.

In this chapter we will review the well-known techniques of successful fashion selling—techniques that will apply to all types of apparel selling to men, women, and children.

A salesperson's duties vary from one organization to another, but nearly all positions involve other activities in addition to selling—some record keeping of both stock and sales, maintenance of stock, responsibility for display, participation in fashion shows, and the interpretation and communication of customer reactions to department or divisional management.

The goal of every business is satisfied customers; they are a company's most valuable asset. Therefore, everything you do in your selling job, and everything the company does in every department of its operation, has but one objective—customer satisfaction. As a fashion salesperson for your company, *you represent the first line of customer contact*. In the customer's mind, *you* are the expert in the store. The way you conduct yourself will determine the opinion your customer will have of you and your company. It is therefore imperative that you as a sales representative become as professional and knowledgeable as possible.

PROFESSIONAL
APPAREL SALES
ABILITY

Fashion Selling

Whether you realize it or not, you are already an experienced salesperson. You have been practicing good sales techniques all your life in your relationships with your family and friends. You already know what satisfies their needs and wants and have acted accordingly. One of your best sales accomplishments will be the selling of yourself to the employer who hires you to sell fashion apparel. Fashion sales ability does not differ markedly from personal sales ability.

Fashion apparel sales ability involves assisting your customers to find what they need and want and then helping them purchase it wisely. This can be a deeply satisfying experience, because of the contribution you can make to customers' well-being. When you do this, you establish a good business relationship that will continue long after your first sale to them.

The Rewards in Fashion Selling

There are many rewards that you will gain from being a professional apparel salesperson. Of course, these rewards are in direct proportion to the amount of effort and enthusiasm you put into your selling job. There are many specific rewards of which you should be aware:

1. ADVANCEMENT. A good sales record is one of the important criteria considered by management for your advancement into jobs of more responsibility.
2. INCREASED EARNINGS. Before you have gained experience, your salary will be about the same starting wage earned in other beginning jobs. As you gain more experience and capability, you may be offered an opportunity to go on a quota-commission basis. Then, your earnings increase because you receive a commission on all sales above your sales quota. Thus your sales income rises in direct proportion to your sales volume. Many salespersons find the rewards of earnings so satisfying that they have very little desire to advance further in the organization or assume other areas of responsibility.
3. JOB SECURITY. The good salesperson has security on the job because all business operations are based on the abilities of their salespeople. High-caliber salespeople are in constant demand.
4. EXCITEMENT. There's never a dull day in selling. Every customer is different and helping with their great variety of different needs adds variety and excitement to your job. Probably the best sale has never been made yet, so there is the additional constant excitement and challenge for improvement.
5. ENJOYMENT. Selling is enjoyable because you bring pleasure and happiness to other people. You can take pride in serving and contributing to others' well-being. You must be sure to be able to tell the fashion story well—you must be a fashion authority. You must know the new seasonal colors and styles. You must build an exciting fashion vocabulary.
6. SELF-CONFIDENCE AND SELF-RESPECT. When you know

you are doing a good job on the sales floor—it's measured by your sales total each day—then you become more confident in your approaches to your customers and in presenting fashion apparel to them. You will also have the respect of your coworkers and of your management. Remember that selling fashion apparel is the main objective of your company's fashion operation, and your quality on the front line determines the success or failure of the entire operation.

The Personality Characteristics of a Good Fashion Salesperson

As we said earlier in this chapter, you have already developed many of the traits that are desirable in good sales ability. You can cultivate others as you realize their importance. A few of the more important traits for your consideration are:

What kind of a person do I have to be to be a good salesperson?

1. COURTESY. Since your customers are your guests while they are in the store, you should treat them with all the courtesies you would extend to guests in your home. You should be friendly, interested, and helpful in every way you can. The very least that your business can expect from you is courtesy to all customers, whether they buy something or not.
2. ENTHUSIASM. You have probably long been aware that when you are enthusiastic about what you are doing and saying others become enthusiastic also. If you really enjoy fashion, be sure to show people that you do.
3. LISTENING ABILITY. Listening carefully to what your customers say helps you learn their buying motives. Then you can help them satisfy their wants and needs more appropriately. Look at people directly with rapt interest and listen to them.
4. GOOD GROOMING. Any job requires good grooming, but in no area is it more important than in the fashion sales position. You must look like a successful fashion consultant. What you select to wear on the fashion sales floor should reflect your sense of correct business attire, its fashion rightness, and your good taste.

   Must you wear the latest fashions? If you are thinking of high fashions, the answer is no. But you must follow fashion trends. If women's skirt lengths are getting longer, then a saleslady would be out of place on the sales floor in a short skirt. If men's suits are featuring wider lapels, the salesman should reflect the trend also.

   Shoes are important. Be sure to wear comfortable well fitting shoes and keep them in good condition.

   Make quality more important than quantity regarding your sales-floor wardrobe. The same customers will probably not see you daily, so variety in your sales-floor apparel is less important than its quality. Avoid extremes in styles and concentrate on classic garments that have a longer wearing cycle.

When diamonds are shown to a customer, they are most often presented on a dark velvet pad to enhance their beauty. So it should be with your sales wardrobe. It should not detract from the apparel you are showing your customer, but be instead a beautiful background for what you are showing.

Your appearance checkup should also include cleanliness and a vital, cheerful, energetic look. These all come from good common-sense grooming and living.

5. IMAGINATION. Without imagination your sales discussions will be colorless and boring. This trait can be developed and improved if you learn to be versatile in meeting each customer's personal requirements. Try to be ingenious, distinctive, and different with each—use creative imagination. Add showmanship to your style of presenting apparel. But don't copy the style of anyone else—observe and study it, but develop your very own style.

6. HELPFULNESS. Get your customer's viewpoint and be understanding of that person's preferences. Give the customer your undivided attention. Think in terms of his or her interests and wants, and be helpful in satisfying them. Make sound recommendations on your customer's apparel selections, and practice the "you" attitude.

7. POSITIVENESS. A positive attitude will enable you to show confidence in yourself, a determination to succeed, and maturity. The mature person has poise, speaks carefully and purposefully, and knows when to talk and when to listen. Be positive and optimistic in your sales conversation.

8. CONTINUOUS LEARNING. Willingness and a desire to learn are essential to continuous learning. Prepare to do a better job every day by studying and reading everything you can about fashion merchandise. Know about fashion trends, new textile developments, the construction of garments, and why your store is featuring a particular style or color in any given season. Study the garments themselves and the hangtags attached to them. They will tell you the fabric content, care instructions, and special treatments the fabric may have had. They may also tell you who the designer was and the resource that produced the garment. Brand names are becoming increasingly important to customers.

Nothing is a substitute for a complete knowledge of the apparel you are selling. You must be able to answer questions your customers will ask and be able to supply facts about apparel that will be of benefit to them. You must be able to tell them, for example, why one garment is more expensive than another. You must be so knowledgeable that you can speak with authority and sincerity because false sincerity or knowledge is easily detected.

9. GOOD HUMAN RELATIONS. Good human relations involve the social qualities and abilities that help you get along well with other people. You should always be courteous and tactful, show a good sense of humor, and maintain a cooperative attitude.

10. PLEASANTNESS. No doubt you have heard "SALESPEOPLE SHOULD SMILE!" over and over. A smile must be sincere—not switched on and off automatically. It includes the eyes and the whole being. Cultivate a pleasant facial expression, and find as many occasions as you can to smile warmly and sincerely at as many people as you can. The warm, friendly, sincere smile is contagious. When you smile, "the whole world smiles with you."

The Customer Approach in Fashion Sales

After a day or two of in-store training on the use of the cash register and store policies and procedures (*systems training*), you will be assigned to a fashion sales floor department to assist customers. Service to your customers always comes first on the sales floor—before stock work, inventory, conversation, telephone calls, or anything else.

SYSTEMS TRAINING

Be alert for all customers entering your department. Then approach promptly and pleasantly with a sincere welcoming smile to set the stage for a comfortable, pleasant relationship. If you are busy with another customer at the time, recognize the new customer by saying, "Good morning, I'll be with you in a moment." Never allow that customer to wait unnecessarily long without further recognition.

Customers usually fall into one of the following groups:

Aren't customers all alike?

1. *Decided customers* (know what they want and why)
2. *Undecided customers* (want something—don't know what)
3. *"Just-looking" customers*

The last two kinds of customers are most frequently encountered. They have need for some kind of wearing apparel but may not be sure what it is or what is available. Be careful not to "pounce" on just-looking customers in your approach, or you may frighten them away from your department. Timing is especially important with the customer who is just looking around. Some sales experts recommend that you watch for the time when they seem especially interested in some apparel and then approach them, giving some information about the garments as you do so.

When they are "just looking," shouldn't I just ignore them?

Whatever you do in your approach to a customer, never start with a question that may get a negative answer. Don't say, "May I help you?" because their reply will likely be, "No, thank you, I'm just look-

CUSTOMER
APPROACH

ing." And what can you say then? If you make such a mistake in your opening statement, you should quickly say something like, "I'm glad you came in today. We've been getting many lovely summer items in, and I'd enjoy showing them to you while you are here." Many times the just-looking customer can be turned into an interested customer by the appropriate presentation of fashion garments.

Successful approaches that are recommended include the following:

1. *The Positive Merchandise Approach.* When a customer is glancing at a specific fashion item, direct attention to some special feature of the garment. You can smile warmly, saying, "These shirts are made of Quiana by Du Pont. They are comfortable to wear and launder especially well." By your actions, make the customer understand that you are offering an invitation to make shopping problems known to you. Be conversational about the garments. This is probably the preferred customer approach in most selling situations, unless the customer is not looking at anything in particular.

2. *A Question to Get Attention.* You can sometimes get attention by asking a question to provoke curiosity. "Hello! We're just getting in our new lines of sportswear. Would you like to see the new spring colors?"

3. *The Name Approach.* This is the best approach of all when you remember the customer's name. A little concentration on learning names pays big dividends—nothing is sweeter to anyone than hearing his or her own name. "Good morning, Mr. Anderson. Let me show you some new suits that I know you are going to like."

During your in-store training, you will be told the customer approach preferred. Regardless of the approach you use, your purpose is to get your customer's interest and attention. It is best to begin showing merchandise and talking about it as you do so.

Determining the Customer's Needs and Wants

It is often difficult to determine whether we *really* need something or need it because we *want* it. Not all needs and wants will result in the purchase of fashion goods, so only those that do result in purchasing are called *buying motives*. It is therefore important to understand the general buying motives that prompt our customers to purchase fashion apparel.

While physical well-being (comfort) is probably the strongest of all human needs, it will rarely be the sole reason affecting the decision of a fashion customer.

The primary buying motives of fashion customers are:

1. Physical well-being (comfort)
2. Recognition (acknowledgment and acceptance)
3. Preservation of self-image
4. Beauty, distinctiveness, originality

As a salesperson, you should be aware of the primary motives of your customers because if the primary motive is not satisfied, there is no sale. To recognize these motives observe the customer's actions and listen to what is said. You will have to interpret what is said, sometimes "reading between the lines." You can also ask probing questions: "For what occasions would you like to wear this suit?"

SECONDARY BUYING MOTIVES (SELECTIVE MOTIVES)

When you recognize the primary buying motive you can look into the secondary buying motives that will sell your apparel over a competitor's. Sometimes a customer may not be conscious of his or her primary motives. The most common selective buying motives are:

SELECTIVE BUYING
MOTIVES

1. Desire for durability
2. Desire for dependability
3. Desire for convenience
4. Desire for versatility
5. Desire for economy

Durability is the ability of a garment to wear well. This motive is directly related to the desire for economy. Durability and dependability are similar because customers want clothing that will last and be ready to wear when they want to wear it. Permanent-press fabrics, or other clothing that requires a minimum amount of upkeep or maintenance is usually most desirable, and economical too.

The versatility motive refers to garments that can be worn appropriately on several different occasions, or in several different ways. Price may not be a prime consideration if a garment has many uses and can be worn frequently. Economy and price may be the selective motive for buying a specific garment. Getting a bargain price pleases a customer, of course, but the garment must have several other characteristics that are pleasing to the customer also.

PATRONAGE BUYING MOTIVES

The buying motives that cause a customer to select one retailer over another are the patronage buying motives. The most important of the patronage motives are the desires for:

PATRONAGE
BUYING MOTIVES

1. Quality
2. Large assortment
3. Fashion exclusiveness
4. Customer services
5. Convenience of store location
6. Price
7. Self-affiliation with other patrons of the store
8. Friendship bias for the store itself

Women and men may buy nearly all of their clothing from the store that generally meets their requirements because of the store's reputation for quality merchandise. Or at least they will shop that store first before going on to another. A wide variety of clothing from which to select is often important to a customer also.

Fashion plays an important role. Customers usually have a desire to buy clothing that is widely accepted as the current fashion, so they shop at the store that offers the latest fashions. Such a store usually has a reputation for being a leader in design. The customer who is looking for "something different" will go to the store that specializes in merchandise that may not be available anywhere else.

Some fashion stores may be patronized because they give more or better customer services than others. They become well-liked because of policies for good alterations, prompt deliveries, credit policies, or other services.

While price, especially when it is low, may be the reason people shop one store instead of another, this factor alone does not guarantee repeat patronage for a store. Other patronage motives are equally important.

Self-affiliation with other store patrons is frequently also a buying motive. Belonging to a certain social group or *wanting* to belong to a certain social group may cause customers to patronize a particular store. Shopping where friends and acquaintances shop, or where a special social segment shops, is self-affiliation.

Friendship bias concerns the motive for wanting to shop in the store where salespeople are known to be friendly, helpful, and dependable.

A convenient location where parking is no problem may be the main appeal to the customer. Before making the trip to another store, a customer will usually look in these stores first.

RATIONAL VS. EMOTIONAL BUYING MOTIVES

Rational motives are based on reasoning, while emotional buying motives are based on personal feelings. The rational reasons for buying include a desire for quality, large assortments, service, convenience, and price. Emotional motives involve desires for fashion exclusiveness, self-affiliation, and a feeling of friendship for a particular store.

Naturally, all customers like to think of themselves as being rational in their buying decisions—careful, analytical, and economical. Even though they may buy for an emotional reason, they will usually try to justify what they have bought in terms of practicality. The woman who buys a fur coat because of a desire for recognition, for example, may rationalize the purchase by emphasizing the durability of the coat, its excellent price, its warmth, or its versatility. The alert salesperson must recognize the rational versus the emotional motives and be able to provide the customer with both—because both are usually present in any single buying decision.

Determining What to Show the Customer

After you have approached your customer, your next duty is to find out what he or she needs and is most interested in seeing. You can do this with a few well-directed questions, but don't bombard the person with "What size? What color? What style? What? What? What?" Usually the customer will give you a clue that he or she is interested in something in particular, and when that happens, answer positively. Say, "Yes, I believe we have just what you are looking for. Let's look over here first." Then, after locating specific clothing items, begin your sales presentation of facts and information. Later, you may show other apparel items which you feel might also serve the customer's need. Do interest your customer in something quickly and watch for further hints about particular needs and wants. Listen carefully.

How do I find out what to show?

Probably in no other area of salesmanship is there more opportunity to present beautiful merchandise with flair and showmanship than in fashion selling. The way you handle your apparel will show your customer how much respect and pride you have for it. Handle all apparel just as you would handle anything valuable. While it is important to show apparel quickly, never yank a garment from the racks.

How do you show fashion apparel?

Try to show the hanging garment in the most attractive way you can. Not all garments have hanger appeal, so it is your responsibility to make them appear as attractive on the hanger as you possibly can. Direct the customer's attention to special detailing of the garment which makes it different and distinctive.

Show a considerable amount of merchandise and watch for your customer's reaction to it. When she or he begins to show a preference for a certain color or style, show more than one garment like that. Offer some choice.

Not all sales experts agree on where you should begin showing price levels of merchandise. Some feel that you should always show the top of the line first. Others believe that you should begin at about the middle of the line, so if your customers object to price, you can show merchandise at a lower price, or if they object to the quality, you can show the better lines. Experimentation with where to begin in your price lines will be beneficial to you in this type of decision.

How much merchandise to show at first is also sometimes debated. Some salespeople believe that you should never show more than three items at first to avoid confusing the customer. However, probably more sales are lost because of a failure to show enough merchandise than because of showing too much. Continue showing merchandise until you begin to get favorable responses. When the customer indicates a dislike for an item, eliminate it and substitute another garment. When he or she seems to show an interest in a particular item, you may stop showing merchandise, and direct the customer to a fitting room to try the garment on.

If you will think carefully about how you like to have merchandise shown to you when you shop, it will help you treat your customers as you like to be treated. Some customers like to see merchandise as it hangs on the racks by sliding the sizes back on the rack, and thus going quickly through the available selections. In this case, be sure to remove any garment from the rack in which the customer shows special interest in order to show it more completely and attractively.

Good Fitting-Room Techniques

Satisfaction with fashion apparel comes mostly from its appearance when worn, so the importance of good fitting-room assistance is apparent. Most customers need help in selecting the most becoming garment, and you should offer advice as appropriate. When you know your stock well, you can easily bring additional garments to the fitting room that would fit better or be more becoming.

The length of time the salesperson spends with a customer in the fitting room varies from one store to another. With better apparel the salesperson remains with the customer most of the time, unless the customer prefers otherwise. When your department is busy you may need to help more than one customer at a time. Do not leave a customer alone for too long; check back frequently to see if you can assist or bring additional merchandise.

Until the garments are tried on, it is difficult to determine fit and wearability. Not all customers fit easily into the standard sizes and some alterations may be necessary. The too-long garment is easily altered, but some garment construction may be difficult or expensive to change. Only the alteration specialist can make this decision and determine the cost for the customer's consideration.

The salesperson's responsibility is to be helpful in getting the apparel to appear at its very best when worn. If it fits well and the customer appears to like it, then mention the positive qualities—fit, color, fabric, and fashion correctness. Begin removing garments from the dressing room as the customer eliminates them from consideration. This helps avoid clutter and confusion.

Making the Sale

Describe the apparel you are showing in terms of what it can do for the customer—its color, lines, quality, fashion-rightness, and versatility. Emphasize the appropriateness of the garment to the customer's probable need for it.

*How can I get a
customer to buy?*

Customers rarely buy fashion apparel just for itself—they want what it can *do* for them. So sell easy care, stylish appearance, and appropriateness for several occasions. Speak of interesting things about the apparel in terms of benefits. Use the "you" attitude throughout your sales discussion. Help your customer envision how it will be to own such a garment; then your customer will sell him- or herself. Speak distinctly and with authority and confidence about the garment so the customer will know you know and believe in it.

TRADING UP

There will be several different prices, fabrics, and styles in the apparel you show an individual, so sell the garments that are best for your customer. A person may not know the differences between the various prices, so it is your job to explain these differences in terms of the benefits. This is called trading up. It means selling on the basis of the value of a garment rather than on the basis of price alone.

What is trading up?

Most salespersons believe that the best method of trading up is by trading *down*. This means that after you have determined your customer's need, you should first show the best item you have which meets this need. Then, if necessary, you can trade down to an item with fewer features and benefits at a lower price. Say, "This is the best garment we have in stock for you, because . . ." If you must trade down because of price, you can show garments with some of the features of the better garment, but not all. Be careful not to speak disparagingly about a garment that is less expensive.

*How does trading up
help?*

There are many reasons why you do your customers a great service by trading up:

1. Customers really want apparel that will do the very best job in meeting their needs.
2. The additional customer benefits of a better garment will increase the value received per dollar spent.

3. Customers remember quality (or lack of it) long after they have forgotten the price.
4. Customers take pride in owning the best available.
5. Trading up increases your personal sales, which is the basis on which your sales performance in the store will be judged.

SUGGESTION SELLING

Does it do any good to suggest other things?

Another important responsibility you have as a professional salesperson is to suggest other apparel or accessories that the customer may need to go with what is being purchased. This is suggestion selling.

The best time to begin suggestion selling is after the customer has tried on several garments and reached a decision about purchasing one or more.

Most apparel items need related merchandise to be enjoyed to the utmost. A new dress may call for a scarf or a jewelry accent. A new suit may call for a new shirt and tie. Tell your customer what you recommend for accessorizing the garment. Remember, you are the fashion expert and you know the best way to complete the outfit. Customers need and want this kind of help.

Specialty-shop salespeople who sell in all parts of the store can do a terrific job in completing an outfit. If you are in a department store, your own department may have limitations, but you should know what is available in other departments and suggest that the customer see and consider it. Often customers may not be aware of what you carry in your store. They may not know, for example, about some special sales and reduced prices. They may be overlooking something that they really need and will appreciate your calling their attention to it. You do the whole store a great service also.

When you suggest an item, try to show it! Don't just tell the customer about it. Get it into the customer's hands, tell of its benefits, and give your customer a reason to buy it. If you sell a woman a pantsuit, don't ask, "Do you have a blouse to wear with this?" Instead, show a blouse, and say, "This is one of the blouses designed to coordinate with the pantsuit you have selected. They look well together and make a beautiful outfit when worn together."

Salespeople, especially newer ones, are often amazed at the way the power of suggestion results in increasing sales. Customers actually receive so little diplomatic help of this kind that they really hunger for such attention. And it is in the area of suggestion selling that a salesperson begins to show his or her real worth to the store and the customer.

CLOSING THE SALE

Sometimes customers will make a decision to buy apparel without your ever having to ask them to do so. When you see that they are getting close to making a decision, you should encourage them to consider a garment or two in particular.

How do you get a customer to say "Yes"?

However, customers generally need help in reaching the buying decision, so the professional salesperson starts planning for the close early in the presentation by getting agreement on minor details of a garment—its color, fit, and attractiveness. You should be persistent but not obnoxious in asking for a buying decision.

These are some successful closing techniques:

1. *Assuming the Close.* "Is there any further merchandise I can show you before I write up this garment for you?" or, "Before you leave the dressing room, let me bring you a lovely new pantsuit that I think will look well on you."
2. *The Delivery Close.* "Would you like to take this with you, or would you like to have it delivered? It could reach you by . . ."
3. *The Credit Close.* "Shall I charge this to your account?"
4. *The Choice Close.* "Would you rather have the white or the green? Or would you like both?"
5. *The Summing-Up Close.* Sum up the reasons for buying the garment and say, "Do you agree that this garment will do all these things for your wardrobe?"

You should, of course, develop your own style of closing a sale. Choose the type of close that fits comfortably with the individual customer. Above all, never tell your complete sales story before you have asked for the sale. Your customer could need further convincing, and you'll have nothing more to add if you've told the entire story beforehand. Trial closings during the sales presentation can help you determine sales objections the customer may have.

SALES RESISTANCE

Even though customers may appear to have found just the apparel they need or want, they may offer sales resistance by objecting to color, style, fit, price, or to buying it at this particular time. Objections indicate that the customer is seriously considering the purchase of a garment and thus offer the salesperson a genuine opportunity to expand on the fashion story.

When they say they don't like something do I just quit trying?

You need to determine whether or not the objection is merely an excuse or if it is a real obstacle to buying. Sometimes even though customers may intend to buy, they will still offer some resistance if only to convince themselves that they are right in purchasing.

You can ask the customer tactfully *why* they feel that way, to help them clarify their doubts. It may be helpful also to ask a customer if there is any other reason than that one for wanting to wait to purchase the garment.

A frequently used method of closing, and an excellent one is the "yes . . . but" technique. For example, if the objection is to price of a garment, the salesperson agrees with the customer by saying, "Yes, the price is higher, but . . ." and then offers sound reasons why the price is justified. Always add the satisfaction to be gained by having the garment and enjoying it now. Say, "Yes, it's true that this garment is more expensive than the other one, but when you consider the quality of the workmanship and the wearing qualities of the fabric, you can easily see that it is well worth its price. Think of the enjoyment you will get from this garment."

When your customer says "yes," stop selling and complete the sale.

MAINTAINING CUSTOMER GOODWILL

Aren't you through when the customer says "Yes"?

The closing is not really the end of the sale. Maintaining the goodwill of the customer after the sale is as important as closing the sale. This is where you reinforce the buying decision by assuring the customer that it was a wise decision. Say thank you, and compliment the customer on the selection. Offer any special instructions that may be essential to the proper wearing and care of the garment. Ask the customer to return again to your department and to you.

Carefully box or wrap the apparel. Prepare the sales ticket quickly and accurately. Some salespeople find it advantageous to add a little descriptive note to the sales ticket concerning the color or style of the garment purchased. Store policy will determine whether or not this is permissible. If it is, a little personal remark at the bottom of the sales ticket might carry your written "Thank You" or "I enjoyed helping you" and your name.

Do use your initiative and creativeness at the end of every sale to encourage the customer to return to you for additional help in the future.

Conclusion

Today's customers are sophisticated and have excellent product knowledge because of modern communications through television, radio, and advertising. The apparel salesperson can further contribute to their knowledge and appreciation of fine clothing by exhibiting an educated floor sales technique and a willingness to be helpful in every possible way.

Selling is challenging, rewarding, and self-satisfying. It takes real teamwork among buyers, management, and salespeople on this "front line" of the business operation.

Since selling is what the entire business organization exists for, then even if everything else is done perfectly, failure on the sales front line means failure for the business. That is why professional salespeople are never in a "dead-end" job, and deserve and secure the high respect of the entire business organization.

Review Questions

1. Define or identify the following terms:
   a. Professional apparel sales ability
   b. "Dead-end" job
   c. Job security
   d. Needs
   e. Wants
   f. Systems training
   g. Decided customers
   h. Undecided customers
   i. "Just-looking" customers
   j. Customer approach
   k. Primary buying motives
   l. Selective buying motives
   m. Patronage buying motives
   n. Rational buying motives
   o. Emotional buying motives
   p. Customer benefits
   q. Trading up
   r. Suggestion selling
   s. Sales resistance

2. What are the rewards available to the excellent fashion salesperson —the fashion consultant?

3. Which sales approach to a customer is best? Give an example of how it should be used.

4. How can you discover your customer's primary buying motives? Secondary buying motives?

5. How can a good salesperson affect a customer's decision to return to a particular store in preference to another?

6. "Trading up is a great customer service." Do you agree? Why or why not?

7. If you have just sold a customer a new suit, or a new dress, what additional apparel could you suggest?

8. If customers offer some sales resistance to buying, what would you interpret it to mean? What should you do?

9. What are the characteristics that you like in salespersons from whom you purchase apparel? What do you dislike?

10. Which method of closing sales do you believe is the most effective? Why?

11. Which outstanding characteristic of I. Magnin policy do you feel has probably contributed the most to the success of the company?

1. Visit two or more departments in a retail fashion store, or two or more different fashion specialty stores. Observe the salespeople carefully. Compare and evaluate their sales proficiency in the following areas:

	STORE #1	STORE #2,	etc.
a. Approach			
b. Friendliness			
c. Interest			
d. Showmanship			
e. Trade up			
f. Suggestion selling			
g. Other areas			

2. Plan a sales-floor wardrobe for a salesman or saleswoman. Emphasize the special requirements of this wardrobe.

3. To enlarge your fashion selling vocabulary, read the copy in several current fashion advertisements in magazines or newspapers. List as many new selling words as you can that describe fashion apparel in an appealing, different, and interesting way.

4. Conduct a small informal survey among your friends. Ask them where they like to shop and why. Check particularly the number of times they answer that they like a store because of the salespeople.

Case 4-1.   Salesperson Jones is with her customer in the fitting room and has helped her reduce her selections to two remaining garments under consideration. Finally, her customer says, "I just can't decide about these dresses. I like them both, but they are much more expensive than I wanted to pay. I'll just have to wait a while and ask my husband's opinion."

1. What should Miss Jones say and do at this point?

Case 4-2.   Salesperson Johnson has been helping his customer in the selection of a suit. They have tried several suits. One coat of a suit is obviously not a good style for the customer—it is double-breasted and increases the appearance of bulk at the mid-waist. The customer appears to be about to buy this, however. Johnson is a conscientious salesperson and wants his customers to purchase garments that are appropriate for them and becoming also. He feels that the customer is making a mistake to buy the double-breasted suit.

1. If you were Mr. Johnson, how would you encourage the customer to purchase the more becoming style?
2. If the customer persists in wanting to purchase the double-breasted suit, what should Mr. Johnson do?

Case 4-3. Mrs. Hardee's customer has narrowed down the selection of garments she has been trying on to three. All are of different prices and all are relatively becoming to her. The more expensive garment has beautiful fabric and construction and would obviously be the better garment for her customer's needs. Mrs. Hardee would like to see her customer decide on that one.

1. How can Mrs. Hardee trade up her customer's selection?
2. If the customer appears to be on the verge of selecting the least expensive garment because of the price factor, what should Mrs. Hardee suggest to her?

Case 4-4. It is a policy in the better dress department for a customer to be approached just as soon as she has entered the department and is examining the merchandise. When Ms. Caldwell approaches such a customer, the customer says almost before Ms. Caldwell has had an opportunity to say anything, "I'm just looking today." She implies that she doesn't like to be bothered by a salesperson when she is looking around.

1. How can Ms. Caldwell let the customer know that she is there to help her in any way she can and make the customer feel welcome in the department? Explain what you would say in this instance.
2. How could Ms. Caldwell direct the customer to garments in her size range to be sure that she is looking at those that will suit her best?
3. What follow-up would you use with this type of customer?

Case 4-5. Ms. Barnett is the department manager of better sportswear. Her department sales have been lower than anticipated, and she strongly suspects that her sales personnel are not using the best techniques of professional salesmanship with the customers. She has observed several bad practices on the floor, also. For example, she has noticed that when the traffic is slow in the department, several of the salespeople stand in little groups and visit with one another. Ms. Barnett is calling a sales meeting in the morning, and is working on the items she thinks she should discuss with her people to improve the department sales figures and to motivate them.

1. What items should she discuss with her sales personnel at the meeting?
2. How can she motivate the salespeople to get to know the floor sportswear stock better during lulls in sales activity?
3. What policies and procedures should she establish for assisting customers?

Chapter 5

Special services offered by fashion stores

Objectives

When you have read this chapter, you should be able to

1. Explain why customer services are a part of store policy and how you can adapt them to your area of sales responsibility
2. Think of and suggest other ways to creatively use store services
3. Discuss why customer services are so important and why so many survey studies have been made
4. Summarize the reasons customers prefer shopping in one store rather than another
5. Find other ways to fit garments expertly, and know when an alterations person should be called
6. Sum up the ways of camouflaging figure irregularities
7. Identify what you feel is the main reason that Harrod's of London has such an excellent worldwide reputation for outstanding sales and customer services

Harrod's was established in 1849 by Henry Charles Harrod and has a world-wide reputation for quality and service. It is the largest department store in Europe, and carries the world's most comprehensive range of merchandise.

Knightsbridge, London SW1X 7XL
01-730 1234

BY APPOINTMENT TO
HER MAJESTY THE QUEEN
SUPPLIERS OF PROVISIONS
AND HOUSEHOLD GOODS
HARRODS LTD LONDON

BY APPOINTMENT TO
H R H THE DUKE OF EDINBURGH
OUTFITTERS
HARRODS LTD LONDON

BY APPOINTMENT TO
H M QUEEN ELIZABETH THE QUEEN MOTHER
SUPPLIERS OF CHINA GLASS
AND FANCY GOODS
HARRODS LTD LONDON

What's so special about Harrod's of London?

Known by shoppers the world over, Harrod's exports over $150 million worth of goods every year, mostly to the United States. Among the interesting and unusual exports have been:

1. a fossil, excavated in Texas, bought by Harrod's, put on display, then bought by a Texan and exported to Texas;
2. an authentic replica of a 1901 Ford sold to an Arab sheik;
3. a handkerchief sent to Los Angeles by Air Freight (air freight charges about $45);
4. sauna bath equipment exported to the Middle East;
5. a Persian carpet sent to Persia (Iran);
6. a one-pound sausage flown to a yacht anchored in the Mediterranean;
7. all breeds of dogs shipped all over the world.

Henry Charles Harrod, a tea merchant, did not foresee how the great company that bears his name would develop when he established his little grocery shop in 1849. When his son took over the business in 1864, the shop was modernized and expanded. By 1880 there were a hundred staff members who worked diligently from 7 A.M. until 8 P.M., paying a fine for every quarter of an hour they were late.

In December 1883, the store, full of Christmas stock, was entirely destroyed by fire. Charles Harrod opened an office next day across the street and Christmas business that year beat all previous records. Perhaps the letter sent to customers on the day following the fire helped:

Did Harrod's have any problems getting started?

Rebuilding was begun immediately, and during the interim the Haymarket stores dealt with the orders, using Harrod's labels. Harrod's business grew and expanded, and in 1898, the first escalator (from America) in a London store was installed. The staff had increased to 4,000 by 1908, and Harrod's was given its first Royal Warrant from Queen Mary. When Charles Harrod retired in 1916, Richard Burbidge became general manager and was subsequently made a Baron by King George V.

Can competitive businesses work together?

FIG. 5-1. One of the largest department stores in Europe, Harrods dates from 1912. It has always been their policy to retain the store's original features as much as possible, despite enlargements and reorganization.

(Courtesy, Harrods Limited, Knightsbridge London.)

Europeans preserve original construction—do we do this in America?

As the store has been enlarged and reorganized, it has always been the policy to retain as many of the original decorations and features as possible. Today in Harrod's, the plaster ceilings are original as are the light fittings on the ground floor. All are of great architectural interest as fine examples of the period. The front on Harrod's dates from 1912.

The staff numbers 4,000 regulars, and rises to 5,000 at Christmas. The great store covers four and a half acres and has thirteen and a half acres of selling space. There is a quarter of a mile of display windows. There are 214 departments, of which 34 are fashion departments. Proud of its reputation for high standards of knowledgeable and

What does Harrod's look for in new employees?

courteous service to its customers, Harrod's looks for trainees with "lots of enthusiasm, common-sense, an ability to get on with people,

```
            Harrods Stores
            101, 103, 105 Brompton Rd.
            7th December, 1883

Madam

    I greatly regret to inform you that, in consequence of
the above premises being burnt down, your order will be
delayed in the execution a day or two.  I hope, in the course
of Tuesday or Wednesday next, to be able to forward it.

    In the meantime, may I ask you for your kind
indulgence.

                        Your obedient servant,




                        C.  D.  Harrod


P. S.  All communication to be addressed to 78 Brompton Rd.
```

FIG. 5-2.   Letter from Charles Harrod to customers

How does Harrod's train employees?

a will to build a sound and interesting career, and good health." The store offers one-year training courses designed to give all employees training in the basic skills of retailing. Trainees are assigned to three or more departments in different areas of merchandise. In addition to job experience, all trainees begin a two-year course of study at the College of Distributive Trades on a part-time basis to obtain the National Distribution Certificate.

Upon completion of the retail trainee scheme, the trainee can elect to become a professional sales assistant in Harrod's or apply for a second year of training. Selection for the latter is based on performance during the first year, and a successful interview and selection test. During the training, retailing skills and knowledge are developed further to prepare the individual to become a buyer's clerk, to apply for executive career training, or to take up a permanent position in a selling or nonselling area. During training, students are taken to visit manufacturers and Harrod's own factories to see the meticulous care involved in the production of high-quality items. Students are also asked to complete projects which involve research into various aspects of merchandise and retailing techniques and trends. After each job assignment, the trainee's performance is evaluated by the department supervisor, and reviewed and discussed with the training officer.

Do they have late shopping nights abroad too?

The store is open six days each week from 9 A.M. to 5 P.M., with late shopping until 7 P.M. on Wednesdays. Employees work a five-day week on a Rota (rotational) system—Monday to Friday one week and Tuesday to Saturday the following week. Paid holidays are two weeks in the summer and, after one year's service, an additional week in the spring and the autumn.

*GOOD BUSINESS—1912**

If I possessed a shop or store,
I'd drive the grouches off my floor;
I'd never let some gloomy guy
Offend the folks who came to buy;
I'd never keep a boy or clerk
With mental toothache at his work,
Nor let a man who draws my pay
Drive customers of mine away.

I'd treat the man who takes my time
And spends a nickel or a dime
With courtesy and make him feel
That I was pleased to close the deal,
Because tomorrow, who can tell?
He may want stuff I have to sell,
And in that case then glad he'll be
To spend his dollars all with me.

The reason people pass one door
To patronize another store,
Is not because the busier place
Has better silks or gloves or lace,
Or cheaper prices, but it lies
In pleasant words and smiling eyes;
The only difference, I believe,
Is in the treatment folks receive.

It is good business to be fair,
To keep a bright and cheerful air
About the place, and not to show
Your customers how much you know.
Whatever any patron did
I'd try to keep my temper hid,
And never let him spread along
The word that I had done him wrong.

EDGAR GUEST

In Chapter Four, we observed that customers develop patronage buying motives for stores that offer the kind of special services they especially like. We will discuss these services in greater detail in this chapter. Your familiarity with all services will make you a more valuable sales associate.

Most retail stores spend huge sums of money on their special customer services and on sales promotion activities to project a store image and personality in order to set the store apart from competitors. How unfortunate it is that a thoughtless salesperson or telephone

* Edgar A. Guest, *Today and Tomorrow* (Chicago: Reilly & Lee Co., a division of Henry Regnery Company, 1942), pp. 62–63.

operator can often cancel the benefits gained from these activities by some careless or misunderstood action.

When you understand and use the customer services you win repeat business for the store and play a vital role in its future growth, as well as your own. In this chapter we will focus on your special skills in developing fitting expertise.

What Are Customer Services?

*Why do people pass
one door to patronize
another store?*

Why customers trade at one particular store in preference to another has been the subject of many a customer survey. Generally these surveys reveal four areas that appear to be the most important in a customer's decision to patronize one store. They are:

1. The kind of merchandise the store carries—and its prices
2. The store location—its accessibility and its parking facilities
3. Special customer services the store offers
4. Informed, helpful, friendly salespeople

As a sales associate, you may not be able to change the kinds of fashion merchandise your store carries. You can offer suggestions to your buyers sometimes, but for the most part it is their responsibility to do the buying as they see fit in accordance with store policies and budget restrictions. Nor will you be able to change your store's location, or even its parking availability. What you can do to influence customers to shop at your store lies in your ability to suggest the many customer services available to them.

Customer services offered by a store are a determination of management and may depend somewhat on the policies of competitors in your area of business. Retailers offer those kinds of services that will contribute the most to the image and profitability of the store. Services vary from one store to another but here is a list of those that a full-service store generally offers. Some or most of the following will probably be available in your store:

1. Credit and layaway privileges; Visa and Master Charge cards honored
2. Prompt, courteous adjustments, and merchandise-return privileges
3. Alterations of clothing—usually free to men, not to women where the alteration may be more involved
4. Delivery—free within a city and suburbs
5. Personal shopping by telephone or mail order; all-night telephone order numbers often available
6. Convenience or accommodation services such as
   a. Rest rooms

b. Strollers for children, children's playgrounds, children's movie areas, supervised nurseries where a small hourly charge may be made by the attendant
c. Mailing and wrapping services for merchandise purchased in the store; post offices for mailing other packages, or purchase of stamps and money orders
d. Sidewalk delivery for telephone or other bulky orders
e. Restaurants and snack bars
f. Fur storage and cleaning
g. Shoe or jewelry repair
h. Checkrooms
i. Parking garages
j. Public auditoriums for use by civic organizations, garden clubs, etc., as well as in-store promotional activities such as fashion shows
k. Beauty salon
l. Gift wrapping
m. Lost and found
n. Merchandise gift certificates
o. Copy machines
p. Notary Public
q. Public telephones

The size and type of store and its policies determine which of these services will be offered. The type of merchandise carried and the target market will also influence the offered services. In addition, customers' income and buying habits can affect the service policy of a store. For example, the higher the income group, the higher its demand for services may be. Customers of smaller fashion specialty stores may expect more personalized services than in a larger store. Specialty stores sometimes have a free coffee bar for their customers. The price of the merchandise may cause customers to expect less service in a "discount" store.

Do all stores offer these services?

Store location may change the policies of the downtown area in comparison to a suburban shopping center. Delivery may be necessary in the downtown store, but in a suburban area where customers are usually able to park closer to the store, it may be less important.

There are other specialized customer services of which you can be a large part. One vital service is fitting expertise. For this you will need to know when to call in the alterations expert. It also involves the development of your ability to show the correct type of fashion to assist a customer in the disguising of figure faults. These will be discussed in the remainder of this chapter.

Are there any special customer services I can offer?

One way you can be of great service to your customers in a special way is to develop your fitting expertise and learn how to assist in camouflaging figure irregularities by the illusionary effects of fashion designs.

Development of Fitting Expertise

FITTING EXPERTISE

Since proper fit in a fashion garment is most important, you must be able to recognize the correct fit through the shoulders and hipline and to suggest an appropriate length. The size of a garment cannot always be the deciding factor in fit, so it may take considerable tact on your part to guide the customer into the correct size requirement. Above all, try to avoid allowing your customer to fit a garment uncomfortably tight. The tight-fitting garment usually reveals figure irregularities and may make a customer appear much larger than necessary. It may also be very uncomfortable, and be subject to excessive wear on seams, shoulders, and hipline areas.

Although there is considerable size standardization, there are still many size differences in garments from one manufacturer to another. Better garments, for example, are generally cut more generously, and sometimes a customer may take a smaller size in a better garment than would be required in a less expensive one.

How can I tell if a garment fits right?

In fitting your customer, consider these questions:

1. Does the garment fit smoothly at the neckline, shoulder, waistline, and hipline?
2. Does it hang straight?
3. Does it appear to fit comfortably?
4. What about the length? Could I place a few pins in a woman's hemline so she could see it at a more appropriate length?
5. Would another size fit the customer better?

ALTERATIONS

Part of your fashion fitting expertise involves knowing when alterations are feasible. When you serve a customer who does not fit easily into a standard size, you have a special problem. Some customers will need clothing alterations in almost any garment they buy.

Do not allow a customer to decide upon a garment that may need extensive alterations until someone from the alterations department makes sure the garment can be made to fit properly and can give an estimate on the cost of alteration. Also, look carefully at the way the garment is constructed—it simply may not lend itself to alteration. Sometimes there is not enough material. Do not make the mistake of encouraging someone to buy a garment that needs a great deal of alteration at the shoulder line. It is probable that such an alteration may be costly, and the final results may never be completely satisfactory because the alteration may completely destroy the original style of the garment. Since your customers expect you to advise them on correct fit, be sure that you do so wisely.

Can every garment be altered?

118

DISGUISING FIGURE FAULTS

119

CHAPTER 5
*Special services
offered by
fashion stores*

The great interest in dieting and figure-control exercising indicates that most men and women are aware of figure problems which they are eager to correct. Clothing can help immeasurably in disguising figure faults.

As a salesperson you can do a great deal to assist your customers by suggesting and selecting garments that will be the most becoming to their figure types.

Designers for ready-to-wear manufacturers are adept at recognizing lines and cuts for various-sized garments. They design clothing so it is generally "wearable" or can be altered comparatively easily. This is fortunate. From season to season, the designers will use these same cuts over and over with only small fashion changes or modifications. Perhaps they never become high fashion, but they are never completely out of fashion either.

Some part of nearly every figure will be too large or too small, too wide or too narrow to relate well to the total body look. While it is important to camouflage figure faults, it is well to remember that the successful garment should have smart styling as well as lines suitable to the figure. Sometimes, by encouraging a customer to choose clothing just to disguise figure faults you may eliminate good design smartness entirely.

There are many elements that play an important role in producing a contour that has style, beauty, and character. They are variously described as quality in the silhouette, proper fit, style, structural detail, texture, color, line direction and movement, composition, rhythm, balance, subordination or dominance. All of these characteristics are a part of a designer's training, and while you won't have to have as much knowledge about them as will a designer, there are some simpler methods of applying the principals of fashion design which you can easily use. The charts presented later in this chapter will help. But perhaps the best way to develop sound judgment of good fashion design is to practice helping customers of various figure types with their particular fitting problems. This is one of the quickest methods to develop your sense of good design.

*Do I need to know
everything about
design?*

We do not mean to imply that you should be overconscious of figure defects or irregularities. Your success in helping customers choose clothing to make the most of their appearance really depends on capturing the elusive qualities of style and smartness, and these factors are fully as important as improving figure irregularities. Three pointers will assist you in achieving the best fit for a customer:

*What can I do to
achieve the best fit for
my customer?*

1. Avoid fitting customers in tight, skimpy clothes that make them appear to have outgrown the garments. Such fitting will make the stout figure appear much heavier. Comfortable fit is most important.

2. Strive for a compact silhouette (profile or outline) without distracting details which may emphasize figure irregularities.
3. Learn what is generally best for the extreme figure types described in the following charts. Figures in between may profit from some of the suggestions as well.

People who experience the most difficulty in clothing selection are apt to be slightly taller or slightly shorter than average. Within each of these classifications, there will be the additional problems of being too fat or too thin. In most of the suggested ways to disguise these figure faults (or play them down, at least) the points will apply to either men or women. In some instances special suggestions for men or women will be listed.

The Taller Figures. Tall, shapely figures are considered to be an ideal figure type. But women who are over 5'8" or men over 6'3" should exercise great care in the selection of a wardrobe that will minimize their height. When people of these heights are too thin or too heavy, they have the additional problem of disguising these figure irregularities.

Unless the tall figure is too heavy, emphasis should be placed on horizontal lines. Since the eye follows a line, it is desirable to direct the eye from side to side rather than up or down. Horizontal lines may be achieved by contrasting belts, jackets, color contrasts between tops and bottoms of apparel, or horizontal stripes. Although simplicity in apparel is always in good taste, it is especially essential for the taller person. (See Figures 5–3 a–d.)

The table that follows will assist you in selecting garments for the taller figure types.

TABLE 5-1. The Taller Figures

Objective: To Achieve an Appearance of Less Height

too slender	too heavy
1. Use horizontal lines to minimize height by broadening and shortening the figure. Avoid parallel lines—diagonal lines or curved horizontals are better.	1. Limit horizontal lines to breaking up areas of vertical or diagonal line predominance.
2. Use of two colors and texture differences between tops and bottoms of clothing helps establish a horizontal rather than a vertical line.	2. One-color apparel is best.
3. Skirt length for women should be average or slightly shorter. Do not allow too much leg to show. For men, suit jackets should be long. Battle jackets will cut height also, in casual clothing. Double-breasted jackets may look well. Cuffs on trousers will give horizontal effect. Be sure legs of trousers are not too narrow.	3. Skirt length for women should be slightly longer. For men, jackets should be on the long side; single-breasted jackets are best. Cuffs on trousers should be avoided—they make the figure appear bulkier.

TABLE 5-1 (cont.)

too slender	too heavy
4. Women should wear skirts with fullness, pleats, or a slight flare. A three-panel skirt with a wide center panel will widen the tall, thin figure. A belt should be added to break the length.	4. Women should not wear too straight a garment, nor should it be so full that it emphasizes heaviness. Dominant center skirt panels hold the eye attention at the center of the garment. But they must not be too wide. A center seam reduces the appearance of width at the hips.
5. Sleeves should be cut fuller. Women should avoid sleeveless garments.	5. Simple, straighter sleeves are best. Try not to emphasize body width. Women should avoid sleeveless garments.
6. Belts that are wider and perhaps in a contrasting color add a good horizontal effect.	6. Belts should be the same color as garment.
7. Bulky, textured fabrics appear to enlarge the figure and are recommended: Avoid any fabric that has a tendency to cling to the body.	7. Softer, flatter-surfaced fabrics are best; bulky fabrics add an appearance of weight. Avoid stiff fabrics, because they too make the figure appear larger. Fabric that falls in close to the body with a flowing line is better.
8. Women's necklines should be rounded or square; large collars are good. Avoid the V-neckline. Also, avoid the low, bare neckline. In men's coats, lapels that come to a low-pointed V-front should be avoided. Three-button suits are desirable.	8. For women, some V-necklines will help reduce the appearance of heaviness. Lapels on men's coats can come to a lower V-point. Long pointed collars are good. Two-button suits are better.
9. Blouson styles, or square, boxy jackets are smart. For women, tunics, peplums, cummerbunds, yokes, sashes, or hemline-bands will add crosslines and appear to shorten and broaden the figure.	9. Less blousy styles that fit closely to the body are best. Women should avoid too much fullness at the bustline, waistline, or hipline.
10. Women's accessories may be impressive in size. Larger pieces of jewelry and handbags are helpful.	10. In women's accessories, moderation should be exercised. Jewelry must not be overpowering.
11. Prints or plaids may be larger and bolder. Plaids emphasize breadth.	11. Some moderation in size of prints or plaids is desirable.
12. Large details are best, such as large collars, cuffs, pockets, and belts. Women can wear high fashion and unusual garments with dramatic effect, such as capes, stoles, muffs, and short jackets. Small, cute, little-girl details are out of character. Clothes should not make a woman appear shortwaisted.	12. Women should avoid clothes with frills, bows, and ornaments. Details should be subtle and more tailored in effect. The tall, majestic woman needs restrained vertical emphasis and rather massive detail. She should capitalize on dignity and commanding appearance. Larger "Junior Miss" dresses will only emphasize her largeness. Long lines and massive spaces—never dainty, fussy detail—complement her height and dignity.
13. Good grooming is a must. Should be neat without appearing prim. Easy fit and freedom of action are important.	13. Good grooming is essential. Particularly if this figure is athletic, easy fit and freedom of action are necessary.

(a) Tall thin woman

(b) Tall thin man

(c) Tall stocky woman

(d) Tall stocky man

FIG. 5-3(a, b, c, d).   The figures on the left of each pair illustrate what thin or stocky tall males and females should *not* wear to emphasize their figure irregularities. The figures on the right illustrate correct styles and cuts to flatter these figure types.
(Drawings by Mary Jane Westbrook)

(e)   Short thin woman   (f)   Short thin man

(g)   Short stocky woman   (h)   Short stocky man

FIG. 5-3(e, f, g, h).   The figures on the left of each pair illustrate what thin or stocky short males and females should *not* wear to emphasize their figure irregularities. The figures on the right illustrate correct styles and cuts to flatter these figure types.

(Drawings by Mary Jane Westbrook)

The Shorter Figures. Women in this group are usually under 5'3"; men less than 5'6". They tend to be petite and slender or at the opposite extreme, stocky and overweight. For the shorter figures, shorter lines and smaller details are in order. It is important that the shorter person's clothing is proportioned correctly.

The vertical lines that are often recommended for the shorter individual to increase the appearance of height aren't always necessarily appropriate because they tend to exaggerate smallness.

For men and women with shorter figures, large, out-of-scale details such as heavy coarse tweeds, big yokes and pockets, or large-patterned prints will be overpowering. (See Figures 5–3 e–h.)

The table that follows will assist you in selecting garments for the shorter figure types.

TABLE 5-2.   The Shorter Figures
Objective: To Achieve an Appearance of Good Proportions and Height

slender	stocky, possibly overweight
1. Clothing and accessories must be proportioned to size.	1. Simple designs, neatly styled, are best. For women, one-piece dresses in one color are desirable. Belts should be of narrow, self-fabric, not cinched in too tightly.
2. Women may use simple, dainty trimmings. There should not be too much gathering or trim, however, because these tend to weigh the shorter figure down. For men, shoulders should not give an appearance of width.	2. For women, material may have easy gathering, but not too much fullness. For men, narrower shoulders and lapels on suits will increase the appearance of height.
3. A smooth silhouette is desirable. For women, princess and empire lines are good.	3. A smooth silhouette should be sought. Women should avoid too much fullness.
4. Soft, light-weight, smooth fabrics should be used. Avoid heavy fabrics and materials that are stiff. Avoid clingy fabrics also.	4. Fabrics that are soft but firm should be used. Dark, solid colors will produce a neater silhouette.
5. Jackets should barely reach the hipbone. Jacket suits and boleros are good for women. Long jackets and tunics should be avoided.	5. Jackets may be slightly below the hipbone. For women, jacket dresses are preferable to suits. They should be the same color throughout with no color change between bodice and skirt. Waist-length jackets should be fastened at the waistline to taper the waistline.
6. Use same color for jackets and skirts/trousers. Don't cut the figure height by a color interruption in the eye-movement.	6. Avoid contrasts in color in the garments worn.
7. Vertical lines should predominate; they should be broken only to cut design into interesting spaces.	7. Slightly curved vertical or diagonal lines, tapering in toward the waistline, are recommended. Unbroken vertical lines tend to make the figure appear older and perhaps too prim and sedate.

TABLE 5-2 (cont.)

slender	stocky, possibly overweight
8. Use narrow, same-color belts. Avoid wide contrasting belts with large buckles or heavy trim.	8. Avoid contrast in belts; narrow, same-color belts should be used.
9. Smaller prints or plaids should be used. Large prints or plaids will be overpowering.	9. Solid colors are best. Garments should be neatly fitted.
10. For women, full-length coats, fitted or boxy, are good. Avoid big pockets and collars. Use small accessories and jewelry.	10. Unfitted coats should be cut to hang as narrowly as the body permits, but not fitted to the body. Use harmonizing accessories and furnishings.
11. Avoid too much fullness in the garment. Straight lines are preferable.	11. For women, there should be only moderate fullness in skirts—but they should not be too straight. Emphasize small accents at the neck or shoulder line. Gored skirts with a slight flare contribute the most to height.
12. For women, extremes in the heels of shoes should be avoided; they should be neither too high nor too flat.	12. Women should avoid extreme in shoes.
13. Some moderate fullness in sleeves and sleeve styles is good for women.	13. Women should avoid too much fullness in sleeves. Slender sleeves are best—no dolmans, puffed sleeves, or batwings.
14. Sleeveless dresses should be avoided. Small bows and crisp, sheer neckline trim is excellent.	14. Women should avoid sleeveless dresses, large collars and bows. Soft, slightly V-shaped necklines slenderize face and neck. They add height and slenderness.
15. Fabrics may be conservatively textured. Should not be very bulky.	15. Dull-surfaced, flat-surfaced fabrics are best, but they should not cling to the body.

Conclusion

Special services that make shopping easy and pleasant within the framework of what is expected of the store are certainly important. As a salesperson you should use them wisely because each service has a cost to the store, and ultimately, to the customer.

You can augment your store services by becoming as expert as possible in the areas of fitting your customers well and attending to good design suggestions.

When you do, you increase your value as an employee, and customers will remember and return to you and your store.

1. Define or identify the following terms:
   a. Store customer services
   b. Store credit
   c. Layaway
   d. Merchandise adjustments

Review
Questions

e. Merchandise return
f. Clothing alterations (men or women)
g. Convenience services
h. Accommodation services
i. Fitting expertise
j. Illusions to disguise figure faults

2. Of the reasons discovered through customer surveys, why do you think customers are most likely to continue to return to a certain store for most of their needs and wants?

3. Why is it important to understand your store customer services if you are a salesperson?

4. Can a salesperson offer specialized customer services in addition to store customer services? Explain what the salesperson can do.

5. Name three important considerations you should use in fitting a customer well in apparel.

6. For people with tall figures, what is your main objective in fitting? How can you achieve it if they are too slender or too heavy?

7. What type of garment should you recommend to the shorter figure that is (a) petite and slender, and (b) stocky and overweight?

8. If the short and stocky or the tall and too-thin person insists on "going against the rules" for his or her figure type, what procedure should you follow?

9. Sometimes, handling figure irregularities gets into very "delicate" areas of sensitivity. What do you think is the most appropriate way to handle the customer who has a figure irregularity?

10. Customer services are what Harrods of London is famous for. How does this business train its sales personnel?

Suggested Student Activities

1. People-watching is a favorite pastime for many people. Sit in a mall or on a busy street and observe what the various figure types are wearing. Especially observe tall figures (slender or stout) and short figures (slender or stout). Report your analysis of how they were dressed to disguise their figure faults or how they ignored the suggestions in this chapter.

2. List all the customer services of selected stores in your area, and compare the amounts of services provided by the high-fashion or department stores with the services offered in a discount store.

3. Classify your figure type. If you have a figure fault, explain how it can be overcome in fashion apparel.

4. Think about the store in which you most like to do your personal shopping. Analyze your reasons for wanting to shop there and why you return there first for a shopping need. If you like several stores for various reasons, analyze which store you really enjoy shopping in most and why.

Case 5-1. Phillip Logan is a menswear salesman for better suits. His customer has purchased a leisure suit and a business suit, and needs the leisure suit for the weekend. The alteration is a simple one. The policy of the alterations department is to promise delivery one week after purchase. The weekend is only three days away.

1. What should Phillip Logan attempt to do to please his customer?
2. If the alterations department refuses to get the leisure suit ready in three days, how could Logan explain the problem to his customer and not jeopardize the sale?

Case 5-2. Christie is a salesperson for a high-fashion women's wear store. The store discontinued its delivery service several months ago because very few customers were using it, preferring instead to take their purchases with them. Christie's customer has just purchased several garments and asks for delivery of them to her address, several miles from the store. She has had delivery service from, the store before.

1. How does Christie explain to the customer that the store no longer delivers customers' purchases?
2. What if the customer says, "Well, if I can't have them delivered, I won't buy them." What should Christie do to help her customer?

Case 5-3. Judy Scott is a salesperson in a ladies' specialty store in a large shopping mall. Among the many customer services available at the mall is a nursery for which there is a small hourly charge. Judy's first customer comes in with two small children—one in her arms, and a toddler. She is tired and distracted by the children, who are restless.

1. How could Judy tactfully suggest to the young mother that she use the nursery service that the shopping mall provides?

Chapter 6

How you can help your fashion business make a profit

Objectives

When you have read this chapter, you should be able to

1. Identify the causes of profit losses in fashion retailing
2. Summarize the causes of shortages in inventory
3. Trace the ways shoplifters work, and explain ways a salesperson can assist store security in detecting them
4. Discuss the main causes of fashion markdowns and returned fashion items
5. Demonstrate methods of eliminating the problems in all of these loss areas
6. Recognize the importance of profit building in business and how you can be a valuable member of the fashion team

The history of Bloomingdale's is closely interwoven with the development and growth of the great city of New York. It began as a tiny store on Third Avenue in 1872.

bloomingdale's

Today, Bloomingdale's epitomizes the ideal of elegance in America.

It was in March 1872 after a cold, dreary winter when New Yorkers came out from under heavy overcoats and wraps to find Bloomingdale's ready to serve them. Central Park was noisy with the sound of children rolling hoops, the skating rink at 59th and Fifth Avenue had melted into a puddle, and all along the avenue people strolled in the spring sunshine. A few blocks east of the promenaders two brothers were opening a store on Third Avenue. One of them, Lyman Bloomingdale, at 31 had already spent most of his life in and around the world of merchants. He had begun his career with a summer job in a drygoods store when he was only 11. Lyman and his brother had been among those who went into business to satisfy the demand of the hoop skirt. The hoop skirt had been invented a few years earlier by the Empress Eugénie of France to conceal her impending childbirth. Because she was known as a stylesetter and trendmaker, women all over the world began to demand hoop skirts. But, as the hoop skirt fashion passed, Lyman and his brother decided to go into business for themselves.

Who started hoop skirts in America?

The brothers were convinced of the value of the Third Avenue address, especially because it had the two best plate-glass windows on the avenue. Lyman, who was one of the earliest to understand the power of advertising, saw in those two windows the best means of showing off their merchandise that money could buy.

Does advertising really help?

Their first day's sales at 938 Third Avenue amounted to the grand total of $3.68. This would have been discouraging to some, but not to the brothers; within a month they had increased sales to such an extent that a partition dividing sales from the area of the stockroom had to be torn down to accommodate new merchandise and new customers.

Change was to become the constant way of life for Bloomingdale's, for whenever physical or social alterations became necessary, the brothers never hesitated to make them.

During the financial panic of 1873, when a worldwide decrease in prices combined with a mercurial rise in stock speculation and overexpansion of the western frontier, the brothers were undaunted by the

[1] *Bloomingdale's 100—Perspectives on a New York Tradition* (New York: Reehl Litho, Inc., 1972).

havoc around them. Analyzing their clientele, they learned that their customers were mainly from the conservative middle class and still held their jobs. So merchandising policy was reorganized to offer the best possible values for the lowest possible prices.

As the depression burned itself out, Bloomingdale's kept growing. A greater variety of merchandise was what customers wanted, and the store met their desires.

With the completion of the Third Avenue elevated train, the brothers acquired a five-story building with good window space on 56th and Third Avenue, and suddenly Bloomingdale's had become a department store. Lyman began running full-page ads in the metropolitan New York dailies, a tremendous investment in the still-experimental field of advertising. But they worked! Bloomingdale's developed into a store with a believable best-value reputation, and the newspaper advertisements were spreading the word, bringing more and more of New York's rapidly increasing population into the store.

How does business location help a store?

As the Third Avenue "El" raced along New York's East Side, Bloomingdale's became more accessible to people living in the northern suburbs, and the sales records of the period showed incredible increases. In 1877, sales totaled $184,184. By 1883, sales had swelled to $851,156. But the "El" wasn't the main reason for the remarkable jump. Lyman's inventiveness, showmanship, and uncanny sense of communications were major contributions to the store's success.

Does it pay to adopt progressive changes as they come along?

For example, less than a year after electric arc lights had gone into production, Lyman had them installed outside the store. In 1883, only seven years after the telephone had been invented, and when there were only 4,500 in service in New York, one of them was at Bloomingdale's.

By 1886, New York and Bloomingdale's were moving into the future at a quickened pace. While Samuel Bloomingdale, 13-year-old son of Lyman, was sailing down New York Bay with the official party to unveil New York's most well-known landmark, the Statue of Liberty, his father was uptown occupied with the opening of a new store at 59th St. and Third Avenue. This was to be their last move, and it eventually became Bloomingdale's block.

Did people like to windowshop?

In an emerging residential neighborhood, the store location meant that more and more people would be strolling by the windows, so Lyman arranged with his architects to construct an unbroken line of windows for the store. Though the term "windowshopping" had not yet been incorporated into the language, Lyman had anticipated it. His promotional skills could not be matched. When elevators were installed in the new six-story building, Lyman named them "sky carriages," thereby attracting people into the store to try out the wondrous conveyances. They *were* wondrous, because they were finished in plate-glass mirrors and fine mahogany. Little upholstered seats carried

131

CHAPTER 6
*How you can help
your fashion business
make a profit*

customers in unsurpassed grandeur from floor to floor. Later, Lyman installed "inclined elevators" from the first to the second floors. They were primitive compared to the later escalators, but they were still one of the greatest attention-getters in New York, and those who came to see the sight stayed to buy.

Bloomingdale's achieved the status of a major metropolitan enterprise, so the brothers set their sights on distant horizons. Interest in almost anything of European origin was directing the retail market toward world trade. French fashions were regularly shown in Godey's Lady's Book, so Lyman sent a representative to Europe for the purchase of foreign merchandise. As the representative, Sam Mayers, crossed the Atlantic, he met Edward C. Blum, and through Mr. Blum, Bloomingdale's initial European connections were established. It was a prophetic meeting between the two men, because Mr. Blum became president of Abraham & Straus, and eventually president of Federated Department Stores, the current management corporation of Bloomingdale's.

Within a short time, Bloomingdale's representatives were crossing the Atlantic three times a year, so a Paris office was opened, soon followed by other offices in Berlin, Vienna, and later all the style centers of Europe. Bloomingdale's was a name overheard in conversations conducted in German, French, Italian, and Spanish, and wherever merchants gathered together.

Sales for Bloomingdale's soared. Lyman's interests led him into civic affairs in New York, and with other business leaders and government officials, the bridge to Queens over the East River was built. Although Lyman did not live to see this dream come true, his incredible drive, imagination, and contributions to the world of his time brought inspiration to those who came after him. Bloomingdale's continued to prosper under the direction of Lyman's son, Samuel, and the annual business in 1905 was in excess of $5 million.

*Did Bloomingdale's
believe in sales
promotions very long
ago?*

With the opening of the 59th Street Bridge in 1909, transportation linkage to Bloomingdale's became a simple matter. In what was the grandest publicity campaign ever "hatched" in New York, the phrase "All Cars Transfer to Bloomingdale's" became as much associated with the New York image as the Statue of Liberty. Richard Outcault, famous for his comic strips of Buster Brown, was commissioned to visually popularize the slogan, and that he did, in songs, slogans, umbrellas, and pictorial extravaganzas to make those five words known to virtually every New Yorker and every visitor to the city. In 1915, the subway that was developed under the sidewalks of New York made that slogan even more meaningful. Bloomingdale's definitely held the transportation advantage in Manhattan.

What had started out as a near-rural outpost store was now a great operation. Bloomingdale's ended the '20s with a sales record of

$24 million. Just before the new decade began, the store joined the Federated Department Stores, Inc. Through this cooperative venture, Bloomingdale's affiliated with other department stores throughout the country and strengthened their position for the dark days of the Depression years.

One way Bloomingdale's weathered the Depression was by changing merchandising methods to make it possible for thrifty people to find what they wanted without having to search through the temptations of higher-priced goods. This policy helped to fortify the image of Bloomingdale's as being the store with values for every customer. When the financial position of the country changed in the late 1930s, those customers whose needs had been anticipated in the depths of the Depression came back to the store that had helped them through the hard times.

In 1947, the exodus from the city to the suburbs was a mere trickle, but Bloomingdale's could see that the trickle would soon grow into a great cascade. In 1949, the branch development program began. It was the same idea that later started the shopping-center constructions that are now part of every major suburban community, but Bloomingdale's acted, opening many suburban stores while most other establishments were still thinking about the idea.

Does Bloomingdale's believe in fashion merchandising?

Today, Lyman would be pleased to see how his enterprise has grown. When fashion exploded during the 1960s, Bloomingdale's helped light the fuse. Styles drawn from a collection of international designers made front-page news, and women went to Bloomingdale's to buy them. Men were not neglected either. Pulling away from the grey flannels and white button-downs, men's fashions evolved into a brightly colored business. A rainbow of shirt hues for the contemporary man appeared in the store's Third Avenue windows, and Bloomingdale's became *the* fashion store in New York.

"It's my favorite store" are the magic words heard all over New York. Yet, the store still manages to keep the range of prices within the financial possibilities of every customer.

There is obviously no end to the Bloomingdale story. Tomorrow, and the tomorrow after that, Bloomingdale's promises never to rest on its laurels, but to unite the past, the present, and the future in anticipating customer needs and initiating fashion trends.

There are many ways in which the fashion salesperson plays an important role in his or her business besides performing sales duties. The three major areas in which losses occur, and that merit the special attention of the salesperson, are:

1. Errors that cause shortages in inventory
2. Theft of merchandise
3. Markdowns and the return of fashion goods

The salesperson who can assist in preventing losses to the company is a valuable asset to the business. This ability also directly affects employees and consumers as well, because a sound profit-making business provides steady, secure jobs and good products for its customers.

Stock Shortages

Stock shortages are of great concern to businesspeople everywhere. When the physical count of the fashion goods you have in your department does not agree with the figures in your books showing what you *should* have, then you have a stock shortage (or overage, a rare happening). It indicates that your fashion goods have disappeared and you cannot account for the discrepancy between what you should have and what you actually have. You know you didn't sell the merchandise, you know you didn't transfer it to another store—you just don't know what happened to it. It represents fashion items which you have paid for and had in your department during the fiscal period—but if these cannot be accounted for, many dollars are lost. Expressed in retail prices, stock shortages represent one of the most serious losses in business. One retailer says that for every dollar that is lost in merchandise, one hundred dollars worth of merchandise must be sold to recover the loss. The three chief causes for stock shortages are errors in inventory, records, and dishonesty.

How does a store know it has a stock shortage?

Why are stock shortages so very important?

What causes them?

ERRORS MADE IN PHYSICAL INVENTORY COUNTS

When you take a physical inventory in your department (this is done periodically in every business), you take an actual count of every item you have. This total is compared with the books. It is important that inventories be taken with great care and accuracy so that they will reflect the true picture of the stock on hand. There are no shortcuts. Every box must be opened and its contents counted, every gar-

PHYSICAL INVENTORY

133

ment on the sales floor and every item in backup stock must be counted. You must be exceedingly conscientious and thorough in taking inventory.

If there is a large discrepancy between your count of the stock on hand and what the books show, sometimes a recount is made, to be sure the first count was accurate and nothing has been missed.

PAPER ERRORS

For the most part errors in paperwork are honest errors. But they do show that someone has definitely failed to do his or her work accurately. Such errors are frequently made (1) in the transfers of merchandise from one store to another, (2) on markdowns, or (3) in the checking of invoices from manufacturers or vendors. Most businesses have a specified procedure for handling all of these activities, but carelessness on the part of employees can be the source of many unnecessary discrepancies.

Transfer Errors. You will probably have some responsibility in the handling of merchandise transfers from one store to another. When you do, you should count and recount the actual items and check the count against the actual entry on the transfer form. For example, if ten suits at $49.50 are to be transferred from the main store to a branch store, check to be sure there are actually ten suits and that the price tags are all marked $49.50. Then check the transfer form to be sure it shows ten suits at $49.50, and sign your name as the responsible person.

When the suits arrive at the branch store, the person there who is marking in transfers should go through the same procedure. Depending on the store system, usually a receiving sheet is written up. It should be signed by the person who makes it out.

If there are any discrepancies between the transfer record and the suits received at the branch store, it indicates that either someone was careless in the main store or there has been a theft in transfer. Always insist on correct figures on transfers to discourage carelessness and dishonesty.

Of course, transfers become much more complicated when a great deal of merchandise at several different prices is transferred. This is frequently where errors in extensions occur. Unfortunately, many people cannot do simple multiplication. Always be sure your records are as accurate as you can make them, and always check the work done by someone else. Then you will eliminate a source of errors that occur so frequently in business.

Markdown Errors. Markdowns in a fashion department are another source of paper errors. The same procedures and the same warnings about count and recount also apply here.

1. Count and recount the number of items being marked down. Be positive of the number.
2. Check the actual entry on the markdown form and be sure it agrees with your count.
3. Check the price tags on all the garments to be marked down.
4. Place the correct markdown price on the price tags.
5. Check the extensions on the markdown form to be sure the correct total appears.
6. Sign your name.

How do you handle markdowns?

When the buyer or department manager pulls several garments from the racks which are to be marked down in selling price, and it's your job to do the paperwork for this, follow the procedure exactly as stated.

For example, suppose the buyer pulls twenty dresses from the racks that are currently marked $50 each. She asks you to mark each of them down to $40. Begin your work by taking all the garments to be marked down to the stockroom or to an office where you will be undisturbed, and keep the garments "off-limits" temporarily to any salesperson, until all the paperwork is completed. This may not be as simple as it sounds. Salespeople, anticipating the markdowns, become especially anxious to start showing the merchandise at the better price, and will try to take them back to the sales floor before the records are completed.

Count the number of dresses that are to be marked down, and count them a second time to be sure your first figure is correct. Check the hangtags to be sure all the prices on the dresses show the selling price of $50. Record the numbers on the markdown form. Then mark all price tickets to show clearly the new selling price of $40. Then complete your paperwork by making the extensions to show that twenty garments selling at $50 each have been marked down to $40 (20 × $10.00 = $200) in markdown total. Recheck all figures on the markdown form and sign it when you determine that it is correct in every detail—date, department, and classification. Then the garments are ready to go to the selling floor.

Is this markdown procedure really necessary?

Small errors can occur in any part of this procedure, as you will be aware. Prices in many stores are not marked in round figures such as our example, and probably there will be much more merchandise marked down at once at several different selling prices. You may think this is unnecessary work and that small errors are really of no consequence. Perhaps this is what causes the vast merchandise shortages that are of so much concern to businesspeople today. They're "people errors," and once they have occurred they are very difficult to trace. If, for example, you had only fifteen garments and assumed you were marking down twenty, that would account for an error of $50. Perhaps in a department that carries an inventory of several hundred thousand dollars this may seem very small, but it only takes a small number of such errors to amount to thousands of dollars in stock shortages and inventory.

INVOICE ERRORS

Can't you rely on invoices to be correct?

Invoice Errors. The receiving department will be the first checkpoint for incoming merchandise from the vendors (the producers or manufacturers of your fashion merchandise). The boxes should be opened and every piece should be counted and inspected to be sure that the amount received is what the invoice states has been sent. The receiving form should then be made out to show the number of items received with any extensions carefully checked. If any of the merchandise is to be returned to the vendor because of flaws or damages, an accurate record must be kept of that also.

When you receive the merchandise into your department, do not rely on the individual in the receiving department to have accurately filled out the report. Count and recount and check all figures and extensions to be sure that the amount of merchandise charged against your department has indeed been received and that all is correctly recorded.

Why do I have to be so careful when I write numbers?

Mistakes often occur because of illegible numbers. Sometimes numbers that cannot be correctly read are the cause of some of the worst errors that occur. Illegible figures are the reason more and more businesses are going to automation in every process that can possibly be converted to machines. If machines are fed the correct information, they are accurate. The problem is that human errors creep into the machines, and no one has yet figured out how to remove the human element! Machines will be accurate, but the information fed into them must be accurate also.

SALES-FLOOR ERRORS

Aren't all salespeople careful on sales slips?

SALES-FLOOR ERRORS

When a fashion department is humming with customers who are buying, poorly trained, uninformed, careless salespeople can cause many errors that later show up as stock shortages.

Poorly written sales tickets, incorrect extensions and totals have caused businesses to go to automated systems on their cash registers just as quickly as they could. (In Chapter Eleven we will discuss electronic data processing and how it has eliminated many sales-floor errors.) With automation, companies can do away with sales slips and the errors they sometimes generate. Studies have found that it is the salespeople who have been with the company the longest who make the most mistakes in writing sales slips. They are good salespeople, but they are sometimes poor on computations. Not only can an electronic register system eliminate errors by guiding the cashier through each sale, but it can also collect information vital to inventory and rebuying.

The sources of all paper errors are *people.* If you will make it a practice to count and recount, check and recheck, and compare your figures with all other figures, you will help to reduce errors that cause shortages in stock.

Theft in Merchandising

The salesperson who is on the selling floor most of the time is in the best position to control the dishonesty that causes stock shortages. Dishonesty that causes stock shortages is of two kinds: internal theft by employees, and dishonest customers or shoplifters.

DISHONEST STORE EMPLOYEES

Internal theft is a universal problem in businesses. Of the nearly $800 million worth of store merchandise that disappeared in one state in a single year, it was estimated that more than half was taken by store employees themselves. As a consequence, businesses nationally are now spending in excess of $15 billion annually for security.

Isn't everyone in business honest?

Businesses have employed security guards in plain clothes, installed burglar alarm systems, called in regular police protection, installed sonic movement detectors, closed-circuit television cameras, and even sophisticated anti-pilferage sensor systems.

About 5¢ of every dollar in the retail price of merchandise is added to take care of shoplifting, employee theft, and protection measures to control both. The cost is being passed on to the consuming public in increasing amounts.

No doubt the immensity of these figures is shocking to you and you wonder what has happened to integrity and ethics in business, to trust and loyalty to employer, and to responsible business employees.

If you ever see, or even suspect, another salesperson or employee of your company in any act of merchandise theft, it is your duty to report it to management quietly, privately, and immediately. You won't be a "tattle-tale" when you do; you will be carrying out your responsibility to your company, and doing just what you were hired to do—protect the company's merchandise.

Shouldn't I just ignore someone who I know is stealing?

Why employees take money from cash registers or steal merchandise is debatable. They may be unhappy about something that is happening in their jobs, or they may feel that the company owes them a little merchandise now and then because their salary is too low. If the latter is the case, such an employee should seek other employment in another job where the salary is more pleasing. At any rate, theft will be discovered sooner or later and there is usually a day of reckoning. Never again will they be trusted to handle money or company property in any other job, because records of dishonesty are recorded and available around the world in minutes.

They don't do anything to people who steal, do they?

SHOPLIFTING

Sooner than you think in a sales-floor position, you will encounter a shoplifter. Knowing what to do when this happens is of utmost importance. It is not always easy to recognize a shoplifter because there are many professionals who have perfected their methods to a sophisticated degree of efficiency. However, the majority of shoplifters, studies have shown, are just ordinary people. Over 50 percent of shoplifting is done by middle-income people, and fully 20 percent is done by upper-income people! Teenagers are the primary offenders, with housewives running a close second. Retailers have found that most of the shoplifters they catch could easily have paid for the item stolen.

Don't all shoplifters look like criminals?

Retailers have gone on a real campaign against such crimes. They will prosecute a shoplifter. A theft of over $200 is a felony, punishable in the United States by imprisonment and fines. Although 18 is considered the legal age for prosecution in most states, there are some states, Texas, for example, where 17 year olds are considered adults—if under 17, they go to juvenile court and the punishment depends on the number of offenses committed, but it does go into the records. Caught in the act of shoplifting, teenagers give various reasons: they are looking for excitement, doing it on a dare, they have heard it was easy to do without getting caught, and so on. The sad thing is that most of them could have paid for the merchandise they stole, and often they are not even stealing something they need.

Why would anyone try to shoplift?

An effective pilferage control depends on the alertness of salespeople, and you should be vigilant at all times. When you approach your customers promptly and stay with them, you make shoplifting difficult. Displays and placement of employees should be arranged so that all parts of a store are under supervision at all times. Good lighting everywhere is important, also. Small, expensive items should always be placed where they will have constant supervision.

If I see a shoplifter, should I try to stop him?

When you detect a shoplifter, under no circumstances confront him yourself—CALL SECURITY. It is not your responsibility to apprehend the shoplifter—it is your responsibility to report it as quickly and unobtrusively as you can. Do note the shoplifter's appearance and anything that sets the person apart from the crowd. Call the operator, ask for a security officer, and give your department and your name. Then wait for the security officer and point out the shoplifter or give the direction in which he or she has gone.

Shopping malls have developed a good system of passing along information on thefts, bad checks, and short-change artists. When one store is "hit," other stores in the mall are notified to keep on the lookout. Thus, the stacks of convictions are high on security desks.

The average shoplifter will hide merchandise on his or her body, in a purse, or in a shopping bag. Some may buy a couple of small items, while they have other items hidden on their person that they won't pay for.

Who should I watch for?

Mothers with little children have been caught shoplifting. Women who appear to be pregnant have been caught with a framework under their clothing full of stolen store merchandise. Just an ordinary-looking coat may contain very deep pockets on the inside, which can carry a huge amount of stolen merchandise. Shoplifters tend to gravitate toward open displays near entrances and exits to the stores. They hope to pick up the merchandise and leave the store quickly without being noticed. The salesperson should watch these display areas very carefully. Beautifully wrapped Christmas packages have been found to be "booster boxes," with a hinged opening at the back of the package that will easily accommodate jewelry, cosmetics, sweaters, blouses, even fur stoles. They are usually held closely to the body so the back opening will not show.

Professionals usually work in teams. They hit the stores or shopping malls and the big stores when they think there will be fewer salespeople on the selling floors. One or two of them will get the attention of the salesperson, while the other makes the move.

Does anyone ever shoplift fashion merchandise?

Year-round, the greatest shoplifting problems occur in women's wear departments. The shoplifters try to get away with merchandise by wearing it out of the store. This usually happens during cold weather, when shoppers are wearing heavier coats and bulging clothing is less noticeable. Such shoppers may take three or four garments into the fitting room, put one or two of them under the clothing they are wearing, and walk right out of the store undetected.

For this reason, many stores have rules about the amount of clothing that can be taken to the dressing rooms at any one fitting. Salespeople should make sure that shoppers come out of the fitting rooms with as many garments as they took in.

Every merchant is in business to make a profit. If a business is overriden with thievery, it cannot absorb the loss completely, and the loss must be passed along to the consumer so a profit can be made. Higher retailing prices are the result, and the innocent, honest consumer pays the costs of the shoplifting of dishonest people.

The best prevention of shoplifting is an aggressive selling program on the part of all the salespeople on the selling floor. Immediate customer approach, fitting-room checks, and constant alertness are the best deterrents. When you do these things, you help your business maximize profits.

TAG SWITCHERS

Tag Switching. A more recent "ripoff" in stores that isn't exactly shoplifting, but is thievery of another kind, is to switch tags on the merchandise. A person may put a $25 label on a $50 item, buy the garment for $25, and leave the store with a $25 merchandise shortage.

Do people really switch tags? Why?

When caught by an alert cashier, such a person's alibi will be, "I found it that way!" You have to actually see the tags being switched to prove otherwise. This person is stealing, and yet may never have shoplifted—may, in fact, consider shoplifting to be dishonest!

Clothing is one of the most popular items with tag switchers in discount and department stores. Any store that uses pens or pencils for markdowns is a real target for the switcher, because a felt-tip pen may be all he or she needs to lower the price on any garment.

Occasionally switchers work in teams. One person goes into a department and does the tag switching or markdown and then leaves the store. A second person comes in soon after and buys the garment with the switched tag. The first person is long gone. Then, the switchers may wait a few days and go back to return the merchandise for a refund using the original tag—the more expensive one.

Can stores catch the price-tag switchers?

Stores are fighting the switching problem. Salespeople are alerted to watch for tag switchers, and some stores offer good rewards to any employee who detects a tag switch at the cash register. Tamper-resistant tags are also being used. A tagging machine that shoots a strong plastic thread through both the material and the price tag has been developed. Removal of such a tag is most difficult—yet some switchers have learned to wiggle them out by some means.

The spread of self-service stores that lack close sales supervision has added to the spread of tag switching, and some shoppers are glee-fully creating instant bargains by pasting low-price labels on high-priced goods. Your best defense against tag switching is to know your merchandise so well that you can tell at a glance if the merchandise being purchased is marked at the right selling price. Knowledge of your merchandise has been emphasized before, and here is yet another reason for its importance.

Returned Fashion Apparel

Another area of great profit loss to any business involves the retail practice of guaranteeing satisfaction to the customer or cheerfully re-funding the money. It is probably the most widely used and abused system in retailing.

Why is there anything wrong in returning goods? It's done all the time.

Almost all stores allow merchandise to be returned because they want to keep the customer's goodwill. They feel that they cannot refuse to allow a customer to return merchandise because they do not want to lose the customer's business. To refuse to accept returned merchan-dise might not only lose the customer forever but lose the entire family and perhaps a number of friends. For this reason, retailers often extend the return privilege to such a liberal extent that it some-times becomes ridiculous.

Most customers have no idea how much cost is involved in repro-cessing merchandise they have returned. While some returns are honest returns, there are many that could be avoided. When you con-sider the costs of rehandling returned goods, you will do your best to prevent this from happening. The worst part of the problem is that returned merchandise is often shopworn or has been mistreated while it was out of the store and cannot be remarked at its original price and must therefore be sold as a markdown. Such expenses become significant for the retailer.

141
CHAPTER 6
*How you can help
your fashion business
make a profit*

You may not be able to stop returns entirely, but you can minimize them if you analyze the reasons. Customers do change their minds. When a garment has only been out for a brief period—two or three days at the most—and is returned in the same condition in which it left the store with all tickets attached, accompanied by the sales check, it is not such a serious problem.

There are many causes of returns, but one of the worst is committed by the salesperson who uses high-pressure methods to make a sale to a customer who really doesn't want the item to start with. Sometimes customers will take an item home only because they don't know how to tell such a salesperson no. How easily and often some salespeople use such phrases and sentences as, "Take it home—you'll be able to see how it looks when you have added your accessories." "Take it home and let your husband see it." "You can return it if you find that you don't like it—we guarantee your complete satisfaction." "You get your money back if you're not happy." All such statements are forced selling and should be avoided.

You will soon learn which customers abuse your returns and adjustments policy and you should deal with them very carefully. The customer is NOT always right, but store policy will have to govern your actions whatever your personal reaction to the chronic problems of customer returns may be.

*Aren't customers always
right?*

Fashion Apparel Markdowns

Naturally, retailers prefer to sell everything they buy at the price originally placed on it. Theoretically, if the right merchandise is bought, is priced right, available at the right time in the right assortment, then markdowns will never be necessary. But this is rarely ever the case, so when an item has been in stock too long the retailer may be forced to make downward adjustments in the selling price to move the merchandise at a faster rate.

Slow-selling merchandise must be disposed of, and there is usually a time limit on how long fashion goods should remain at the original selling price before being marked down. You can do your part in eliminating the need for a markdown on many fashion items if you will make it a practice to know your older inventory and try to show customers garments that may have been in stock longer than the newer ones.

It is also a good practice when you are studying your stock of fashion apparel to think of each garment in relation to the type of person the garment was designed for, and on whom it would be most becoming. Some stores give a small incentive in the form of an award to the salesperson who sells a garment that is about to become a markdown. Salespeople who are new in a department often sell more older garments than salespeople who have tried unsuccessfully to sell those items on several occasions. They become bored with the garment, whereas to the new salesperson the entire stock seems new and attractive. It helps if you try to see your stock each day as new and exciting with many sales possibilities.

For example, one good floor salesman for men's suits makes it a practice during slow-selling periods to study his stock of suits. He tries different combinations of suits together for mix-match combinations and picks interesting combinations of shirts and ties to go with them. In this manner he builds up more enthusiasm for the suits and when a customer comes in, he can quickly show the two suits together and quickly assemble furnishings for both. The result is often a sale of two suits rather than one. There really doesn't ever have to be a dull moment on the sales floor.

Conclusion

This chapter has dealt with the major sources of profit loss that exist in the fashion business today. Through your personal accuracy in everything that you do and your integrity and loyalty to your company, you can help prevent these big losses. You can be instrumental in helping your business make a profit—and this will also benefit you as the employee and the consumer.

Review Questions

1. Define or identify the following terms:
   a. Physical inventory
   b. Stock shortages
   c. Merchandise transfers
   d. Markdowns
   e. Invoice errors
   f. Sales-floor errors
   g. Tag-switchers
2. How do the greatest causes of profit losses occur in fashion merchandising?
3. If physical inventory differs from book inventory, what is the cause?
4. How do errors on paper occur? What should you be careful to avoid in causing errors on paper?
5. Why do you think many businesses have gone to automated sys-

143

CHAPTER 6

*How you can help
your fashion business
make a profit*

tems in special cash registers to eliminate "people errors" on sales slips?

6. If you suspect a fellow employee of merchandise theft, what is your responsibility as a salesperson? How can you report it diplomatically?

7. Is it easy to recognize a shoplifter? Who are the worst offenders in shoplifting? Do retailers prosecute them? What should you do as a floor salesperson to prevent shoplifting?

8. Why is it important that the salesperson be alert and aware of the number of garments that a customer takes into the fitting rooms?

9. What is the best method of helping your store avoid tag switching?

10. How can you prevent fashion merchandise from being returned? Why should you be sure that each sale is a final sale?

Suggested Student Activities

1. Visit several different kinds of retail stores in your community and observe what, if anything, they appear to be doing to prevent merchandise shortages. Drug stores, supermarkets, and department stores now generally use rather sophisticated electronic equipment, closed-circuit television cameras that are monitored, convex mirrors, and numerous kinds of sensor-tagged merchandise devices which sound an alarm if the merchandise is carried past exist barriers without purchase. Make a list of the methods you observe in use.

2. Ask a police official in your area how shoplifting crimes are handled locally.

3. Ask the manager of a store about the kinds of instruction given to employees in the handling of suspected shoplifting cases.

Case Problems

Case 6-1. Margaret is alone on the sales floor of the sportswear department just before the lunch hour—usually a quiet sales period in the department. Three women suddenly come quickly into the department. One requests that Margaret get something for her that is kept in the stockroom, a second selects several garments from a rack and heads for the fitting rooms. The other woman moves toward the suede pantsuits and takes a few of them off the racks for closer inspection. Margaret suspects that there is something not quite right in the behavior of the three women.

1. Whom should she alert to the situation?
2. How could she make a telephone call without making it obvious that she is reporting the behavior of the women?

Case 6-2. Mrs. Peters is the manager of a women's specialty store in a large shopping center. Word has just come to her that a major shoplifting has just occurred several doors down from her store. She calls her salespeople and alerts them to be on the lookout for the suspected individuals. No sooner has she done this than she sees the described women enter her store.

1. What procedures should Mrs. Peters and her salespeople follow?
2. Should she make any attempt to confront the women herself?

Case 6-3. Bill is a new employee in the men's furnishings department. He feels that he is being watched by a customer and each time Bill looks toward the customer, he finds the customer staring at him. Bill is busy with another customer at the time, as are all the other salespeople. The customer who keeps staring at Bill is wearing a bulky all-weather coat; his hands are out of Bill's line of vision near the display of better ties and leather accessories.

1. Should Bill excuse himself from the customer he is serving, and approach the customer near the ties?
2. How could he alert the other salespeople that he suspects the man's behavior?

Case 6-4. Jane is quite sure she saw a young woman quickly whisk some silver chains and bracelets off the counter into her purse. As Jane walks toward the young woman, she quickly turns and heads for the front door of the store, where she joins a young man.

1. Should Jane follow the young woman out onto the street?
2. If not, what can she do to keep the young woman under surveillance until help arrives?
3. Is it possible that Jane might find herself in danger if she approaches the young woman too closely?

Case 6-5. Mr. Perry only works on Saturdays in a menswear specialty store, so he is not too familiar with the new merchandise arrivals each week. While Mr. Perry is helping at the cash register on one busy Saturday, he is handed a cashmere sweater by a customer who is obviously in a big hurry to pay and leave the store. When Mr. Perry begins to write up the ticket for the sweater, he notices that the price on the sweater is much less than he thinks a sweater of that quality is usually marked in the store. The customer urges him to hurry with the sales transaction, but Mr. Perry hesitates.

1. What, if anything, should Mr. Perry say to the customer about the price of the sweater?
2. Should Mr. Perry make sure that the price on the sweater is correct? How could he check the price?
3. If the sweater is indeed marked incorrectly, how can this be explained to the customer?

Chapter 7

Showing management you are ready to advance

Objectives

When you have read this chapter, you should be able to

1. List the traits and abilities that are most often rated formally or informally in employee evaluations
2. Explain why each characteristic is important for serious consideration, and the interrelationship that one characteristic has with another
3. Give examples of how each rating factor can be applied in a fashion job situation
4. Determine which traits and abilities you need to improve, how you might accomplish improvement, and why you should begin that development immediately
5. Chart your own direction for advancement on a fashion job
6. Explain why some people succeed in the fashion business while others remain at about the same level of the organization at which they began
7. Realistically evaluate yourself for those efficiency-builders that determine advancement in fashion merchandising

YOUNKERS
SATISFACTION ALWAYS

Iowa had been a state for only ten years in 1856 when the three Younker brothers, Lytton, Samuel, and Marcus, fresh from Poland, opened the first Younkers store in the Mississippi River town of Keokuk. Because of its strategic position on the river, the town was one of the most important and prosperous in Iowa. The rapids on the Mississippi north of Keokuk were swift and treacherous, so the town was a terminal for freight on packet boats up from St. Louis, Missouri.

The merchandise for the new Younkers store first came from the East by a circuitous route through Pittsburgh, down the Ohio river, and up the Mississippi by way of St. Louis to Keokuk. Of further importance to Keokuk was its location at the mouth of the Des Moines River. It led up through the rich center of Iowa, a new territory just then being opened for development. As yet, no railroad served the middle of the state, and difficult as navigation was on the Des Moines River, it did serve as an avenue for freight movement during some months of the year.

ITINERANT MERCHANTS

Using the store in Keokuk as their headquarters, the brothers were at first itinerant merchants, carrying packs of merchandise out through the country in all directions from Keokuk. They explored the Des Moines River valley and secured much business from it. They ate and stayed with farmers along their route, and always paid for their "keep" with merchandise from their packs, thus planting the first seeds of goodwill for the store.

The Civil War came with its trying days, and money was uncertain. But in the face of adversity, Samuel Younker placed the store's first advertisement in the Daily Gate City newspaper in the fall of 1864. The small one-column, three-inch ad was printed daily without change of copy from October 14 to December 31:

What was early store advertising like? Did it help?

Have on hand and for sale at the very lowest market prices the best selected stock of

DRY GOODS

comprising Black and Colored Silks, Merinos and Alpacas, Shawls and Cloaks, Blankets and Quilts, Yarns and Hosieries, Carpets and Oil Cloths, which will be sold at prices to correspond with the late decline in gold.
Special Notice is given that our store will be closed on every Saturday. Younker & Bros., 82 Main St., next to Anderson & Co.'s Bank.

Construction of 162 miles of railroad between Keokuk and Des Moines began in 1856, but because of the Civil War, it was not completed until ten years later. Samuel Younker had the distinction of being on the first passenger train to enter Des Moines; this was an arrival that was the occasion of great celebration.

Herman Younker, a younger brother, was attracted by the rapid growth of the capital city, so in 1874 he was sent to Des Moines to open a branch store there. Marcus Younker wrote in his memoirs:

*Can you start a store
with $6,000 capital
today?*

> We found ourselves too large for Keokuk, our business had outgrown the town, which at that time, along with all other river-front towns, was on the decline, and, ever being ambitious to attain a firm foothold in the business world, we took out $6,000 of our capital and invested in a branch store in Des Moines, which was said to be the promising center of commerce in Iowa.

The new Des Moines branch was opened in a one-story room measuring 22 by 60 feet. The new store ran its first advertisement in Des Moines on October 3, 1874:

> We have come to live here and mean to do what is right. If you want honest goods at bottom prices, call at Younker Brothers.

Ever progressive, in expansion and innovation, Younkers was the first store in Des Moines to employ a woman in 1881. Women in department stores today do not realize how this timid woman paved the way for them. Ways and attitudes have changed since that day, but for the first few days of her employment, Mrs. McCann was anything but happy. She kept herself discreetly in the rear of the store, feeling entirely strange and out of place in this business world dominated by men. However, in a short time, women customers were seeking her out because they liked the idea of being waited on by a woman. Mrs. McCann's success was so decided that much jealousy developed among the men. For about a year, however, she was the only woman in the store.

*How did one of the first
women employees in a
department store get
along?*

In 1899, the Younkers brothers made a "foolhardy move," so their competitors thought, by clearing a space for a new building "way up on Seventh and Walnut"—a whole block out of the then retail district. It proved to be anything but a foolhardy move, however, and from then on a series of great store purchases, expansions, and mergers took place.

Younkers was among the pioneer merchants in transforming the oldtime drygoods stores into department stores, with all the merchandising services and special promotional activities. In 1913, the firm made department store history by opening its Tea Room, which is now a social center in Des Moines. Later the Tea Room was open for dinner in the evenings with an orchestra for dinner dancing.

Almost every year after that, Younkers made news with a major remodeling project, or with the purchase of additional stock, or with modernization.

FIG. 7-1. Younkers's interior displays during their fall 1974 promotion of the British Fair, featuring merchandise from Great Britain throughout the store and in many of the fashion departments.
(Courtesy, Younkers, Des Moines, Iowa)

1936—The store was completely air-conditioned. Iowa has cool spring and fall weather, so air-conditioning was a rarity in the 1930s.

1938—A large warehouse was purchased.

1939—A new electric stairway was installed from the first to the second floor.

1943—The cycle billing system was inaugurated.

1947—Electric stairways were completed throughout the store.

The first branch store of the Des Moines store was opened in 1941 as a little shop in a city just north of Des Moines in Ames, Iowa. So successful was this first little shop that it was expanded within a year to a full-scale branch store. From that time on, branch stores were established throughout leading cities in Iowa, and extended into surrounding states. Today there are twenty-two stores in eighteen major metropolitan areas, comprising 1,600,000 square feet of space. There are over 4,000 employees.

Is it good to have a low management turnover in a store?

Younkers is one of America's largest independently owned and operated prestige department stores, consistently ranking among the nations' top profit performers. The store enjoys one of the lowest management turnover rates in the country, partly because of the generous profit-sharing plan. "Satisfaction Always" is Younkers's policy.

FIG. 7-2. Letter of introduction from Younkers

WELCOME TO YOUNKERS

You are now an associate of one of America's finest department store organizations.

From this very day you are one of the persons behind our slogan "SATISFACTION ALWAYS."

Whatever your job or responsibility . . . . salesperson, auditor, deliveryman, window trimmer, credit adjustor, advertising copywriter, artist, baker, stockkeeper, workroom artisan . . . . . ALL of us are "selling."

Selling is the foundation of our business. Without it there is no business — and no opportunities for ourselves.

In order to sell ourselves, our firm and our merchandise we must be friendly, considerate, kind, honest, ambitous, alert and thorough.

By applying these attributes and principles to our everyday work, we are able to give "SATISFACTION ALWAYS" service to our customers, gain the respect of our suppliers and work in harmony with our fellow Younkerites.

As president of Younkers I congratulate you on choosing this dynamic business for your future. You can go as far as your talents and ambitions dictate. Start today to build your own future on the solid foundation of selling the "SATISFACTION ALWAYS" way.

MUCH SUCCESS TO YOU!

Charles Duchen
President

Isn't it strange
That princes and kings
And clowns that caper
In sawdust rings
And common people
Like you and me
Are builders of eternity?
Each is given a bag of tools,
A shapeless mass and
A book of rules;
And each must make,
'Ere life is flown,
A stumblingblock
Or a steppingstone.

R. L. SHARPE

The material in this book emphasizes the important job characteristics that will make you more efficient and successful in a fashion merchandising position.

Am I graded on my job?

**EVALUATION
RATING SYSTEMS**

In this chapter we will look at some of the specific characteristics that are the basis of formal or informal *rating systems* used by modern executives periodically to evaluate their employees. The ratings become a part of the permanent employment files and are considered when openings for advancement occur.

People who move ahead are those who strive for excellence in everything they do. They know when they are doing a good job and they strive continually to do better. Probably they are aware that they can do "just enough to get by," but they do more because they get a genuine satisfaction out of doing their very best. They are motivated workers who take pride in achievement. They are intellectually and emotionally satisfied by the challenge of their jobs. They are *goal-oriented*. They set realistic, purposeful goals and work toward their achievement.

**"JUST ENOUGH
TO GET BY"**

Isn't "just enough to get by" enough?

GOAL-ORIENTED

Success and advancement in everything we do is almost entirely up to us. It is no accident that some people succeed and advance while others stay where they are, never moving ahead. This chapter will review some things which you intuitively know; if these "efficiency-builders" are utilized, they can help you achieve success and advancement in fashion merchandising.

What Is "Work"?

151

CHAPTER 7
*Showing management
you are ready
to advance*

Before we discuss the qualities you will want to develop to become a good fashion merchandising employee worthy of advancement, we should have something to say about work itself.

Work is an individual thing that we do by ourselves or in the company of a group of people. It becomes a very personal thing, to do well with or to neglect, to improve or degrade.

The *work ethic* is one of the most written-about subjects in today's editorial comment. Some feel that the work ethic is dead—that the "oldtime worker" no longer exists. Perhaps it is true that productivity suffers because of the lack of dedication to the job on the part of workers. Some people don't have the compelling urgency for work that our forefathers had. In times past, most people had to work long and hard just to survive.

However, most successful "workers" consider work to have an ethical value in their lives. Most believe that work is good in itself. Work makes a contribution to society. Most "workers" are better persons by virtue of the act of working. Many people believe that they are not participating in the process of living unless they are doing some meaningful and challenging work.

The human motivators for work are many: the possibility of advancement, the responsibility of the work itself, recognition, and the sense of achievement it gives. To some people satisfaction in simple work comes from just doing a job well. It's the attitude that you take toward work that counts. For example, one man chipping rocks might be consumed with self-pity because of the drudgery in his job. Another man working right beside that man may be proud to be chipping rocks because he is helping build a great cathedral.

We want job satisfaction from our work. The ideal job is the one that gives us a purpose in life and makes us a part of the world around us. We want to be proud of our work. We are challenged by the opportunities to develop our strongest skills and talents. Our interest and abilities are stimulated through the variety of tasks our jobs provide. We appreciate being given the freedom to make responsible decisions. Increasing our decision-making authority satisfies our ego needs. We like opportunities for self-expression. Our work becomes an intimate expression of us, ourselves.

Management has a great responsibility for making work more desirable and for giving individual workers an opportunity to live up to their fullest potential. But every worker has obligations of equal importance to him/herself and to his/her company.

*Isn't the "boss"
responsible for making
us work?*

Today's progressive worker is far different from the worker of the past who depended upon his luck or his personal winning ways to get him what he wanted out of his job and his life. Today's worker knows that the basic truths about work are

1. What the job requires of you and where you stand in it
2. How to fill your position efficiently
3. How to remain in a state of growth and interest
4. How to respect quality performance

5. How to keep a cheerful, optimistic, *positive attitude* about work
6. How to value and use your time well at work

When opportunity for advancement or improvement in a job knocks at the door, it usually is wearing "working clothes." The *pursuit of happiness* means work; *freedom* means being able to work for things we want; *independence* means standing on our own two feet free from dependence on others; and *self-respect* comes from working for what we get.

Therefore most people work because work is an economic necessity and they aren't content to live on charity. They believe that work is their social obligation. They also understand that work is a basic human right. Work is self-fulfillment through its meaningful, challenging activities.

Quality Rating in the Fashion Business

The qualities and personal characteristics rated in fashion businesses do not differ markedly from factors that are usually rated in other kinds of businesses. You can use the list of qualities we present here to evaluate yourself honestly in each category. Use a continuum of from one to five points—poor, fair, average, better, best—with the best receiving the highest number of points.

First rate yourself on the qualities given in the following list. Then read the rest of the chapter, in which these qualities are described for your benefit. You may want to rate yourself again when you have finished.

In the formal rating, the sum of the scores on such qualities and characteristics as these become your total efficiency score. Whether you are formally rated or not, some or all of these qualities will be the basis for consideration on how you are doing in the world of fashion business.

- Accuracy in everything done
- Rapidity of accomplishing acceptable results—persistence
- Evidence of constructive planning
- Orderliness and neatness exhibited
- Observance of business politics and regulations

- Acceptance of change and ability to learn new activities quickly
- Promptness in meeting deadlines
- Appropriate use of individual creativeness, originality, and initiative
- Efficient management of time
- Demonstration of leadership abilities and potential for growth
- Maturity in judgment—self-confidence and resourcefulness in handling demanding situations—mature insight
- Appropriate personal appearance, including neatness and cleanliness, social alertness, and enthusiasm
- Correct usage of business vocabulary, including ability to express ideas concisely, briefly, and persuasively; and spontaneity, conversational ease, and social responsiveness
- Development of interpersonal skills, including ability as a team worker, cooperativeness with associates, personal integrity, willingness to accept suggestions, enthusiasm, acceptance of delegated responsibilities

INTERPERSONAL SKILLS

How to Rate Highly in Your Job

At this point we will discuss individually all the qualities you will need to develop in order to do your job well and put yourself in a position for advancement, self-fulfillment, and value to the fashion merchandising business that employs you.

ACCURACY

You are expected to learn the correct techniques in your work. You should also learn *why* they are important. Watch and listen carefully when you are trained in how the work is to be done. If you don't understand completely, ask some intelligent questions. Then, once you understand, believe that you *can* do the work accurately, and take pride in doing so.

Any job involves a sequence of related activities. You must remember and do all necessary details. Sometimes it is folly to trust your memory completely. You will profit from writing down some of the directions soon after your initial training. In the very act of writing them down, you will improve your memory for doing them.

Some people make a game of learning a new job by keeping score on their progress. In the beginning, check and recheck everything you do to be sure all instructions have been carried out exactly as you were told.

How can I ever learn all the details on a new job?

EFFICIENCY AND PERSISTENCE

While it is desirable to accomplish results as rapidly as possible and persist until you do, in the beginning you may actually deter your efficiency by trying for speed. The trick is to learn all the details in the sequence of job activities so thoroughly that you have almost overlearned them. Then they will become an almost automatic routine for you. It helps to practice repeatedly any task that slows you down. Your objective should of course be to increase your speed as you improve your ability, and to increase the amount of work that you can accomplish, but never at the expense of high-quality work.

Almost every new job in almost every kind of occupation will have some stress and strain involved, which may be a source of frustration. We just have to train ourselves to be as personally efficient as possible. Then speed will follow as we strive for ultimate results.

CONSTRUCTIVE PLANNING

CONSTRUCTIVE PLANNING

Do I have to have any plans for my work days?

Constructive planning of work involves setting objectives and then determining how best to achieve them. It is deciding in advance what needs to be done, how it should be done, and when it would be best to do it.

Planning bridges the gap from where you are to where you want to be. By planning, you can accomplish things that would not otherwise happen. While it is a basic management function, planning exists at all levels in a business organization, from executive positions right on through to your level. For example, if your department manager has plans to achieve certain sales goals, you should find out what they are and then plan your work in accordance with them. Without planning on the part of everyone in an organization, nothing can really develop efficiently.

Why have plans?

Organizing your work may not become an immediate necessity at the very beginning of a new fashion job because you will be told what to do. However, as your ability and responsibility increase, you will want to show organizational ability through advance planning.

How am I ever going to get organized?

Perhaps the best advice on planning and organizing work is "don't put off doing the hardest job!" If you are not given a deadline for accomplishment, then set a due time for its completion on your own—plan how you will complete it—and go to work on it. Whatever you do, don't be a "pencil-sharpener"! A pencil-sharpener is someone who spends all his time getting ready to work but never actually gets going on it. Try to work on the hard job the necessary time every day to complete it by the date you have set.

"PENCIL-SHARPENER"

SHORT-RANGE PLANS
LONG-RANGE PLANS

In organizing your work, you need to make short-range plans and long-range plans. Short-range planning should be consistent with, and a part of, your long-range planning. Be careful in choosing your objectives to be sure they are reasonably attainable. They should "stretch" your abilities and cause you to reach to achieve them, but they should never be completely unattainable. Allow yourself a degree of flexibility in your planning also.

ORDERLINESS AND NEATNESS

Neatness and orderliness in work does not necessarily come easily to anyone, but it is a habit worth cultivating. Do keep your department and work area neat and orderly. If you keep everything you work with in a definite place, where you can find it quickly when you need it, you will be well on your way to doing neat, orderly work. Above all, don't succumb to borrowing. Anticipate, plan, and evaluate your work needs and provide for them in advance.

As long as I get the job done, who cares about how neat I am?

Not all job activities can be easily measured for neatness and orderliness, as stockkeeping can be. You may be able to judge your neatness and orderliness better than anyone else. Be sure to keep your standards high, and remember that "good enough" is never really good enough. Personal quota setting in your work will help. Time budgeting is also a form of setting personal quotas. Quotas will make you more systematic in your work. Without some kind of time quota, you may never get enough time to do all the things you want to accomplish in a working day, let alone being neat and orderly in doing them. (We will discuss efficient management of time later.)

How will I ever get everything done that I want to do?

You will increase your motivation and make better use of your capabilities when you work toward goals and quotas. But, again, aspirations should never be too high. Reasonable goals are stimulating —wishful ones may cause undue stress, causing you to feel frustrated and give up entirely. If you do not let your self-confidence dwindle, then goals and quotas can be extremely useful stimulants to realistic accomplishments. Your work will result in neatness and orderliness of accomplishment also.

OBSERVANCE OF BUSINESS POLICIES AND REGULATIONS

There is a strong interrelationship between accuracy in performing work and the observance of specific business policies and regulations. Both are expected of you on any job you perform. But it is not enough to just know what the business policies and regulations are. What you must watch out for is never to allow yourself to become so accustomed to doing the "same old thing in the same old way" that you become habit-bound.

When you are goal-oriented and have a serious occupational direction, you find yourself looking for better ways to do work—ways to improve current methods. An "old rut" is such a safe, secure place to be in that it can sometimes be a real hindrance to advancement. So, never let an old habit hold you back. Make it a new habit to compare what you are doing today with what you were doing a month or so ago and decide whether you are currently doing your work more efficiently.

Why should I set up future goals when I've only started on a new job?

ACCEPTING CHANGE, LEARNING NEW ACTIVITIES

Why do I have to change?

It is an axiom of business today and a universally recognized truth that you must be moving forward all the time just to keep up with the competition. Sometimes, you almost have to shock yourself into wanting to learn new methods on job details and accepting changes. If you don't, you are already standing still and will soon be moving backwards instead of ahead.

Accepting change and learning new activities have some good aspects and some bad aspects. For example, at first you may learn quite rapidly. Then, suddenly, your learning may slow up, or you may actually seem to be going backwards. If you hit a standstill period in your learning and you seem to be getting nowhere, it is time for you to

I can't seem to learn this new job. What am I going to do?

analyze what you are doing. Try to remain confident that you can improve, analyze your methods to see if they can be improved, and keep on trying. Often, a breakthrough will come just about the time you are ready to give up. It helps if you get excited about learning something new. An example of one of the changes taking place today in many businesses is the new automated cash register technique—it can be a difficult but exciting new aspect of the business to learn.

MEETING DEADLINES PROMPTLY

Why are deadlines so important?

You have undoubtedly heard, "When you are given a job to do—do it!" This means finishing your work by keeping at it steadily, doing a consistently good job throughout, and doing it as rapidly as possible. Avoiding errors, and sticking with the job no matter how hard or boring or degrading it may seem to you, is also a part of it.

Why do I have to do all the little jobs?

Keep in mind that the job given to you to do would not have been assigned to you unless you were capable of doing it. Doing little jobs well means that the big jobs will almost automatically follow. Of course, it helps immeasurably if you know the reason why the job has to be done by a certain deadline. Try to ascertain what this reason is before you start—then tackle it and get on with the work.

How can I do six things at once?

Often, meeting a deadline means that you will be working under pressure. You may need to keep several other things going at the same time. Since this can cause frustration, try to remain calm. As pressure begins to mount, stop for a moment and analyze why you feel pressured. Then begin the job again and complete it.

What's wrong with wanting to leave work on time every night?

If it takes you a few minutes after closing time to complete a job, try to concentrate on how glad you are to see the job completed. While it wouldn't be advisable to keep the security people waiting every evening for you to complete your work, it isn't good to be the first person off the job all the time, either.

CREATIVENESS, ORIGINALITY, AND INITIATIVE

Doing the right thing at the right time in the right way without being told probably best describes what is implied in our advice to use appropriate individual creativeness, originality, and *initiative*.

Using initiative? What's that? How can I show initiative?

You cannot exhibit these qualities until you have had some experience on your job, learned the company policies and procedures, and found out why jobs are done in a certain way. After you have had some experience on your job, you will begin to see possible ways of improving certain activities. When you think you do, you should discuss them with your manager for suggestions as to their adaptability. By studying your job carefully, you will be able to discern ways in which you can do some parts of it better. Probably these characteristics can be best portrayed by showing a spirit of wanting to improve current methods when it is possible to do so.

Also, sooner or later, on any job, a situation will arise requiring you to make a decision on your own. When this happens, think the situation through carefully, do not panic, and make a decision based on the facts. Use your resourcefulness, which simply calls for your being able to look ahead at the consequences of two or more possible actions and choosing the one most likely to succeed. Then proceed with confidence. Remember, it's permissible to be wrong once in awhile— just not all the time. Use care and restraint and mature judgment, and you'll be all right.

The boss is off the floor—do I ever have a problem! I've got to do something, but what?

APPROPRIATE PERSONAL APPEARANCE

Personal appearance is valuable for its own sake for all those who meet the public. What we discussed in an earlier chapter in relation to appropriate appearance for the job interview also applies when you are *on* the job. Probably, in no job is it more important to be dressed becomingly, conservatively, and in good taste than when you are in fashion merchandising.

Is my job appearance important to my job?

During the first few seconds after a stranger meets you, he/she has made a judgment about the kind of person you are, and the kind of firm you represent. Clothing, grooming, and facial expression have much to do with initial impressions. It also raises your self-confidence to know you are appropriately dressed, and you can easily direct your attention toward the other person and away from yourself.

EFFICIENT MANAGEMENT OF TIME

Effective personal time management is an area in which almost everyone can improve. To do so, you should carefully analyze what it is that you are doing and how long it takes you to accomplish certain job activities.

If you are like many people who reach the end of a day, unable

I just never have enough hours in the day. What's wrong with me?

to account for their time, saying to themselves, "Where did today go? I don't feel that I accomplished anything!" then you may not be investing your time wisely. You should ask yourself, "What have I been doing all day?" You may discover that your day was not goal-oriented. Or perhaps you need to establish some performance standards for yourself, and time quotas for their accomplishment, as we discussed in an earlier section.

Planning in advance helps you arrive on the job in the morning knowing what it is you want to accomplish during that particular day, and which activities have priority over others. Sometimes it helps to jot down the five most important objectives that you have for that day, and manage, schedule, and control your work time so that you do accomplish them. When you do, you will be running your job—it won't be running you! Time can be managed successfully through careful planning.

DEMONSTRATION OF LEADERSHIP ABILITIES AND POTENTIAL FOR GROWTH

Since all growing businesses need large numbers of managers in their organizations, it becomes exceedingly important to identify the people within the organization who show ability for possible growth and who have potential leadership abilities.

I want to become a manager. How can I do this?

Leadership is not easily defined because it is not fully understood. However, there do appear to be several traits and characteristics which all the better leaders have in common. You are already familiar with many of these traits, and we have discussed them in relation to success, advancement, and job satisfaction. Therefore, we will simply list several of the more important characteristics for your further consideration.

What is leadership?

Good leadership potential is shown by the person who

1. Likes to work with other people and understands the importance of good human relations
2. Listens willingly to others and offers them help with a problem
3. Has faith in other people's abilities
4. Is tactful and uses persuasive suggestions—never tries to force his or her own opinion
5. Shows sincerity, honesty, straightforwardness, and fairness to all people
6. Is self-controlled, not easily frustrated, and acts with mature judgment—not impulsively
7. Accepts responsibility, keeps promises, enjoys challenging activities
8. Is highly appreciative of any help given, and shows it
9. Shows high morale, sets a good example for associates, and encourages others

158

10. Shows a high level of inner motivation for achieving self-realization through long-range goals

MATURITY IN JUDGMENT, SELF-CONFIDENCE, RESOURCEFULNESS, AND INSIGHT

As we all know, age does not determine maturity. Psychologists explain that even though you are physically "grown up," you are not necessarily mature in your judgment and insight. Many of the characteristics of the person with good leadership abilities and potential are also characteristics of maturity. A mature person will exhibit the following characteristics:

self-control
self-confidence
sincerity
sense of purpose
self-direction
supportiveness to others

USAGE OF BUSINESS VOCABULARY

Words have great power. Try to always use words that can be understood—clear and positive words. To be positive in your statements, say what you *can* do, not what you cannot do.

In conversation with another person keep your voice alive and look at the person to whom you are speaking. Cultivate a voice that has a smile in it—a voice that is warm, friendly, sincere, and interested.

If you are aiming toward executive work it is especially important that you develop a good, usable vocabulary because it is one of the principal tools in management. Famous people—successful people—have all made a conscious effort to improve their word power. They have developed the dictionary habit.

It is worth your while to develop the ability to express your ideas concisely, as briefly as possible, and persuasively. Everyone enjoys conversing with a person who exhibits spontaneity and can carry on a conversation pleasantly and in a clear, interesting manner.

DEVELOPMENT OF INTERPERSONAL SKILLS

More people lose good jobs for reasons of lack of human relations ability—effective interpersonal skills—than for lack of job skill. A reason often given for this is lack of cooperation, or difficulty in getting along with others. Almost all definitions of good personality emphasize the effect one person has on another person. Because interpersonal skills can and should be developed for job success, we'll discuss them here.

Ability as a Team Worker. We are all members of a team, and we must pull our load of job responsibility with the team and never against it. Above all, we must be cordial and friendly when we do.

All efforts should be coordinated toward the goals of the team. Ideas should be accepted and solicited from others in the work group also. When you have respect for others, pay attention to them, and use a friendly attitude of helpfulness, you are well on your way to becoming a good team worker.

Cooperativeness with Associates. There is an old axiom that the best way to win a person's cooperation is to build up his self-esteem. We truly like the person who helps us to like ourselves—this builds up our *self-esteem*. We are more likely to follow their lead also. The more popular person is the one who, by his or her manner, makes others feel pleased with themselves and happier for having been with that person. In no way are we trying to imply using lavish praise or insincere flattery. We are talking about the importance of building up the other person's self-esteem by sincere friendliness, warmth, optimism, and cooperation.

Should I talk about
confidential business
matters at home?

Personal Integrity. As an employee you have a moral and ethical responsibility, and a legal obligation, to protect the business secrets of your company. What you learn about your company is not to be discussed with your friends or relatives.

Businesses are able to make a profit and develop a marginal edge over their competition through a particular method of operation, through doing some phase of the work a little better or differently than others in the same field of work. Betrayal of such secrets would be the worst act of disloyalty you could commit.

If you ever leave one firm and go to another, be sure you don't take or use any of the business secrets of your previous employer. You may involve your new firm in a lengthy and expensive litigation, if you do. Many lawsuits result from the fact that an employee didn't realize he was doing something wrong in discussing his previous company. If you are ever in doubt about what may be discussed or used, then it would be better to remain silent.

In your business life you will learn a lot about different members of your organization—their habits, conduct, and their past history. All such things are confidential, and should not be shared with others.

When they tell me how
to do something, aren't
they really just
criticizing me?

Willingness to Accept Suggestions. When your manager makes suggestions for your improvement, it is a clear indication that your potential growth and advancement with the company are being considered carefully. When you show an attitude of sincerely wanting to learn, more and more suggestions for improvement may be made to you. Do not feel that you are receiving a criticism for former work, but rather that this is a positive interest in your future. If you make a mistake (and who hasn't?) the best policy is to admit it, and determine that it will never happen again. You will be respected for doing so.

Enthusiasm. Is anything as contagious as enthusiasm? When you are interested and enthusiastic and excited about what you are doing, your associates will get interested, enthusiastic, and excited also. Dropping a little pebble of enthusiasm into everything you do causes waves of enthusiasm to spread on and on until they engulf your whole department.

Should I suppress my excitement on the job about what I'm doing?

Acceptance of Delegated Responsibilities. Accountability in your work implies dependability in all that you are given to do. So when you assume a responsibility, be sure that you understand it thoroughly, and can do it correctly.

Occasionally you will be asked to handle more responsibilities, so you must have the capacity to respond in harmony with the policies of the company. In this way, you can begin assuming more and more responsibility, and become a much more valued associate in your company.

When will they give me more responsibilities?

Conclusion

The manner in which you develop all of these frequently rated efficiency traits and abilities will determine how soon you rate "better" or "best" in your job evaluations. When you really consider how many opportunities there are in a good fashion job, you will be glad to work on improving your work performance.

All of us need to think about these characteristics and measure our accountability frequently. We must use knowledge and general intelligence in the true sense of the work ethic 100 percent of the time in everything we do.

1. Define or identify the following terms:
   a. Itinerant merchants
   b. Evaluation rating systems
   c. "Just enough to get by"
   d. Goal-orientation
   e. Interpersonal skills
   f. Work ethic
   g. Positive attitude
   h. Constructive planning
   i. "Pencil-sharpener"
   j. Short-range plans
   k. Long-range plans
   l. Initiative
   m. Maturity
   n. Self-esteem
   o. Accountability

Review Questions

2. Do you feel that the characteristics that are usually the basis of formal or informal evaluations of job performance are important? How do formal and informal evaluations differ?

3. Is job appearance any more important for the fashion merchandising person than for those in other kinds of work?

4. Why is "just enough to get by" never enough in the working world, regardless of what you do?

5. To those who really enjoy working there is a great deal of satisfaction in their jobs. Why do they feel this way?

6. On a new job, what must you do to show your associates that you are going to be a valuable person in the department?

7. For what purpose would a manager take the time to carefully explain a correct procedure to a new employee—merely to criticize? Or for other reason?

8. Do more people fail on a job because they don't know how to do the job, or is there another reason? Explain the importance of the latter in any job situation.

Suggested Student Activities

1. Rate yourself (independently and confidentially) on the qualities usually rated in fashion businesses. Use a point system of 1–5.

	1 Poor	2 Fair	3 Avg.	4 Better	5 Best
Accuracy					
Efficiency and persistence					
Constructive planning					
Neatness and orderliness					
Observing procedures					
Learning new things					
Deadline promptness					
Initiative					
Time management					
Leadership					
Maturity					
Appropriate apparel					
Neatness and grooming					
Pleasantness on the job					
Enthusiasm					
Ability to express self					
Social responsiveness					
Conversational ability					
Teamwork ability					
Cooperativeness					
Integrity					
Willingness to accept suggestions					
Enthusiasm					
Acceptance of responsibility					
TOTAL SCORE					

2. Time management is an important aspect of our total lives. Most of us have no idea what we have done all day unless we have planned the day carefully in advance. To provide an idea of how you spent yesterday, use 15-minute blocks of time from the time you got up until you retired, and write down exactly what you were doing for those 15-minute segments. The results may surprise you, and perhaps you will discover blocks of time when you may not really have been doing anything. This is not to imply that it is not good to relax occasionally or have some form of different activity. But many people discover that they are not using their time as efficiently as possible. It's an interesting experiment for us all.

3. Just as you rated yourself on the qualities for success in fashion businesses, likewise give yourself a rating on your maturity level, as suggested on page 159.

4. Select several current fashion magazines and write down a list of the descriptive words used to explain a new fashion or fashion trend. Also read a few pages from the *Wall Street Journal, U.S. News & World Report, Barron's,* or any of the financial publications, and notice and write down the words with which you are not familiar. Look up their definitions in a dictionary. Then reread the articles. Do they have more meaning to you on the second reading?

Case Problems

Case 7-1. Gary has been working almost all day in his brand-new job in the stockroom, and nobody seems to know he is there. His job-buddy came by at lunchtime and took him to the cafeteria for lunch, but otherwise, after the department manager explained the job to him, no one has paid him any attention. Bill knows he is doing a pretty good job because the stockroom has really needed attention. It was a mess when he started, and now it is beginning to look better organized. But he's a little discouraged, and wishes somebody would notice the difference.

1. How do you think Gary is doing on his first day on the new job?
2. If the stockroom didn't show improvement after he had worked all day in it, do you think anyone would notice?

Case 7-2. The department had many customers waiting to be served when Joan walked on to the sales floor. Joan had just started on the job that morning and hardly expected the department to be so busy. She made her first sale—several items of different prices. She started to ring up the sale on the electronic register, when suddenly she realized she didn't know which button to push to begin the tape. She tried to collect her thoughts and remember what she learned in training but she was close to pressing the "panic button."

1. What would you do if you were Joan?
2. Do you really think the department manager or the other sales-floor people expect Joan to be thoroughly proficient and rapid in this circumstance?
3. On her own time, would it be advisable for Joan to go back to the training room after a day on the floor and practice using an electronic register?
4. Should she make any comments to the customer about her hesitancy with the register? What would you say to your customer if it was noticeable that you didn't know what you were doing?

Case 7-3. Rick Perkins is concerned. He has been with his company for over a year and a half, and feels that he has been doing his work just as efficiently as has a close friend of his on the job. The friend has just been selected for management executive training by the company, and Rick compares himself with his friend, wondering why he wasn't given a similar opportunity.

1. If you were Rick, what are several questions you would ask yourself about your job qualifications?
2. If Rick still feels that he and his friend are equal in all areas of work, what would you recommend that he do?

Part Three

Advancing in the World of Fashion Merchandising

Chapter 8

The importance of fashion sales promotion

Objectives

When you have read this chapter, you should be able to

1. State why fashion sales promotions are important to the field of fashion merchandising, and how you might contribute to their success
2. Outline the necessary steps to prepare a well-organized fashion sales promotion plan
3. Explain why a good store image is important and how it is achieved
4. List the kinds of media available for advertising fashion items, and comment on their effectiveness or limitations, for large or small stores
5. Plan a fashion show, paying specific attention to details that were not readily apparent to you before you studied them
6. Discuss the effectiveness of point-of-sale displays in a fashion store
7. Analyze fashion sales promotions that you have observed, or in which you have participated, stating why you think they were successful or why they failed

Neiman-Marcus

Probably no other store has had as colorful a growth as this world-famous fashion specialty-store chain of Dallas, Texas. There are many now-famous legends about the growth, fame, and image of this business. Its unusual and excellently conceived sales promotion activities rank as its most important assets.

When Carrie Nieman and Herbert Marcus started their first store in a two-story building in downtown Dallas, they advertised in the *Dallas Morning News* on Sunday, September 9, 1907, that they would be bringing the Southwest the "finest assortments of ready-to-wear from all parts of the world" to be sold with "the highest degree of personalized service ever offered," for "complete customer satisfaction." These were not idle words, because this first advertisement created the philosophy that was to be carried out through the years. Legend has it that the very idea of bringing high fashion to the agricultural Southwest was thought to be sheer folly by other fashion experts of this time. However, the store showed a profit from the very beginning, proving that the founders' ideas and good taste were not only right for the area but right for the times as well. So Neimans grew with the city of Dallas, which increased from 80,000 cattle-raising and cotton-growing townspeople in 1907 to the great metropolitan area that now includes over a million people.

The discovery of oil the same year the store opened seemed of little consequence at the time, because it was still just a horse-and-buggy world. But this later proved to be one of the greatest growth assets in the area.

The store had its share of misfortunes—including a fire that completely destroyed the store and its contents in 1913. Then followed a drop in cotton prices—war in Europe prevented cotton shipments across the submarine-infested Atlantic Ocean and the cotton farmers became nearly bankrupt. Discouraging as many of these misfortunes were, they never dimmed the founders' belief in their store and its future. Rebuilding programs, enlargement, and expansion with several additions of new departments continued. By 1917, west Texas oil was discovered, and thus began a new source of wealth in Texas and a new surge of interest in the fine quality of Neiman-Marcus merchandise.

In 1926, when Stanley, son of Herbert Marcus, came home from college and entered the business, the store became known for its many fashion sales promotions. The stockmarket crash of 1929 and the great Depression that followed gave Stanley a chance to experience business the hard way. Soon after, another great oil discovery was made in east Texas, and another new group of millionaires bolstered the store's business. The reputation for always making sure the customers got what was just "right for them" spread nationwide. Advertising in

FIG. 8-1. Portrait of the late Carrie Marcus Neiman, who with her brother, Herbert Marcus, Sr., founded Neiman-Marcus in 1907. (Courtesy, Neiman-Marcus, Dallas)

national fashion consumer magazines created additional interest and attention.

A department of public relations that was separate from the advertising department helped create news by playing up the unusual happenings in the store. There were always many of these, always expertly handled by the staff. Perhaps the most unusual request came from a man who, wanting to save his marriage, asked Nieman-Marcus if it would be possible to reproduce the window displays in the store's four main windows on his front lawn on Christmas Eve. The Neiman-Marcus display staff complied, and on Christmas Eve, his lawn was ablaze with luxury. At last report, the marriage was flourishing. There are literally hundreds of stories like that in Texas—all spreading the Neiman story far and wide.

What does a public relations department do?

FIG. 8-2. Often called the merchant prince of Dallas, Stanley Marcus, son of founder Herbert Marcus, was responsible for the great expansion of Neiman-Marcus stores.
(Courtesy, Neiman-Marcus, Dallas)

But aren't there lots of Christmas catalogs?

Perhaps the most famous Neiman-Marcus activity is its annual Christmas catalog. Many fabulous and unique gifts—gifts found nowhere else in the world—are featured in the catalog. In years past the catalog has featured such things as "his and her airplanes," an ermine bathrobe, white mink cowboy chaps (a few were sold, but not to Texans), a "steer on the hoof," "his and her submarines, the ultimate in togetherness," "his and her bison" for anyone who has a home where they'd like buffalo to roam, a Chinese junk imported from Hong Kong, and one year, for the person who wanted to spend a million dollars, a list of beautiful furs and jewels plus a few Neiman's coins to spend in the stores in case something had been overlooked. All these his and hers gifts make news and are carried by newspapers and television newscasts. To most people they are merely amusing items, but the publicity that the store gets because of them is invaluable to Neiman-Marcus. While such items would be considered outrageous in the catalogs of other stores, they are accepted in Neiman-Marcus catalogs because of the image of the store and because the press and the public are well prepared to expect these items yearly. Only rarely are these unusual gifts sold, but sometimes there is a buyer who wants a conversation piece or a gift for "someone who has

FIG. 8-3. The downtown Dallas Neiman-Marcus store. The famous Fortnights are held here, and during these events the exterior of this store is often transformed to resemble the country being featured. In one British Fortnight a bobby directed traffic on the corner and double-decker buses were parked on the streets. (Courtesy, Neiman-Marcus, Dallas)

everything." This is just one way that Neiman-Marcus tells its own story.

Another outstanding annual promotional feature—the Fortnight—was begun in 1957 by Stanley Marcus. Fortnights are usually held the last two weeks in October, and people travel long distances to view merchandise that is featured from a specially selected country each year. Several months in advance of the Fortnights, leaders of the city are invited to a luncheon to hear about the plans in advance, and thus the events become citywide affairs. The museums bring in special exhibits of fine paintings and sculptures from the country featured, theaters run films about the country, supper clubs feature entertainment

Is there anything different about the Fortnights?

FIG. 8-4. Japan Fortnight shopping bag, 1974. Special shopping bags are designed for all Fortnights and are known as an instant status item.

(Courtesy, Neiman-Marcus, Dallas)

from the selected country, civic clubs invite speakers from the guest list attending the Fortnight by special invitation. The French Fortnight in 1957 brought in 200 French visitors on a special charter by Air France. That year, the event was opened by the mayor of the city and the French ambassador. In the evening, there was a gala ball in honor of the visitors.

The store is transformed for the Fortnights—visitors feel as if they are in the "guest" country while they are in the store. Frequently there is craftwork being done on the spot by a native craftsman. Fashion designers often are included. Since the French Fortnight of 1957, in

173

CHAPTER 8
*The importance of
fashion sales promotion*

conjunction with the fiftieth anniversary of the store, many other foreign countries have been featured yearly including Great Britain, Italy, Switzerland, Denmark, Austria, Ireland, South America, Hong Kong, and Japan.

Every new employee who joins the Neiman-Marcus Company is given a booklet about the store, which begins with these words:

> So glad you're here . . . your smart appearance, your warm friendliness, your interested efficiency . . . these are Neiman-Marcus. They make up what is referred to as "The Neiman-Marcus personality," a compelling quality that causes many of our customers to call Neiman-Marcus simply "The Store," as if there were no other. The Neiman-Marcus personality is expressed in: A porter's welcoming smile . . . a salesperson's interested concern . . . a fitter's pleasant understanding of figure problems . . . an executive's personal greeting . . . a credit man's interest in a family's budgeting . . . a packer's loving care of merchandise . . . a delivery man's extra courtesy . . . and in you, our newest staff member. You are now "what we're famous for."

Neiman-Marcus constantly reminds employees of the image the store is attempting to maintain. Thus employees feel very close to their store. Fashion buyers in the stores hold short daily meetings with salespeople to go over new arrivals of fashion apparel, explaining why the items were purchased and what special fashion features each has. Thus salespeople are well-informed about their stock.

The Neiman-Marcus stores are now in many areas of the United States—Atlanta; St. Louis; Chicago; Bal Harbour, Florida; and several Texas cities as well. They are a part of Carter Hawley Hale Stores, Inc., of Los Angeles, a group that acquired the Neiman-Marcus stores in 1968.

In December 1976, Stanley Marcus celebrated his fifty years in retailing with an informal party given by the employees of the Fort Worth store. Marcus would be the first to admit that to young people, fifty years in a store sounds like a lifetime sentence. But, he said, "I never got over the excitement of the people you meet—your customers, and the people who work in the store."

Neiman-Marcus customers are inclined to agree with Oscar Wilde, who said, "I have the simplest of taste—I am always satisfied with the best."

FIG. 8-5. The Neiman-Marcus image for beautiful store interiors is expressed in this Bal Harbour, Florida store.

(Courtesy, Neiman-Marcus, Dallas)

Sales promotion actually exists in all areas of business and production, but probably it is most exciting and offers the most opportunity for creative activities in the sphere of fashion merchandising.

In this chapter we will discuss the objectives of fashion sales promotion and the many popular ways in which it is practiced in fashion merchandising today. Since the most successful sales promotions always involve everyone in a retail store, you should be aware of exactly what is involved in sales promotion and what it is designed to accomplish. Even though you are a student, it is assumed that you are interested in advancing in the fashion merchandising world. Consequently, you need to know about sales promotional activities as if *you* are directly involved in planning and executing them.

Actually, sales promotional activities are becoming increasingly important in the successful fashion stores because competition grows continually greater and customers are becoming more and more selective in their buying.

What Is Fashion Sales Promotion?

Fashion sales promotion consists of all the functions and activities within a store that are developed and used to influence the sales of its fashion merchandise. These activities include personal selling, displays, advertising, fashion shows, and many other supplementary selling activities designed to increase sales of apparel.

SALES PROMOTION

Successful fashion sales promotions do many other things also. They build continuing customer loyalty to the particular store and they communicate the image that your store wishes to be known among its customers. Sales promotion efforts enlighten the public about new trends in fashion; inform the public of advanced methods of merchandising that will make it easier and more convenient to shop; and announce special merchandise events or special prices. The promotion is always aimed at attracting more customers and new groups of customers who may not have been shopping in the store. Fashion promotions frequently attempt to establish and continue to enforce a particular store's fashion leadership and authority. In effect, the store is saying, "See us first for all your apparel needs!"

What do fashion sales promotions do?

Who is responsible for planning fashion sales promotion events depends on the size of the organization. Larger businesses usually create special departments to plan promotions and assign the responsibility to specially trained individuals. These people work with all the departments in the store—merchandising, advertising, display, and publicity departments. The jobs are variously known as public relations, advertising and promotion, and so forth, but all are creative

Could I, should I, plan a store promotion?

FIG. 8-6. Bicentennial 1976 was a dominant theme in the sales promotion activities of many retailing businesses. This design by Woodward & Lothrop, Washington, D.C., was a major part of its display and merchandising efforts. It appeared on awnings, shopping bags, and wrapping paper. Loomed in fabric, it appeared on walls, display cabinets, and tables. It is illustrative of the effort the store made to create pride and awareness in Americans regarding their Bicentennial celebration. (Courtesy, Woodward & Lothrop.)

positions with the responsibility of promoting the store and its fashion apparel. In smaller stores, the promotion activities may be planned by the store manager or assistant. Actually, any store associate may present a sales promotion plan for consideration. Regardless of store size, the plan must be presented to top management for final approval, so we will discuss how to plan a fashion sales promotion and how to present it.

Planning a Fashion Sales Promotion

Individual fashion sales promotions must be a part of the total year's plans, so they are usually spaced apart on a planning calendar. They are designed to emphasize the seasonal apparel and to level out the peaks and valleys of fashion sales periods.

SALES PROMOTION CALENDAR   There are certain traditional department store activities that are generally associated with the long-range sales promotion calendar, and we will mention a few. You can probably think of many more.

JANUARY:	White sales (emphasis on linens and bath accessories—sometimes called "pink sales")	I know about these. Are they fashion promotions?

JANUARY: White sales (emphasis on linens and bath accessories—sometimes called "pink sales")
Fashion clearances—holiday fashions and fall and winter apparel

FEBRUARY: Introduction of "fifth-season" apparel (cruise clothes, early spring apparel)
Emphasis on Valentine's Day and patriotic holidays —red-white-blue colors

FIFTH-SEASON APPAREL

MARCH: Easter apparel featured

APRIL: Spring and summer apparel

MAY: Vacation apparel

JUNE: Brides and trousseaus

JULY: Post–4th of July clearances

AUGUST: Back-to-school; transitional (from summer to fall) apparel introduced

SEPTEMBER: Fall and winter apparel lines in peak assortment

OCTOBER: Halloween

NOVEMBER: Thanksgiving
Bride's trousseaus

DECEMBER: Christmas and holiday apparel
Apparel appropriate for gifts
Early spring apparel lines may be introduced

Interspersed with these traditional events, stores will hold store-wide anniversary sales, harvest sales, and many other special fashion sales promotion events.

GENERAL FASHION SALES PROMOTION CAMPAIGN PROCEDURES

1. Determine what the campaign is to do. What are the objectives?
2. Choose a central theme or idea to enhance its appeal.

How do you start? What do you do?

3. Decide to whom the campaign will be directed. Who is to be the target market?
4. Decide how you can best influence your target market and select the promotional activities that will best accomplish your objectives. (Advertising, special events, store displays, publicity, and any other store activity that will contribute to the effectiveness of the campaign.)
5. Develop a timetable and assign definite responsibility to the individuals who will carry out each of the activities. Decide who will be accountable. Schedule events.
6. Prepare the budget. Get approval—discuss the campaign with all executives concerned.
7. Execute the plans. When ready to begin, introduce it in a "kickoff" sales meeting to create enthusiasm and understanding among the sales personnel. Offer incentives to them.

177

8. Follow progress of the campaign closely. Be flexible if necessary to keep momentum going.
9. Evaluate the results. What benefits were accomplished? Decide if the costs were in line with the results.
10. Make recommendations for future campaigns of a similar nature.

In the remainder of the chapter we will discuss each of these fashion sales promotion campaign procedures.

DEVELOPING OBJECTIVES

Aren't all promotions for the purpose of increasing sales only?

Generally, your main purpose in developing a promotional campaign will be to increase sales of fashion items to more and more customers. When you evaluate the campaign effectiveness in the end, you will carefully analyze the point-of-sale results.

All fashion sales promotions and special events should be in conjunction with the long-range objectives of the business and its policies. They are directed toward impressing customers with the fashion leadership of the store, and projecting the best store image possible. Image

What is a store image?

has to do with what used to be referred to simply as "reputation." Today it concerns the total appearance or picture that a store has in the eyes of a fairly large group of the people with whom it does business. Actually a store presents its image not only to its customers, but to its employees, its vendors, and to its stockholders. It also projects its image to its city, its state, and perhaps the nation. The quality of the sales promotions that it develops play an important role in projecting the best store image to all people.

STORE IMAGE

Store images are not alike, even though two stores standing side by side may carry the same kinds of apparel at about the same prices, and look very much alike. Their store images will be as different as

How is a good store image achieved?

people are. Creating the image of your own store cannot be accomplished by copying anyone else. Like an individual, each store must have its own personality and its own method of expression. A clear-cut definition of a store's character is the first step in image projection and is essential to the objectives of its sales promotion activities. These activities must accurately mirror all that the store stands for in services, values, quality, assortments, taste, and fashion aggressiveness.

Why do some stores have a bad image?

Some stores project a mixed-up image to the public because the management doesn't have a clear understanding of what they stand for, or because their ideas change from month to month, or year to year, as they experience the ups and downs of business.

So, the objectives of all fashion sales promotions must accurately reflect why your store has value and deserves respect; these promotions should project your store image honestly and forcefully to increase your fashion sales, to keep your customers coming back to your store, and to keep your public interested.

CHOOSING A CENTRAL THEME OR IDEA

Above everything else, the theme of a sales promotion should be as attention-getting, as new and fresh an approach as you are capable of making it. It must be believable and completely honest in keeping with your store image.

The theme should emphasize the customer's point of view, and emphasize the benefits the customer will receive. A customer doesn't buy a dress or a suit—he or she buys what the dress or suit will do for him/her in terms of attractiveness, fashion smartness, and so forth.

The business that is highlighted in this chapter, Neiman-Marcus, was chosen because it has always done such an outstanding job of fashion sales promotion. Because of its clear understanding of the image it wants to project and its ability to express this image through long-range fashion promotion, this is one of the most respected high-fashion stores in the nation.

Once you have selected a specific theme and decided how you want to present it, then do so as well as you can. Use every possible means of creativity—do it dramatically.

SALES PROMOTION THEME
What must a promotion theme be like?

Why is the Neiman-Marcus label so prized?

CHOOSING THE TARGET MARKET

Your target market is the group of customers you wish to reach through your sales promotion. You will need to analyze these customers—are they present customers, or are you trying to reach an additional group or groups? What ages are they? Are they men and/or women? Do they belong to any special income group? Do they generally own their homes or live in apartments? How near do they live to your store? How fashion conscious are they? Are they high school graduates or college graduates? What are their occupations—professional or semiprofessional?

The answers to these questions will decide how you will proceed with your sales promotion activities, and will determine the media that you will use for most effectively reaching your desired target market.

TARGET MARKET
What should you know about your customers?

Once you know about your customers, what can you do with this information?

REACHING THE TARGET MARKET

Once you have decided to whom you are addressing your special fashion promotional campaign, you need to choose the kinds of events and advertising media that will most effectively reach these people. Usually, you will select several that will be supportive of each other, but all media should be selected for a well-defined purpose.

Newspaper advertising appears to be a leading choice for most retail stores, although many of the larger stores use magazine advertis-

NEWSPAPER ADVERTISING

ing and are developing television spots and using radio advertising more frequently. The particular way your store chooses to reach its target market depends on the amount of money available in the budget for use, and also on the verified circulation—readership or listening audience—of each of the media. This information is available from newspapers, magazines, television and radio stations. Because these media are in a highly competitive market, they are as anxious as possible to maintain their readership or listening audience. They subscribe to many rating services and do a great amount of target audience surveying as well.

Do radio and TV stations know anything about their audiences?

Newspapers are generally read by 80 to 90 percent of the people, and unquestionably provide a good communication channel by which potential customers can be reached. The size and position of your advertisement is an important consideration. Preferred positions (in the women's section if advertising is directed to women, or in the sports section, if your advertising is directed to men, for example) are more expensive than run-of-the-paper positions. Preferred positions are not always available, because they are given first to the stores that contract for a particular space over a long-range period. Color gets more reader attention, but it is more expensive than black and white. Your objective is to *reach* as large a readership as possible, advertise as *frequently* as possible, and be as *consistent* and *continuous* in projecting your fashion story as possible.

Why do so many fashion stores advertise in newspapers?

Good newspaper advertisements contain the following parts, and all are generally necessary:

What should a newspaper ad contain?

Headline. Gets the attention of the reader and clearly shows the intent of the advertisement

Copy. Descriptive of the apparel or sales event being advertised

Illustration. Should do what the copy says—setting the mood for the advertisement, and projecting store image to a large extent

Logo. Store name and location

Radio advertising is an excellent means of attracting the attention of people—we have radios almost everywhere we go. They wake us up in the mornings, and they may be the last thing we hear when we go to sleep at night. There are an estimated 350 million sets in use in the United States, and about one-third of these are FM or stereo sets.

I like to listen to radio on my way to work. Isn't that the best time to advertise?

Cost of radio advertising is determined by the length of the announcement and the time the announcement is made. The important times for various "target audiences" are:

Drive Time: 6–10 A.M. and 3–7 P.M.
Housewife Time: 10 A.M.–3 P.M.
Evening Time: 7 P.M.–12 midnight.

181
CHAPTER 8
*The importance of
fashion sales promotion*

Radio advertising differs from newspaper advertising, because when you buy newspaper space, you are more assured of circulation. You can't be sure your advertising will be read but at least you know the number of subscribers to the newspaper. Radio advertising coverage and audience is less certain. So, when you buy radio advertising time, you are really only buying the air time of a certain station. You cannot be sure how much of the radio audience will listen. A radio station may have a very large coverage but a relatively small audience. Radio stations are very conscious of their coverage and reach, so audience studies are conducted regularly. They plan their programming with specific audiences in mind—the teenager, the housewife, or their drive-time listeners, for example. When they accomplish their programming goals, the retailer can pick the most desirable market time to accomplish specific objectives of a sales promotion event. However, radio advertising has one limitation in fashion apparel advertising that makes it less desirable than television advertising—television can actually show the fashion apparel in action.

**RADIO
ADVERTISING
SPOTS**

Radio advertising is a growing medium for advertising, in spite of its limitations, and the friendly announcer can deliver your selling message at a low cost for each thousand listeners. It is a medium available to small as well as large retail advertising promotion events.

*Isn't radio advertising
expensive?*

**TELEVISION
ADVERTISING**

Television advertising is becoming increasingly more important in fashion sales promotion. It has been estimated that over 90 percent of American homes have TV sets and they are viewed on the average of about five hours every day per person. Commercial time are sold in 10-, 20-, 30-second or one-minute spots. As with radio, the time that TV commercials are run determines the cost, and choice time spots on national broadcasts can run into several hundreds of thousands of dollars, for example.

Evening hours between 7 and 11 P.M. are considered prime time because these hours have the largest viewing audience. One hour before and after prime time is fringe time, which is somewhat less expensive. The local television station usually has a coverage of approximately 100 miles and is an effective way to reach a mass audience through sight, sound, and motion.

*How do you get a TV
commercial made?*

Producing a good television commercial must be considered. Production costs need not be prohibitive. Some of the larger retail institutions have their own personnel for the purpose. Others use a small production company, write their own copy, and supervise the production through their advertising staff. Independent advertising agencies produce effective commercials, and television stations themselves are also excellent producers, eager to assist their advertisers. But many advertising dollars must be committed when the decision is made to go into television advertising.

While television advertising has some limitations, especially in holding the attention of the viewer long enough to help him remember the merchandise you are advertising, the usage and expenditures for it are growing by large percentages each year. Improvements are reducing some of the costs of production also. It is well worth considering as a part of a fashion sales promotion plan. There is probably no more exciting and glamorous way to reach the greatest number of people at any one time.

DIRECT-MAIL ADVERTISING

Where do you get your best mailing list?

Direct-mail advertising is usually the first form of advertising that a fashion firm uses. When you consider how much direct-mail advertising you receive through your daily mail, you can readily see that it is an extremely popular form of advertising. It also produces outstanding results.

Charge customers are an excellent source for direct-mail advertising because store advertising can be sent to them along with monthly statements. Statement enclosures such as these are designed to get mail or telephone orders, and to stimulate people to come into the store for special sales events.

But mass mailings are costly, too, when you consider the cost of printing and postage on a list of charge customers that can run into hundreds of thousands for some stores. However, the results can be astounding, because customers consider direct mail to be personal attention, and are favorably inclined toward buying and visiting the store.

FASHION SHOWS

What are the ingredients for a really good fashion show?

Of all special events used by fashion stores, the *fashion show* is one of the favorites—of the fashion buying public as well as the stores themselves. The successful fashion show needs to be carefully planned; there must be excellent advance publicity to assure that an audience worth all the time and effort involved will be secured. An appropriate theme for the season you are promoting should be chosen, and all garments shown should emphasize the theme, through color, fabric, and styling details. It is best to choose some "smash conversational" garments for the beginning and end of the show especially. Garments should be grouped into natural categories, which ordinarily are daytime clothes, sportswear, travel clothes, sleepwear and lingerie, or after-five and evening clothes—all of which are easy categories with which to work.

The models should typify the specific audience group to which you are addressing the show—college group, career women, clubwomen, high school students; or if you have a mixed or dissimilar group, you should use models of several types. If you anticipate that men may be present for the show, then present some suits or leisure clothes for their interest.

Never overlook the appeal that child models have, especially in an audience of young mothers or grandmothers. Train the models to move gracefully and somewhat rapidly so that all the garments will be presented to their best advantage and to keep the show fast-moving.

183

CHAPTER 8
The importance of
fashion sales promotion

Commentators sometimes do not use notes for their commentary, but those who are unsure of their stage presence should have some notes available. The commentary should be brisk, brief, and fast-paced, but it should point out the main features of the garments and any unusual or noteworthy detail. Live music is desirable when possible for background, but it should always be subdued so that your audience is barely aware of it.

*How can you make sure
your show will run
smoothly?*

The stage setup and runway—including scenery, lighting, microphone, and entrance and exits—should be checked well in advance of the start of the show to assure a smooth-running program from beginning to end. Dress rehearsals are well worth the time and expense involved. Audience seating arrangements should be carefully planned to assure comfortable viewing.

One of your main objectives in giving a fashion show is good after-the-show sales. Therefore, be sure you are stocked in depth on all featured show garments and accessories. It is also a compelling reason for having the fashion show within your own store if at all possible. If this isn't feasible, try to hold the show as near to your store as you can, being sure that adequate parking space is available.

The appearance of celebrities at fashion shows is valuable not only in securing a good viewing audience but also because this creates publicity for the event and for your store, which we will discuss presently.

SPECIAL EVENTS

All *special events* are for the express purpose of increasing store traffic and giving your ready-to-wear greater exposure. There are many kinds of special events used in modern retailing today for these purposes. They include flower shows for the garden clubs, trunk showings by designers, informal modeling of fashion apparel in tearooms, customer contests, parades at Thanksgiving and Christmas, fashion advisory boards, gift-wrapping events, schools of instruction on sewing techniques in fabrics departments, and a host of others. Any time that a special event creates publicity for your store, you gain an additional advantage.

*Planning big events must
be a lot of trouble. Are
they really worthwhile?*

PUBLICITY

Publicity for your special events in the form of news releases in newspapers or on television are an important kind of advertising for your store for which you cannot pay, and over which you have little actual control.

Publicity departments prepare press releases and send them to the advertising media—newspapers, radio and television stations—in the hope that they will be of such news value that they will be featured. Actually, such publicity-seeking events are carefully planned happenings.

*How can you get some
publicity for your
fashion store?*

No doubt you have seen much publicity concerning fashion.

Fashion innovations are generally newsworthy and secure wide, interested reading or viewing audiences.

*Lots of stores prepare
Christmas catalogs.
Why don't they get
publicity?*

As you have already read in our Neiman-Marcus feature, this store's Christmas catalog probably receives more publicity than any other store catalog. This is because it always features what to give the person who "has everything." The gifts—usually for "him and her"—are always unique and fabulous, and many of them cannot be bought anywhere else in the world. Because of their unusual nature, these items make news—first-page stories in the newspapers, on radio and television newscasts. They're items that are always discussed by people in the vicinity of the stores, and are "right" for Neiman-Marcus because of its unique store image.

*How important are
point-of-purchase
displays?*

Store displays are another important influence in attracting your target market. It is true that "goods well displayed are half sold." Both the window and interior displays should tie in directly with your store promotions and advertising, and should be as carefully planned in advance as any other activity.

Studies of the shopping habits of today's customers have clearly shown that display merchandise has less than seconds to catch the attention of a passing customer, so packaging and display techniques are receiving increased emphasis.

An attention-arresting store window can stop the window-shopping customer and bring him or her inside to look around. Once inside, the person must be further exposed to buying suggestions by way of strategically located island, floor, or ledge displays. Mannequins have the advantage of being three-dimensional and show how a garment will appear when worn and accessorized for the total look. Someone in the fashion department should be assigned the responsibility of checking floor displays at frequent intervals during the selling day to make sure they are not in disarray.

How often fashion windows and interior displays should be changed will depend on the frequency of the individual customer's visits to the store. Generally, it is recommended that windows be changed about once a week, and interior displays more often.

DEVELOPING A TIMETABLE; ASSIGNING RESPONSIBILITIES; SCHEDULING THE EVENTS

Adequate planning time before the beginning of a fashion sales promotion plan is most essential. Contracting for advertising space in newspapers or time on radio or television must be arranged, and the time and space must be bought, in order to maximize the investment in advertising media. Usually, advance preparation requires six weeks.

Once you have contracted for the advertising medium to be used, prepare a schedule of the pattern of time and space usage and assign

185
CHAPTER 8
*The importance of
fashion sales promotion*

the responsibility for each to a specific person in the organization who will be accountable for seeing that all deadlines are met.

How long any specific fashion sales promotion should last is determined by a number of factors:

1. What your objectives are
2. The interest value that will be generated among your customers
3. Allowing a reasonable amount of time for the campaign to be known, but not to become boring to customers or salespeople
4. Enough time for all interested customers to be able to come to the store
5. How much time it will take to accomplish your objectives
6. History of similar promotions in the past

It is a matter of judgment when the time length of a fashion campaign is set. It should have a definite beginning and a definite ending. It should be timely, and the advertising should peak during the beginning of the campaign period.

Special clearances usually last for three days. They are announced in Sunday newspapers, for example, and allowed to run for the first three days of the week. Or they are announced in the Wednesday evening papers, to run on the last three days of the week. Weekends may allow more customers an opportunity to take advantage of special sales. Storewide anniversary sales may run for a week or longer.

Fashion sales promotion plans should never be allowed to run so long that they lose their momentum. Depending on the amount of involvement the promotion has, and the extent of the results in increased sales anticipated, it might run for a week or ten days.

Note that the Fortnights for which Neiman-Marcus is famous run successfully for two weeks.

PREPARE THE BUDGET—GET APPROVAL
FOR THE CAMPAIGN

Once the planning is completed, then an exact cost figure for every aspect of executing the plan should be prepared and presented to the executive or the executive committee authorized to approve it.

The budget should be detailed to show a breakdown of how much each activity in the campaign will cost, the exact dates of advertising frequency and the cost, with a final total of expenses for the entire campaign.

*When you have
formulated a plan,
when can you start?*

When the budget is presented, an estimate of sales expectations should be given and justified. It may take a carefully planned sales presentation to gain approval for the plan. Adequate time should be allowed for questions and suggestions from the executive committee.

If it meets approval, or modifications are made, such as deletion of certain expenditures, agreement on the final cost should be secured, and the planned fashion sales promotion is ready to be executed.

EXECUTING THE PLANS

Why have a sales meeting?

When everything is in readiness and the time nears for the campaign to begin, it is time for the "kickoff" sales meeting with all the sales associates in the fashion department.

An interesting meeting must be planned. Skits showing good fashion selling vs. poor fashion selling might be included. Or a skit about how to overcome sales objections would be beneficial. Clever stunts can keep interest high, but these must be fast-moving—never draggy. Some training materials should be passed out summarizing the main points brought out in the meeting, as the meeting closes.

How can you keep a sales meeting interesting?

Your main objective is to generate lots of enthusiasm for the new fashion sales promotion. If there are to be sales contests or special sales incentives, they should be announced and explained.

Perhaps no area of your entire planning is as important as this sales meeting. If the salespeople fail, then the best of sales promotions are of no avail—they fail also.

FOLLOWING THE PROGRESS OF THE CAMPAIGN

The sales promotion job is only half accomplished if the salespeople fall back to doing their routine daily duties, forgetting all about the campaign. Daily reports on the campaign progress should be given in order to keep everyone involved motivated to action. Credits or awards for outstanding sales performance should be given periodically.

How can you keep the sales force excited?

The momentum and interest must be maintained so the campaign never slows down. If some flexibility is required, adjust to it and proceed until the very end.

EVALUATING THE RESULTS

Why should you summarize the results?

At the end of the promotion, as soon as sales figures are available, the results should be carefully analyzed. Were the costs of the campaign justified by the results? Were the objectives met?

Everyone who participated will be eager for the results also. This is the time to show appreciation for the enthusiasm shown by the participants; this should be done as dramatically as any other part of the campaign.

MAKING RECOMMENDATIONS FOR THE FUTURE

For the benefit of all future fashion sales promotion planning, it is essential that the results of the campaign are carefully written.

What were the most successful parts of the campaign that should be repeated? Could anything have been eliminated? Should anything be added for greater emphasis in future campaigns? Were the planned objectives met? Why or why not? Were the costs justified? Was the timing and scheduling appropriate?

Are the recommendations of any value in the future?

Recommendations and general observations about the success of the campaign justify the time in careful preparation, and are of great value in all future planning. They should be made as soon after the close of the campaign as possible so no detail is overlooked. The successful campaign will be repeated!

Conclusion

Opportunities for interesting and worthwhile fashion sales promotion campaigns are almost unlimited, regardless of the amount of budgeted money that is available.

Creative, well-planned fashion promotions accomplish tangible results of sales increases and customer traffic. They often accomplish intangible results that are not as easily measured, too. They generate enthusiasm and interest among your customers, they project an aggressive image for your store's fashion position, and they encourage your store personnel by creating glamor and excitement in their jobs.

Review Questions

1. Define or identify the following:
   a. Sales promotion
   b. Store image
   c. Point-of-purchase displays
   d. Radio advertising spots
   e. Television advertising
   f. Newspaper advertising
   g. Publicity
   h. Direct-mail advertising
   i. Store displays
   j. Sales promotion calendar
   k. Fifth-season apparel
   l. Sales promotion theme
   m. Target market
   n. Fashion shows
   o. Special events
2. Name traditional sales promotion events usually used in the promotional calendars of department stores. Can you name additional ones used in your community which may not have been mentioned in this chapter?
3. Trace the development of a well-organized fashion sales promotion

plan from beginning to end, using all ten points discussed in this chapter.

4. Is it important for a store to define the image it desires to project in its community? How is good store image achieved?

5. Most department stores feel that they are wasting good potential postage if they do not include some enclosures of a sales promotion each month when they send out the customer billings. Do you agree? Why is it a good idea?

6. If you were selected to coordinate a fashion show, what organization would you develop?

7. What should always be done at the end of a sales promotion campaign? Why is it helpful and important to the store?

8. Why do you think Neiman-Marcus has achieved its position of fashion leadership?

Suggested Student Activities

1. Observe and name fashion sales promotion events that may be going on right now in your own community. What are the stores promoting? How do the campaigns seem to be progressing?

2. List as many sales promotion events as you can that are being promoted through national television advertising or on radio or in magazine advertising.

3. Plan a fashion sales promotion campaign for a local (or imagined) store. Be sure to follow the steps for successful planning.

4. *Reach, frequency, and continuity* are three very important terms in fashion sales promotion. Define each, and classify the events you selected in activity #1, for the impact of each in your community.

Case Problems

Case 8-1. After reading her newspaper, a customer calls a prominent local department store, and inquires of the operator about a special item of interest to her that has been advertised that day. The operator replies, "Oh, are we advertising dresses at that price?"

1. How does this sales promotion campaign fail in an important area of the planning function?

2. Should the telephone operator be held responsible for reading the store's advertising each day?

3. Does any responsibility for her lack of knowledge about the store's advertised specials have anything to do with those who planned the specials in the first place? Who should be held accountable?

4. Have you ever had an experience similar to this one? Did it affect your opinion (image) of the store?

Case 8-2. The following conversation took place between two women who were just leaving a fashion show. "I couldn't see below the models' waistlines, could you?" "No, and I wonder what kind of shoes the model wore with that jumpsuit." "Could you hear the commentator?" "Yes, most of the time, but she talked so much—I really didn't listen to her all the time." "The music was good. I really liked the violins. Did you notice the trumpet player?" "How could I help it—he played so loud!" "It seemed quite long, didn't you think so?" And, on and on.

1. What areas of fashion show planning were obviously overlooked in this presentation?
2. How would you plan a show to improve at least these three or four criticisms?

Case 8-3. Jim opened his letter from the department store which contained his bill for the month. As often occurs in circumstances like this, his first reaction was, "How could I have purchased this much?" Then his eye fell on several enclosures that came along with the statement. His interest in purchasing the items displayed on the enclosures immediately gave him his answer.

1. Why do you think Jim's charge account surprised him? Do you think Jim was buying from a good department store? Why?
2. What are some of the values of statement enclosures?

Case 8-4. Mrs. Sims read with considerable interest several pages of good department store advertising in her newspaper. Early the next morning she went to the store prepared to select a new fall wardrobe in the departments that had advertised. First she went to the shoe department, which was bustling with activity. Evidently others had been attracted by the advertising also. Since she was not immediately assisted, she moved around in the department hoping she would see the advertised shoes on display and be able to examine them more closely. She couldn't find them.

1. What do you think may have happened in the fall wardrobe promotional plan that caused the shoes not to be on display? Who was accountable for the problem?
2. How could this problem have been avoided?

Chapter 9

The creation of fashion apparel: fibers to fabrics to garments

Objectives

When you have read this chapter, you should be able to

1. Explain how the history of fabric development is interwoven with developing civilization and why it is important to fashion merchandising
2. Discuss the extent of textile fiber consumption today, and explain the areas in which textiles are used most extensively
3. Discuss the significant developments of the natural fibers from primitive times to the present
4. List some of the memorable dates in the history of cotton, showing how these events were significant for fabric production in general
5. Explain how man-made fibers were discovered, how long they have been in existence, and how they differ from natural fibers
6. Classify the important laws that have been passed for fabrics and explain the purpose of these laws
7. Explain the processes that fibers undergo to become yarn and finally cloth, as carried out in our present manufacturing methods
8. Show the time sequence involved in getting fabrics made into garments and on their way to the consumers, with emphasis on the need for speed in the procedures
9. Explain how the great apparel marts under one roof have made buying trips much more pleasant and efficient

Often called the "nat-
ural buying center of
America . . . where
you can see every-
thing under the sun,"
the Apparel Mart of
Dallas is a vibrant
softgoods market. It
has been growing
every year, as more
and more buyers from

coast to coast and from at least fourteen foreign countries realize the
ease and convenience of seeing almost 8,700 lines of apparel concentrated under one gigantic roof. Merchandise categories include
ladies' apparel, children's apparel, men's apparel, ladies' accessories,
men's accessories, shoes, and textiles.

Built in 1964 at a cost of over $15 million, the Apparel Mart was
an instant success. It was expanded in 1968 and again in 1973 to accommodate the demand for more showroom space by manufacturers.
It now encompasses a space of 1,300,000 square feet, and still the demand for space continues by the many producers of fashion apparel
who want to display their goods to the growing thousands of buyers.

In the center of the mart is a Great Hall, which serves as a mam-
moth hub for the Apparel Mart, with overhanging balconies from the
lobbies on every floor. It is a room so large that it could by itself hold
a large building. There are staging facilities for major fashion shows
which are marketwide reviews open to all registered buyers at each
show. Four thousand people can be seated auditorium style, or 2,400
banquet style in its opulent space graced by fountains, live greenery,
and flowers.

The Apparel Mart is a part of the huge Dallas Market Center
Complex which also includes the Trade Mart, Homefurnishings Mart,
Market Hall, World Trade Center, and Decorative Center. Annual
sales of the market center are in excess of $5 billion, of which over
one-third represents apparel. There are never less than five major
women's/children's/textile shows per year, plus two major shoe markets
and five menswear markets.

Shows are planned as long as ten years in advance to assure adequate housing for out-of-town buyers. There is parking space adjacent
to the Apparel Mart for 7,800 cars.

There is a strong showing of many New York and Los Angeles
couture houses in the Dallas Mart. Previously, some of these couture
houses had held shows in downtown hotels, but with their move to the
more convenient, concentrated location at the Mart, they realized

FIG. 9-1. During a market as many as 8,700 cars are parked adjacent to the Dallas Apparel Mart. Licence plates from almost every state in the United States can easily be found. (Courtesy, Dallas Apparel Mart)

their greatest growth potential for any market outside their cities. They are most enthusiastic about the Mart because of the volume of new accounts they have opened and the subsequent repeat business they now enjoy.

In 1977, during the women's and children's early fall market, the Apparel Mart featured Fashions International, a showing of import lines, many of which were appearing in the United States and Dallas for the first time. The collections of fashion apparel and accessories from France, Spain, England, Italy, Rumania, Israel, Brazil, Canada, Hong Kong, Germany, and other countries were available throughout the Mart.

For buyers, the import show eliminated the necessity of traveling abroad as many had been doing in the past. Long travel commitments and the time involvement away from places of business constitute a large expense. The show also eliminated many of the shipping and communications problems buyers have often experienced with imports in the past. For buyers who either have not regularly traveled abroad on buying trips, or do not go at all, the showing was an exciting opportunity to view and select the latest in import merchandise.

FIG. 9-2. This 42,000 square foot Great Hall is terraced on seven levels and features natural planting, fountains, and overhanging balconies. The Hall has complete stage facilities for fashion shows.

The success of Fashions International will probably assure its becoming a feature at the Apparel Mart in the future.

How fortunate we are to be living in the century that has seen so many advances in the textile and apparel manufacturing industries. When we ponder that for five thousand years the only fabrics—natural fibers—known to man were made of wool, cotton, silk, or flax, it is almost unbelievable that today we have such a vast choice.

Fabric development goes back several centuries before recorded history. The early Stone Age pictures scratched or painted on cave walls show that early human beings had discovered that the fleece of sheep was softer, warmer, and more comfortable than the skins of other wild animals. The romantic history of silk begins more than

NATURAL FIBERS

How long has clothing existed?

4,000 years ago, and weaves its way like a gleaming thread through tales of Oriental splendor and Western majesty down to the news stories of today's latest fashions. In 5,000 B.C., cotton was cultivated and used in the Tehaucan Valley of Mexico. Scientists have determined that fiber and boll fragments found in this area were about 7,000 years old. The flax plant that contains the long, strong fibers that make linen cloth is known to have been raised by the Egyptians more than 5,000 years ago.

MAN-MADE FIBERS

It was in this century of ours that *man learned to make fibers!* The first man-made fiber, rayon, was introduced in the United States in 1911. Acetate followed in 1925. Although rayon and acetate were the first "synthetics," they are in fact only partly man-made, since both are rebuilt from cellulose, the basic ingredient of vegetable matter.

The first true "man-made fiber" to become a commercial reality was nylon, introduced by Du Pont in 1938. From that time on a full fiber spectrum followed. Today, there are so very many that it becomes increasingly difficult to answer the question, "What fiber is best for a specific purpose?"

When we consider how slow and time-consuming it was to produce even a small amount of cloth centuries ago, and how expensive and valuable it was, it is almost impossible to believe that now about 23 billion square yards of fabric are produced each year. Today, cloth is still exciting. It is high fashion, moon suits, nose cones, inflatable buildings, artificial arteries, and more new and exquisite fabrics. Cloth is all of these things, and yet some methods of constructing fabric are still used that have been around for hundreds of years. Only the speed and machinery have changed. Today, fabric making is computerized, electronic and modern in production. It's market- and style-oriented. Cloth can wind up as anything from a bikini to a portable bridge.

What uses does cloth have?

In this chapter we will explore parts of the fascinating history of fabrics, discuss how they are produced, and suggest recommended ways to care for them. And we will discuss how fabrics become the garments that consumers buy in retail stores. This chapter is only an introduction to fabrics. Do take a course in *textiles*—it will be interesting and valuable.

Textile Fiber Consumption Today[1]

The 23 billion square yards of fabric produced each year are made from the natural fibers—cotton, wool, silk, and flax—and from man-made fibers—nylon, rayon, polyester, acrylic, and a number of others.

[1] *All About Textiles,* American Textile Manufacturers Institute, Inc. (Charlotte, N.C., 1976), pp. 1–9.

Textile Fiber Consumption (in pounds)		
	1976 (Est.)	**1975**
Man-made	**8.0 billion**	7.4 billion
Cotton	**3.4 billion**	3.1 billion
Wool	**128.0 million**	132.0 million
Silk	**1.0 million**	1.0 million
Total	**11.5 billion**	10.6 billion

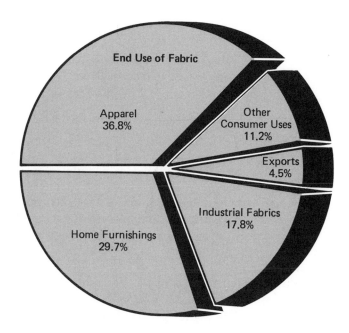

FIG. 9-3. These charts explain the textile fiber consumption and end use of fabrics.

(American Textile Manufacturers Institute, Inc., *All About Textiles*, North Carolina, 1976.)

Throughout the history of the American textile industry, cotton was king until the 1960s, when man-made fibers outpaced it in use. Today the textile industry consumes about 11.5 billion pounds of fibers annually. Of these fibers, over 69 percent are man-made, while

Which is the most important fiber today?

29 percent are cotton. About 2 percent are wool and silk. The average American consumes around 59 pounds of fibers a year, with the same percentage breakdown.

Where does fabric go after textile plants have produced it? (See Figure 9–3.) More of it goes into the making of apparel than into any other type of product, although home furnishings run a fairly close second. Everyone is familiar with the products in the latter category— clothing, sheets, and pillow cases, drapery and towels, carpets and upholstery. Three million Americans depend on textiles and apparel for their jobs.

Textile Fiber Consumption
(in pounds)

	1976 est.	1975
Man-made	8.0 billion	7.4 billion
Cotton	3.4 billion	3.1 billion
Wool	128.0 million	132.0 million
Silk	1.0 million	1.0 million
Total	11.5 billion	10.6 billion

All About Textiles, American Textile Manufacturers Institute, Inc. (Charlotte, N.C., 1976), pp. 1–9.

Throughout the world, the textile industry is immense. Production of textiles and apparel in the United States alone accounts for one job in every eight. No other industry makes such a massive contact with people, in millions of jobs, and billions of items.

Do we know how much
we depend on textiles?

Yet most of us do not realize how important textiles are to us. When we brush our teeth first thing in the morning, chances are that the brush bristles are made of synthetics produced by the textile fiber industry. Even the newspaper we read could never have been produced without textile conveyor belts and meshes.

The clothes we put on represent the accumulation of the talents of thousands of years of spinning, weaving, knitting, printing, or dyeing. When we drive our cars we feel secure knowing that its tires are held together by textile fibers.

When the astronauts went to the moon, their voyage was made possible by a textile-cased nose cone that withstood the heat of re-entry and allowed them to return alive. Many people are alive today thanks to artificial heart vessels developed through textile science.

Fabrics are a part of our heritage and our history—they have been the object of intercontinental trade and economics, conquests and wars have been waged because of them, they have been coveted, worn, and loved. Textiles are a necessity, a luxury, a way of life, an art, and a science.

197

CHAPTER 9
*The creation of fashion
apparel: fibers to
fabrics to garments*

When we try on a handsome, doubleknit suit or a pretty print dress, we are seeing the newest advance in an old art. To appreciate better where we are today, we must look back to where we have been.

*Who were the first
weavers?*

We know that at least 4,000 years ago the Egyptians were making fine cloth from cotton or linen spun by hand, as fine as the best made by modern machinery. Undoubtedly the skill of weaving started long before that, but we don't know when people first learned to weave. Even in the Stone Age, the prehistoric Lake Dwellers of Europe wore woolen clothing. Perhaps man's first attempt at weaving could have been in the crafting of baskets or fishing nets, or as he interlaced tree limbs to form his shelter.

At any rate, early man produced a crude cloth that was in some respects similar to what we see today. Always, though, it was a product of handwork, done at the cost of much labor and for an isolated, limited purpose. Cloth was a prized possession and in great demand.

Where there has been demand, human beings have always found methods of increasing production. Individual weaving continued past the times of Greece and Rome until shortly after the birth of modern England, when the Lancashire area of that country became the center of the great handicraft textile industry. Fabrics were produced there up to the beginning of the Industrial Revolution, 200 years ago.

*What caused cloth
production to improve?*

Then, new methods of increasing production began to appear on the scene, cutting down on man-hours: a fly shuttle to eliminate the need for a weaver's helper and quicken the pace of hand weaving; a spinning jenny and then a spinning frame to spin many ends of yarn at the same time; and ultimately a power loom to speed up the process of weaving. Finally, all these processes were combined into one mill that would begin with raw materials and end with cloth.

Who was responsible?

The names of men like Arkwright, Cartwright, Jacquard, and Whitney still live today in many modern processes. The processes took hundreds of years to develop, but today, a shirt or a blouse, once a great luxury, is a modern bargain. Furthermore, that shirt or blouse is finer today than those fit for a king only 100 years ago, and they don't cost a king's ransom, either.

Fibers Today

There are two families of fiber used to make fabric today. One family consists of fiber from nature itself—such as cotton, wool, silk, and flax—which remains pretty much in the form in which it is found. The

[1] *Textiles from Start to Finish,* American Textile Manufacturers Institute, Inc., 2nd printing (Charlotte, N.C., 1974), pp. 1–21.

other, man-made fibers, are produced from other substances, such as oil and wood cellulose. Increasingly, today's modern fabrics use combinations of natural and man-made fibers, known as blends.

TABLE 9-1.   Textile Fibers

generic names for man-made fibers
(as defined by the Federal Trade Commission.)

Acetate and Triacetate	Metallic	Rayon
Acrylic	Modacrylic	Rubber
Anidex	Nylon	Saran
Azlon	Nytril	Spandex
Glass	Olefin	Vinal
Lastrile	Polyester	Vinyon

natural fibers most widely used

Asbestos	Flax	Silk
Cotton	Jute	Wool
	Mohair	

Burlington Industries, Inc., *Textile Fibers and Their Properties* (Greensboro, N.C., 1970), p. 4.

Natural Fibers

WOOL[1]

Sheep have walked along with men through the pages of written history. Wool gave the primitive hunter warm clothing and protective tents which extended his range into extreme climates. As we follow the wool development from that first raw fleece worn by the hunter to the luxurious fabric in the suit of the jet traveler today, we are retracing man's long journey from the cave to the present.

Why was wool called the "golden fleece?"

Wool is one of the very first commodities with enough value to make international trade necessary and desirable. Wool garments were worn in Babylon (which means land of wool) as early as 4000 B.C., and archeologists have found inscribed seals from that period which indicate that trade in wool had begun. Clay tablets from 2500 B.C. indicate that Mesopotamia had developed an important sheep industry, and there also are accounts of Sumerian merchants who were apparently selling the "golden fleece" to surrounding nations.

The first tailored suits are credited to the horsemen of the nomadic hordes from the Asian steppes who wore pants and coats made of wool as they made their successive invasions into the Near East during the year 2000 B.C. These barbarians were herdsmen on a large

[1] American Wool Council, Wool Education Center, *The Story of Wool* (Denver, Col., 1968); pp. 2–21.

scale and they brought with them wool carpets as well as "tailored" clothes.

Phonecian traders spread wool, wool fabric, and the art of weaving throughout the Mediterranean area and are said to have taken the first sheep to England. References which reflect the pastoral life of the times are found in the literature from the Homeric Greeks and the early Latins.

The Romans took sheep to Spain, because they considered the climate there ideal for raising them. From this first scientific breeding came the Merino sheep, one of the foundation breeds of the world. Spanish wool was, in fact, considered to be the best in the world at that time, and the death penalty threatened anyone taking a Merino out of Spain. It was the wool trade wealth that helped finance the explorations of Columbus and the Conquistadores.

Did wool have something to do with the discovery of America?

When the Romans conquered and occupied the British Isles in 55 B.C., they brought the craft of wool textile production with them. The craft became an art from which grew the great British Empire. By 1660, wool textile exports comprised two-thirds of England's foreign commerce. When the English developed wool manufacturing machinery, the demand for wool cloth grew so rapidly that new sources of raw wool were needed. The supply was found in the dominions of South Africa and Australia, where the climates favored the development of sheep flocks. From these early Merino sheep have sprung the herds that make Australia the principal wool-producing nation of today.

Where is the best wool grown today?

When Columbus made his second voyage in 1493, sheep were among the livestock he brought with him, and so sheep came to the New World.

Wherever the early explorers and conquerors traveled, they took sheep with them because the sheep were an ambulatory supply of food and clothing. Thus sheep were spread across Mexico and the southern area of the United States from coast to coast.

Why were sheep taken nearly everywhere?

The sheep population grew sharply and, by 1698, there was considerable trade in wool and fabric among the early colonists. There is little doubt that the action of the English monarchs, in attempting to suppress the growth of wool production and manufacturing in the colonies, was actually one of the foundation stones which eventually led to the American Revolution. Then, wool became a symbol of patriotism and protest, and many colonists who could afford the fine English broadcloths of the time wore the rougher homespun instead. Home spinning, weaving, and knitting were encouraged.

Throughout the 1800s, as people moved across the fertile middle-river valleys of the United States, the sheep population moved with them. Today, there are sheep in every one of the fifty states, and they grow the fiber that is the raw material for a great industry. The

Is wool still important?

simple sheep that fulfilled the needs of the Stone Age master fills the needs of modern society today.

Wool is sheared from the sheep and taken to the mill. At one end of the mill are the huge bags and bales of raw or grease wool; at the other is the rainbow of color and beauty that is the finished fabric; and in between is the incredibly complex maze of giant machinery. The manufacturing of wool is similar to the methods used in other types of fabric production, so the processes will be discussed later in the chapter.

The Wool Label. The label on the wool garment or fabric is placed there to help the customer buy and the salesperson sell more wisely. The Wool Products Labeling Act of 1939 states that its purpose is "to protect producers, manufacturers, distributors and consumers from the unrevealed presence of substitutes and mixtures in spun, woven, knitted, felted, or otherwise manufactured wool products. . . ." A tag, stamp, label, or other marking telling the wool content, and the condition or type of wool, must be affixed to all fabrics containing wool. Wool is the fiber from the sheep; also from Angora and Cashmere goats, camel, llama, alpaca, and vicuna.

Are there different kinds of wool fiber?

Virgin, or *new wool,* refers to wool converted into yarn or fabric for the first time. *Reprocessed wool* is made from samples, cutting-table scraps, and mill ends that are collected and made into other fabrics. Such wool has never been worn or "used." *Re-used wool* is just what the name implies—old rags and clothes that have been worn are collected, cleaned, and converted into fabric, usually by blending with some new wool to provide necessary strength.

Look for this label on wool garments.

COTTON[1]

No one knows exactly where cotton originated or when. Early Egyptians used it in clothing, imports came from India. It was grown in Mexico in 5000 B.C. We know that it is one of the oldest and most versatile of all fibers and its good properties blend well with other fibers.

In the United States, cotton is grown in nineteen states and is a major crop in some fourteen states where it averages a third of all crop marketings. (See Figure 9-6.) The Cotton Belt stretches across the southern part of the country from lower Virginia to California.

Why does everyone like cotton clothing?

Cotton meets the three major demands of a textile product: appearance, performance, and comfort. Its good appearance is accounted for by its ability to hold bright, lasting colors, the wide variety of weaves and textures, and its adaptability to many different kinds of

[1] The National Cotton Council of America, *COTTON—From Field to Fabric* (Memphis, Tenn., n.d.), pp. 1–16.

PURE WOOL

FIG. 9-4. (The "Wool-mark" is a certification mark owned by The Wool Bureau, Incorporated.)

IT'S A NATURAL WONDER

FIG. 9-5. (Courtesy, The National Cotton Council of America.)

finishes. It keeps its good looks because it can take the fastest dye, holds its shape, launders exceptionally well, won't fray easily or pull apart at the seams, and can be given the new finishes for special freedom from wrinkles and mussing.

Its dependable performance comes from its durability and strength. Tests have proved that it has the highest abrasion resistance of any fiber suitable for comfortable apparel. It takes naturally to laundering because it becomes stronger when wet, can be bleached, and can accept the strongest dyes, resists heat and alkalis, and can stand the hottest water.

It is a most comfortable fiber because it does not irritate the skin, is not sticky or clammy, can be woven tightly for warmth or loosely for coolness, and is free of static electricity, which causes fabrics to cling.

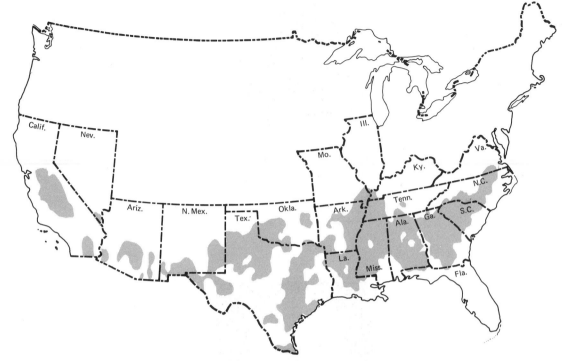

FIG. 9-6. Cotton is grown in 19 states and is a major crop in some 14 states where it averages a third of all crop marketings. Cotton, furthermore, is big business for the nation as a whole. It forms the basis of a $24 billion industry in terms of investment.

(Courtesy: The National Cotton Council of America, *COTTON—From Field to Fabric.*)

Cotton is absorbant to body moisture; it transmits it through the fabric, and allows it to evaporate and cool the body.

In determining the value of cotton, samples are taken from each bale and classed according to staple, grade, and character.

Isn't all cotton alike?

Staple refers to length of the cotton fibers. Sea-island cotton has the longest fibers, sometimes two or more inches. It can be spun into fine, strong thread and woven into delicate or very strong fabrics. It grows best in a hot, humid climate near the sea. Egyptian cotton is related to the sea-island type. Its fibers are fine, lustrous, and strong, of about 2 inches in length. Pima, a variety of Egyptian cotton, grows in Arizona. Upland short-staple cotton makes up about nine-tenths of the crop in the United States, and is from ½ to 1 inch long. Cotton of the same variety will produce fibers of about the same length but may vary somewhat within a bale, so the staple designated by the "classer" is that which he believes most of the fibers in the bale to be.

Grade refers to color and brightness, the amount of foreign matter, and ginning preparation. Standards for grading are established by the government.

Character refers to the diameter, strength, body, maturity, uniformity, and smoothness of fibers and to all other qualities not covered by staple and grade.

Perhaps there is no more beautiful drive than to travel through cotton country during harvest time. Vast fields of cotton bushes about 3 to 4 feet high, glossy with green leaves, covered with snowy white cotton bolls, stretch into the horizon endlessly. On the road, you pass hundreds of wagonloads of clean-picked cotton on its way to the gin. It all represents the basis of a $24-billion industry in terms of investment in America.

Here are a few of the memorable dates in the history of cotton:

5000 B.C Cotton was cultivated and used in the Tehaucan Valley of Mexico. Fragments of fiber and bolls found in this area were about 7,000 years old, scientists have determined.

3000 B.C. Spinning and weaving of cotton was practiced in Pakistan —evidenced by discovery of cotton fabrics from excavations at Mohenjo-Daro.

500 B.C. Cotton was used in Zuni and Hopi ceremonies in Southwestern U.S.

327 B.C. Alexander the Great invaded India and returned with robes of printed cotton.

1328 A.D. King Edward III (England) encouraged Flemish weavers to settle in Manchester—this was the beginning of the Lancashire spinning and weaving industry.

1492 Columbus found cotton growing in the Bahamas.

1556 Cotton was planted in Florida.

1600 British East India Company traded in cottons with the Orient.

1607 Colonists planted cotton in Virginia.

1730 The first cotton yarn was spun by machinery in England.

1764 The spinning jenny, the first practical spinning frame, was invented by James Hargreaves (England).

1769 Richard Arkwright patented the roller spinning method in England. He is called the father of the modern textile industry.

1785 Edmund Cartwright, Oxford graduate, made the first power loom.

1790 Samuel Slater established a mill in Pawtucket, R.I., reproducing Arkwright's spinning machinery from memory.

1793 Eli Whitney invented the cotton gin, revolutionizing the cotton industry because it solved the problem of removing seeds from cotton lint. By hand, the process had been producing only about a pound per day. Whitney's gin stepped up output to 50 pounds per day.

How did a cotton gin help?

1813 The spinning and weaving processes were combined under one roof in Waltham, Massachusetts.

1850 The first patent for a cotton picking device was granted to Samuel Rembert.

1898 Mercerization was introduced to give cotton yarns greater luster, more strength, and better dyeing qualities.

1920 Equipment was installed for controlling humidity in textile mills, contributing significantly to manufacturing efficiency, yarn and fabric quality.

1930 The Sanforized process was used commercially to control shrinkage of cotton textiles.

1955 Wash-wear cottons appeared in significant volume.

1963 Stretch cottons became available in ski suits and other apparel.

SILK[1]

The romantic history of silk begins with its discovery, more than 4,000 years ago in China. It has been a symbol of elegance and beauty ever since Empress Hsi Ling-shi first unraveled the secret of the silk cocoon.

For nearly three thousand years, the Chinese successfully guarded the secret of the silk cocoon. Death and disgrace faced the traitor who disclosed the origin of silk to the outside world. In 300 A.D. Japan somehow penetrated the mystery of silk, and still later, India learned to grow the worm and reel the thread to weave silken cloth.

Caravans transported silk on camel over the perilous old silk routes across the heart of Asia, and eventually silk found its way to Rome. Julius Caesar restricted it to his exclusive use and to the purple "roman stripes" on the togas of the officials he favored. Roman women began robing themselves in silks so extravagant in sheerness and in price (silk was worth its weight in gold) that the Roman Senate attempted to ban its purchase. Succeeding emperors forbade their wives to wear silk garments, refusing to exchange good "Roman gold for spider webs." But silk purchase was never curbed.

By the twelfth century, Italy became the silk center of Western Europe, and the ecclesiastical silks woven during the Italian Renaissance remain among the art treasures of the world. By the seventeenth century, France was challenging Italy's leadership, and the silk looms then established in Lyons are still famous for the beauty of their weaving.

The silkworm never flourished in the chill English air, and the raw silk was imported at enormous cost. England made determined but futile efforts to encourage the culture of the silkworm among the American colonies. However, weaving was not encouraged, and it was 1810 before the first silk mill was erected in America.

Today, America imports more raw silk than any other country in the world, and some of the most beautiful silk fabrics are woven on American looms. The magnificent silks that once were reserved for

Silk—worth its weight in gold?

Do we use much silk in the U.S.?

[1] Grace Beller, *What Is Silk* (New York: International Silk Association, n.d.).

205

CHAPTER 9
*The creation of fashion
apparel: fibers to
fabrics to garments*

the adornment of kings have become available to almost every American who wants them.

   Qualities of Silk.   Silk may be woven on any type of loom made, into fabrics of any degree of crispness or softness, thickness, or transparency. It is the strongest of all natural fibers. A filament of silk is stronger than a similar filament of steel. It is supremely lasting. The beautiful fabrics remaining with us from ancient days attest to silk's almost uncanny resistance to aging. It is also elastic, and will stretch 20 percent and more beyond its own length without breaking, and return to its original length. This elasticity gives silk fabrics their resistance to crushing and ripping. Its insulating properties give it a cool feel in summer, a warm feel in winter. Its absorbency prevents it from feeling clammy or damp.

Man-Made Fibers[1]

While natural fibers have been in use for thousands of years and no one knows when they were first woven into cloth goods, we have more specific knowledge about the origin of man-made fibers.

   Production of man-made fiber on an experimental basis started around 1850. In 1884 a Frenchman named Count Hilaire de Chardonnet received his first patents on a fabric he called "artificial silk." It is what we know today as rayon.

*Who found out about
"artificial silk" first?*

   What the count did was to figure out just what the silkworm found in mulberry leaves to manufacture real silk. The "secret" substance Chardonnet found in mulberry leaves was cellulose, hence the name cellulosic fiber.

CELLULOSIC FIBERS

   Originally, cellulose was made commercially from the short fibers of cotton called "linters." Today, cellulose for production of rayon and other cellulosic fibers such as acetate and triacetate is derived from spruce and other soft woods.

*Are man-made fibers all
completely man-made?*

   Rayon was first produced commercially in the United States in 1911, but it was not until 1939 that nylon, the first of the noncellulosic fibers, was introduced. Nylon, like most noncellulosic fibers, is made from petroleum products called "petrochemicals." About 1 percent of our nation's petroleum is used in the production of fiber.

**NONCELLULOSIC
FIBERS**

   Nylon was followed by other noncellulosic fibers, including acrylic, polyester, olefin, saran, and spandex, each with its own individual characteristics of strength, wrinkle-resistance, washability, and ease of dyeing and printing. Then there are glass and metallic fibers for uses requiring the special characteristics of these substances.

   Most man-made fibers are manufactured in basically the same way. The chemicals are reduced to a syrupy solution similar to

*What's in man-made
fibers?*

[1] *All About Textiles,* American Textile Manufacturers Institute, Inc. (Charlotte, N.C., 1976), pp. 1–9.

molasses. This substance is then forced by pressure through tiny holes in a spinneret, then solidified to form stringlike fiber. The fiber is later stretched and joined. It may then be twisted with other fibers to form multi-filament yarn. Or it may be cut into short lengths as "staple" and processed like natural fiber to form yarn.

Since they can be stretched and shaped so many ways, man-made fibers are exceptionally versatile and are often combined with natural fibers with excellent results.

Man-made fibers are the newest members of the many generations of fabric materials and new and better ones are being produced every year. Until ninety years ago the choice of fabrics was up to nature. Today, thanks to modern technology, the future offers limitless possibilities.

FACTS ABOUT MAN-MADE FIBERS[1]

How many kinds of
man-made fibers are
there?

The properties of fibers used in fabrics greatly influence the behavior of a finished garment. We will discuss the ten generic man-made fiber groups most widely used for consumer goods. Acetate, triacetate, and rayon fibers are termed "cellulosic" because they are made from cellulose, a fibrosous substance found in all plants. The remaining fibers are completely made in the laboratory, and are called "noncellulosic."

Each fiber has different properties that add to the performance and esthetics of end-use products. However, these desirable properties cannot be assured unless the fibers are properly used, the fabric construction is right, the colors are fast to washing, and the garment or end-product is put together with the right thread, zipper, and lining.

The Celanese Identification Program helps to assure consistency of these properties. A sample of every fabric identified with the Celanese Arnel trademark is rigorously pretested for its intended use before the trademark appears on a fabric.

POLYESTER

POLYESTER—STRONG, WRINKLE-RESISTANT

Trademarks: Fortrel (Celanese), Dacron (Du Pont), Kodel (Eastman), Trevira (Hoechst)

Outstanding Characteristics:

1. Superior wrinkle-resistance in laundering, wearing, and packing for travel
2. High strength and abrasion resistance for durability

[1] Celanese Fibers Marketing Company, *Facts About Man-Made Fibers*, New York, 1976.

3. Colorfastness in washing and sunlight
4. Resistance to bagging, stretching, and shrinking, especially in knit fabrics
5. Blending abilities with cotton and rayon for permanent-press garments
6. Holds pleats
7. Available in all weights of fabrics, from light to heavyweight

207

CHAPTER 9
*The creation of fashion
apparel: fibers to
fabrics to garments*

Care: Usually machine-wash in warm water (approx. 110°F, 40°C), except where trim prevents. No ironing of permanent press or doubleknits needed when tumble-dried at low temperature. Static electricity may be reduced by using a fabric softener in every third or fourth washing. Check hangtag or label for care instructions, with special attention to prohibited cleaning additives.

Primary Uses:

Apparel—Women's slacks, shirts, dresses; doubleknits for dresses, women's and men's suits and men's and boys' pants; men's underwear, men's sportcoats, rainwear, dress and sport shirts; PolarGuard fiberfill for outerwear.

ACETATE—ELEGANT, VERSATILE

ACETATE

Trademarks: Celanese Acetate (Celanese), Lanese* (Celanese), Acele (Du Pont), Estron (Eastman)

Outstanding Characteristics:

1. High luster
2. Flexibility, making for softness and drapability
3. Vivid colors
4. Moth and mildew resistance

Care: Dryclean. Some acetates can be hand-washed or machine-washed, gentle cycle. Press with a cool iron on reverse side. Check hangtag or label for care instructions with special attention to warnings against specific cleaning additives.

Primary Uses:

Apparel—Wide variety of dress fabrics such as embossed satins, crepes, taffetas; tricot for lingerie and backing for bonded fabrics

TRIACETATE—WRINKLE-RESISTANT, COLOR STYLING

* Lanese is a core-bulked or "fluffy" yarn that achieves unusual esthetics as well as performance because of its unique composition. A core of Fortrel filament polyester is surrounded by acetate, and both are texturized to produce high bulk without weight in a single yarn. The polyester core delivers strength and performance while the acetate sheath furnishes beauty and color fidelity.

TRIACETATE

Trademark: Arnel (Celanese)

Outstanding Characteristics:

1. Excellent colorfastness to washing and sunlight, retains color clarity in prints
2. Quick-drying; shrinkage-controlled
3. Excellent pleat retention
4. High wrinkle resistance in washing and packing for traveling
5. Resistance to glazing when ironed
6. Comfort in wearing

Care: Machine-wash in warm water at shortest cycle. Jersey knits generally need no ironing; woven fabrics need only touch-up with steam iron. Check hangtag or label for care instructions. Fleece fabrics need no ironing and retain their lush appearance through countless wearings and washings.

Primary Uses:

Apparel—Dresses, blouses, men's sport shirts, jumpsuits, jackets (especially when combined with nylon), women's slacks and pants outfits, fleece robes, pleated garments.

NYLON

NYLON—STRONG, RESILIENT

Trademarks: Celanese Nylon (Celanese); Caprolan (Allied); Antron (Du Pont); Qiana (Du Pont); Enka (American Enka)

Outstanding Characteristics:

1. Lightweight strength; excellent stretch and recovery capabilities
2. Excellent abrasion resistance provides long wear-life
3. Dries quickly
4. Is often combined with acetate, triacetate, or other man-made fibers

Care: Machine-wash in warm water (approximately 110°F, 40°C), except where trim prevents. Iron, if necessary, at low temperature. Knitted fabrics require no ironing after tumble-drying. Static electricity may be reduced by using a fabric softener in every third or fourth washing. Check hangtag or label for care instructions.

Primary Uses:

Apparel—Lingerie, hosiery, ski pants and jackets, golf shirts, swimwear.

ACRYLIC

ACRYLIC—WARM, RESILIENT

Trademarks: Creslan (American Cyanamid), Zefran (Dow Badische), Orlon (Du Pont), Acrilan (Monsanto)

Outstanding Characteristics:

1. Wool-like feel and warmth
2. Lightweight bulk and fluffiness in pile fabrics which resemble fur in appearance
3. Resistance to shrinkage and wrinkling
4. Blends well with wool, rayon, and cotton

Care: Wash in warm water (110°F, 40°C), except where trim prevents. Some garments may be machine-washable. Static electricity may be reduced by using a fabric softener in every third or fourth washing. Check hangtag or label for care instructions.

Primary Uses:

Apparel—Sweaters, knit dresses, socks, slacks, pile fabrics

MODACRYLIC—FURLIKE, CRUSH-RESISTANT

Trademarks Verel (Eastman), Elura (Monsanto)

Outstanding Characteristics:

1. Bulky and crush-resistant; resembles fur in appearance and warmth
2. When used in blends, provides increased flame resistance

Care: Wash in warm water (approximately 110°F, 40°C), except where trim prevents. Some garments may be machine-washable. Static electricity may be reduced by using a fabric softener in every third or fourth washing. If touch-up ironing is desired, use lowest iron temperature setting. Check hangtag or label for care instructions.

Primary Uses:

Apparel—Fake furs, fleece fabric for dresses, pile lining for coats

SPANDEX—LIGHTWEIGHT, ELASTIC

Trademarks: Lycra (Du Pont), Monvelle (Monsanto)

Outstanding Characteristics:

1. Excellent stretch and recovery. Can be stretched 500 percent without breaking
2. High strength and abrasion resistance
3. Resistance to damage from body oils and perspiration

Care: May be machine-washed and dried at low temperature. Fragile garments should be hand-laundered. Wash whites separately.

Do not use chlorine bleach. Check hangtag or label for care instructions.

Primary Uses:

Apparel—Foundation garments, support hose, swimwear, ski pants, lace

RAYON—VERSATILE, ECONOMICAL

Trademarks: Avril (Avtex), Fibro (Courtaulds)

Outstanding Characteristics:

1. Soft and pliable; comfortable to wear because of high moisture absorbency
2. Takes dye easily in vivid colors
3. Provides more uniform quality than cotton does in polyester blends; also blends well with triacetate

Care: Some fabrics wash well; more require drycleaning. Check hangtag or label for care instructions.

Primary Uses:

Apparel—Linenlike fabrics for dresses, slacks; blends with polyester in permanent-press fabrics, linings

Fabric Finishes and Special Treatments

Most fabrics have one or more chemical finishes applied during the final steps of processing. Consumers often ask about some of these finishes.

PERMANENT-PRESS

How is apparel that never needs ironing made?

PERMANENT PRESS—A resin applied to polyester/cellulosic blends. It is heat-set onto the fabric to improve its resistance to wrinkling in wearing and laundering, provided care instructions are strictly heeded. Alterations may be difficult because of the permanence of hemlines and creases which are heat-set when the finish is applied.
Polyester knits are sometimes referred to as permanent-press fabrics because of their excellent wrinkle resistance and no-iron characteristics, even though no finish is applied.

STAIN-RESISTANT

STAIN-RESISTANT—Makes it easier to lift off or sponge away spills of food, water, and other substances. Scotchgard and Zepel are trade names for stain-resistant finishes.

FLAME-RESISTANT

FLAME-RESISTANT—Helps to slow the rate at which a garment will both catch fire and burn, but does not make a fabric fireproof. This finish may need renewing after laundering or drycleaning. Examples of fire-retarding yarns, currently available, are all modacrylics, Celanese Acetate ADA, Triacetate DDC, and Du Pont's Nomex nylon.

When polyester, acetate, triacetate, acrylic, or modacrylic are used in flame-resistant fabrics, the special-care instructions should be followed to assure the flame-resistant characteristics will be retained.

WATERPROOF—Fills the pores of a fabric so water cannot pass through.

WATER-REPELLENT—Causes fabrics to shed water in normal wear, but does not make them completely waterproof.

The Label and the Law

1954—THE FLAMMABLE FABRICS ACT

The Flammable Fabrics Act, effective on June 30, 1954, was amended on December 14, 1967. The purpose of the Act is to protect the public against flammable textiles that can cause either bodily injury or death.

Are fire-resistant garments desirable?

Basically, the Act makes it unlawful to manufacture for sale any article of wearing apparel or fabric that is dangerously and highly flammable. Originally the Act covered only wearing apparel or fabrics intended or sold for use in wearing apparel. But, by its amendments, the Act now includes home furnishings as well.

Standards have been issued for carpets and rugs, children's sleepwear (sizes 0–6X and sizes 7–14), and mattresses and mattress pads. The Consumer Product Safety Commission has jurisdiction over the Flammable Fabrics Act.

1960—THE TEXTILE FIBER PRODUCTS IDENTIFICATION ACT

This law requires that textile fiber products bear stamps, tags, labels, or other means of identification clearly showing the constituent fiber or fibers in the product, designating each by its generic name in the order of predominance by weight; the percentage of each fiber by weight; the name or other identification of the manufacturer of the product; and the name of the country where the product was processed or manufactured, if it is an imported textile fiber product.

Why are there so many hangtags and labels on garments?

1972—PERMANENT CARE LABELING RULE

Most garments must have care and maintenance instructions permanently affixed to them. Retailers must also supply care labels to home sewers who buy piece goods.

TRADEMARKS

Manufacturers may choose to give consumers more information on the hangtag than the law requires. They may, for instance, add the trademark name for the fiber used. An example would be Arnel, the trademark for Celanese triacetate produced by Celanese Fibers Company. However, this kind of information must not be given in such a way as to be false or misleading, nor may it interfere or conflict with the generic fiber content information that is required by law.

Fibers to Fabrics

Before fiber, either man-made or natural, can be woven into cloth, it must first be made into yarn.

Just how is cloth made?

Some yarn is produced by the man-made fiber industry simply by twisting several continuous strands of fiber to form multi-filament yarn. However, if the man-made fiber is to be blended with natural fibers such as cotton or wool, which have relatively short length, continuous-filament yarn is usually cut into shorter lengths called *staple*.

BLENDS

The staple, which looks very much like natural fiber, is then processed and blended with natural fibers in preparation for spinning into a blended yarn.

Then the fibers move through ducts to the carding machines. In the carding machine, the fibers are moved between a moving slat and cylinder covered by fine teeth, which parallels the fibers, cleans them of impurities, and condenses them into ropelike strands called *slivers*.

For the fiber sliver to be changed into yarn, it must be twisted slightly to achieve strength, and wound onto spools. The next task is to twist and stretch these strands into tightly twisted thread, much smaller in diameter but also much stronger. The process is much the same for all fibers, but there are many variations. For example, wool must be washed (scoured) to remove grease and other foreign materials before the carding process begins.

Once either man-made or natural fibers have been spun into yarn, they are ready to become fabric. This is achieved in a variety of ways.

Is there really more than just one kind of weave?

Weaving is the oldest method and has three basic designs: *plain, twill,* and *satin.* Although modern methods of weaving are fast and complicated, the main function of weaving is very simple. (See Figure 9-10 on page 214.)

First, a number of threads or yarns are placed lengthwise on the loom. This parallel row is known as the *warp* and today there may be as many as 15,000 threads arranged this way. The hand weaver today, as in the past, then pushes a shuttle carrying the thread at right angles to the warp, first over one of the parallel threads, then under the other, depending on the weave desired. Once the *filling yarn* has crossed the warp, the hand weaver reaches up and pushes that yarn up against

FIG. 9-7.   Blending of fibers—mixing man-made and natural fibers together—
is done in the opening room.
(Courtesy, Burlington Industries, Greensboro, N.C.)

FIG. 9-8.   Carding—fibers move into the carding machine where they are
cleansed of impurities and condensed into slivers.
(Courtesy, Burlington Industries, Greensboro, N.C.)

FIG. 9-9.   Yarn spinning—fiber slivers are twisted slightly and wound onto spool.
(Courtesy, Burlington Industries, Greensboro, N.C.)

Fabric Construction

Weaving is the oldest method of construction and has three designs: plain, twill, and satin.

(a)   (b)   (c)

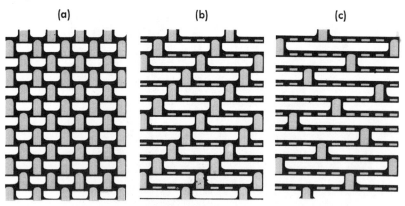

FIG. 9-10a, b, c.   (a) *Plain* weave—the pattern is the same as on a tennis racquet. The up and down strings are called warp—the ones running across are called filling, or woof. (b) *Twill* weave—the filling and warp yarns are intermeshed in such a manner that a raised diagonal line is left on the cloth. (c) *Satin* weave— the least common weave. It is not strong, but it produces a fabric with a soft, smooth surface. Either the warp or filling yarns dominate the face of the cloth with fewer intermeshings of the threads. (See discussion on page 212.)
(From: *Textiles from Start to Finish*, American Textile Manufacturers Institute, Charlotte, N.C., 1974, p. 7.)

FIG. 9-11.   Warping—placing yarns lengthwise on the loom preparatory to weaving.
(Courtesy, Burlington Industries, Greensboro, N.C.)

FIG. 9-12.   Weaving—shuttle carries thread at right angles and over and under the warp.
(Courtesy, Burlington Industries, Greensboro, N.C.)

the previous yarn at the end where the warp is attached, and begins the same motions again. Modern industry does in seconds what it takes a hand weaver hours, days, and months to do, attaching many yarn ends to huge beams and using power-actuated shuttles in the place of the weaver's hands. The shuttles move across the warp at tremendous speeds. It has been said that the movement of a shuttle in a conventional loom represents the greatest acceleration man has ever achieved by mechanical means.

Other modern looms have an even faster method of weaving done by the shuttleless loom. In this type of loom, the filling yarns (crosswise) are carried through the warp threads by steel bands attached to wheels on each side of the loom.

Plaid, for example, is one of the oldest patterns known to the weaver's art. The machine that this cloth is made on is called a *box loom,* and the shuttles carry different colors of yarn. Another famous loom for the making of fancy or intricate patterns is the *Jacquard loom.* The pattern for the fabric is programmed on a series of punch cards similar to modern computer cards. The cards manipulate the warp yarns, raising or lowering them to create the desired pattern.

Knitting is new?

KNITS

Knitting is a familiar process for producing fabric also, but it is relatively new compared to weaving. It was first introduced during the sixteenth century, and it differs from weaving in that knit fabrics are formed by intermeshing or interlooping yarn loops. There are a variety of methods to accomplish different fabrics, but regardless of the type of knit, all are done in the same manner. A loop of yarn is pulled through another loop.

If cloth isn't woven or knit, how does it stay together?

The majority of fabrics are manufactured by weaving and knitting, but today more and more materials are being manufactured that use, instead of these traditional methods, simple processes such as heat, pressure, and mechanical bonding. One of the oldest of such materials is the felt often used by the makers of hats and carpet padding. Felt is usually composed of cotton, wool, or animal hair that has been subjected to heat, moisture, and friction under high pressure. As the pressure and friction are applied, chemicals are added to interlock the fibers and create a usable, solid fabric.

After fibers have been turned into yarn and yarn has been woven or knitted into fabric, there are many more steps left before the cloth can go to the marketplace, including *finishing, dyeing,* or *printing.*

GRAY GOODS

The new fabric (called gray goods) may be bleached if white goods are wanted. If color is wanted, dye is added and fixed to the yarn or cloth. There are many different types of dyes, some that work better with some fibers than others. Some come from natural sources, and some are man-made. They are applied according to what kind of fiber is being used and what kind of result is desired.

The basic dyeing processes are *stock dyeing, yarn dyeing,* and *piece dyeing.* In stock dyeing the fiber is dyed before it is spun into

(a)   (b)

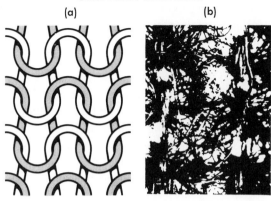

FIG. 9-13a, b.   (a) *Knits:* While weaving is the oldest
art, knit goods have become very popular in modern
times. In knit goods, regardless of the appearance, one
loop of yarn is pulled through another loop. (b) *Nonwoven:* Nonwoven cloth is made by interlocking or
bonding fibers through chemicals, heat or mechanical
means, or through a combination of these.
(From: *Textiles from Start to Finish,* American Textile
Manufacturers Institute, Charlotte, N.C., 1974, p. 7.)

yarn. In yarn dyeing the dye is applied after the fiber has been spun
into a yarn. In piece dyeing the dye is applied after the yarn has
been woven or knitted into cloth. This is the more frequently used
method.

After the fabric has been dyed, the utility finishes are added.
Some of these special finishes were discussed earlier in the chapter.
The most common processes in finishing are *mercerizing, durable
press, calendering* (which imparts a glaze, shine, or embossed design),
heat-setting (by which man-made fibers such as nylon can be set to
any desired shape such as pleats), *napping* (which gives the fabric
added warmth and smoothness), and *sanforizing* (to preshrink the
cloth so that it won't shrink or stretch more than one percent during
home laundering).

Fabrics to Garments

Fabric designers and stylists actually work from one to two years
ahead of the time that a finished garment reaches the retail stores
for sale to the consumers. To understand this better, ask yourself if
you could forecast what styles, colors, or fabrics will be in demand

*How can a fabric
designer possibly
figure out what we'll
like so far in advance?*

one or two years from now. It isn't easy to anticipate what consumers will be wanting in one or two years, but fabric designers are sensitive to fashion trends, which they observe closely. For example, these are some of the things they watch:

1. What the buyers of their fabrics are saying. These are the apparel manufacturers, and they listen carefully.
2. What fashion magazine editors are saying.
3. What's happening in the world, politically and economically.
4. Where people are going on their vacations, and what types of recreation they are enjoying.
5. What people are wearing in foreign countries—particularly Europe.

Don't we always like the new colors?

The fabric designers and stylists travel abroad when possible and carefully observe the people. Finally, they do not make any startling changes in color from year to year, but follow traditional color patterns. For example, navy and white are good, traditional spring colors. So, each spring, there is some navy and white—sometimes with touches of red, another year bright green, and another year touches of yellow. Designers know from experience that consumers take several seasons to adjust to a sudden change in colors, so they introduce them gradually. They are good trend observers, and they are sometimes trend-setters as well. What the fabric houses offer will be the basis of what the apparel manufacturer uses to make ready-to-wear garments for each of the seasonal markets.

Why so much speed in apparel production?

The momentum of fashion begins to pick up steadily from the time the fabric is ready until the garment is finally produced and shipped to the retail stores. If you will look at the market dates scheduled by the Apparel Mart of Dallas, which is one of the leading markets where retailers go to purchase their new seasonal merchandise, you will notice that there are five shows a year. The apparel manufacturers must have their new seasonal lines at the shows for viewing by their retail buyers. Major markets try not to schedule their showings at the same time, because retail buyers sometimes like to go to two or more markets. For example, a buyer might go to the markets in New York the week before the Dallas market, then fly to Dallas for that market, and fly on to California for the markets there. (Or he/she might go to Atlanta, Chicago, New Orleans, or other places.)

If we look at the time sequence involved to get ready for the midsummer market in Dallas, for example, this is what has happened. Remember that customers do not see the midsummer garments in the retail stores for two or three months following the market showing. (The dates are approximate.)

January 1975	Fabric houses are designing and styling midsummer 1977 fabrics, to be purchased by apparel manufacturers. (From one to two years ahead of a market.)	*As much as two years from the beginning of clothes?*
November 1976	Designers for apparel manufacturers are preparing their style lines for the midsummer market for 1977. (Two to three months before market.)	
Midsummer Market January 29–February 3, 1977	Apparel manufacturers show their midsummer ready-to-wear collections to retail store buyers. They place their orders.	
April 1977	Midsummer apparel arrives in the retail stores and appears on the racks for consumer buying soon after. (Two to three months after market.)	

When you remember that there are five markets a year, you can readily see that fabric houses and apparel manufacturing firms are very busy places. No sooner is one market over than another is coming right up.

DESIGN AND GARMENT CONSTRUCTION

As we noted in the time sequence chart, the apparel manufacturer must begin work on a new collection two or three months before the new seasonal collection is to be shown at market.

What goes on in a garment factory?

The design comes first, of course. It may be an original design, or it may be a copy that has been purchased. Sometimes, it may be a design that is similar to a best-seller of the former season—with different color, trim, or fabric.

When the designs have been selected for the upcoming season, actual garments are made up in muslin or in the fabric of the garment. Company executives then view the garments and analyze them for their potential salability, their costs to produce, and profit margins. Some may be rejected, some will be modified, and some will go directly into the new seasonal line.

Those designs chosen are given style numbers, and turned over to a patternmaker, who makes a pattern for production in the firm's sample size. Garments are then made from the patterns, tested, approved, and made into as many samples as will be needed to show the line.

Depending on the policies of the firm and how confident it is of the new season's designs, production could begin at this point or be de-

FIG. 9-14. The Apparel Mart's market dates for 1977.

PATTERN GRADING

layed for market reactions—orders. If production is to be begun at once, and this is advantageous because the apparel manufacturer will be ready to ship the garments soon after market, the patternmaker grades the pattern by sloping it up or down in the size range in which the garment is to be made. Once the sizes have been made, a marker is prepared. The marker is a long, heavy paper guide that shows the layout for all the pieces required in the garment in all its various sizes, for the use of the cutter. Economy of fabric use (as well as bias and straight garment pieces where needed) is the purpose of the marker.

The cutter rolls out layers of fabric on a long table, puts the marker in place, and, using electrically powered knives, cuts through them. Several thousands of garments of a style can thus be cut at one time. Once cut, the pieces are bundled separately, identified by name, and readied for the sewing processes.

If the sewing is done by the apparel manufacturer (known as an "inside" shop), the pieces are delivered to the sewing area. If the sewing is done outside the firm, it is trucked to an "outside" shop—a contractor—who completes all the sewing required and returns it to the apparel manufacturing firm.

The garments are then inspected and pressed. Shipment to the retail stores soon follows.

Retail buyers usually buy slowly and in small quantities at market to start their seasons because they want to see which garments will sell more quickly. Once they determine which are popular with their consumers, they reorder quickly. Thus, the apparel manufacturer must be able to refill orders while the demand for a garment is at its peak. There's a real speed factor involved at this point, because this is where the manufacturer usually makes his margin of profit. The firms eliminate their slow sellers at this time, and concentrate on their reorders.

The fashion industry differs from other industries in its method of distribution. Some industries distribute their products through several middlemen and wholesalers on their way to the consumer. The fashion industry distributes apparel direct from manufacturer to retailer. The reason for this is that fashions are sometimes so short-lived that there is no time for a middleman to operate efficiently.

Why don't retail buyers do all their buying and get it over with?

Conclusion

Fashions for men, women, and children require a massive group of industries to serve their needs. The United States is noted for its rapidity in producing and distributing fashion garments. American designers have been recognized worldwide for their creativeness, but this only began about the time of World War II. Up to that time, everyone thought that the only really fashionable clothes came from Paris. But today, the United States takes its place in the fashion world proudly. Just as the history of civilization itself is written in the tapestry of textiles—from the simple beginning to the greatness of today—so is American fashion moving toward a greater tomorrow.

1. Define or identify the following:
   a. Natural fibers
   b. Man-made fibers
   c. Blends
   d. Cellulosic fibers
   e. Noncellulosic fibers
   f. Polyester
   g. Acetate
   h. Triacetate
   i. Nylon
   j. Acrylic

Review Questions

k. Modacrylic
l. Spandex
m. Rayon
n. Permanent-press
o. Stain-resistant
p. Flame-resistant
q. Plain weave
r. Twill weave
s. Satin weave
t. Knits
u. Nonwoven cloth
v. Gray goods
w. Pattern grading

2. What fabrics were the only ones known to man for the first 5,000 years of civilization? Do you think fabric development has anything to do with advancement in civilization? Why?

3. Name as many uses of textiles outside the clothing industry as you can.

4. Textiles contribute to your lifestyles, and this is not always recognizable to us. Name a few textiles that you may not have really thought about before.

5. How did some famous inventors add to the increase in textile production? Who were they?

6. Can you look at a fabric today and easily tell what it is made of? Why?

7. Why do you think the laws and labels acts were enacted?

8. Explain fibers-to-fabrics-to-garments processes.

Suggested Student Activities

1. Visit several fashion stores in your area, look carefully at the new seasonal merchandise. and report the differences that you are aware of between this year's offerings and those of about a year ago. Do you detect any new trends? Do you think they will be long-term or short-term trends? Are some garments similar to last year's? How do they differ?

2. While you are in the fashion stores, examine the fabrics to see if you can identify what they are made of. Check your guess by looking at the hangtag or label in the garment. Why is it difficult to identify fabrics today?

3. On a map of your state, locate areas where natural fibers are grown. From library resources try to find out the locations of any man-made fiber industries in your area, and locate them on your map also.

4. Visit a fabric store in your area. Notice how many blends there are in comparison to pure fiber contents. Do you find a predominance of man-made or natural fibers in the textiles?

Case 9-1. Mrs. Davis is hurriedly shopping for a casual, comfortable, and tailored traveling outfit to wear on a trip to a warmer climate for the holidays. She spots just what she thinks she is looking for, talks to the salesperson about the trip and what she wants, then tries the garment on, likes it, and takes it with her. Forty-five minutes later, Mrs. Davis is on the telephone telling the salesperson to have the garment picked up as soon as possible, and admonishing her for not informing her that the garment was made of 100 percent wool. Thus it will not be appropriate for the trip.

1. How might the salesperson have been more helpful in encouraging Mrs. Davis to try a more appropriate fabric for her trip? Should the salesperson have been more explicit about the contents? Would a better knowledge of fabrics, their contents, and uses have been beneficial for the salesperson?
2. How was the store's image damaged for Mrs. Davis?
3. If a salesperson is not sure about the contents of the fabric in a garment, how can it be quickly found?
4. Would the 100 percent wool garment have had some features that would have made it a satisfactory garment for the trip?

Case 9-2. Mr. Morgan tells the salesperson that he wants a good-looking pair of trousers that can be washed but that would be appropriate to wear to the office. The salesperson takes Mr. Morgan to the rack where this kind of garment is hung, and Morgan selects two pair that he will buy. Subsequently, Mrs. Morgan washes the first pair of trousers and dries them in the dryer, only to discover that they have shrunk unbelievably. She is aghast, and in explaining to her husband says, "But you told me they were washable, and I just did what I ordinarily do."

1. Does the store have a problem? Whose problem (in the store) is it? Why is it important for salespeople to know the contents of the fabrics in their garments and what the care instructions are, regardless of where they are hung?
2. If the salesperson had been more familiar with his stock might he have avoided the error? What should he have checked for sure even if he thought the garment was washable?
3. Is this an example of why the laws and labels were put into present use? Does it make the warning "caveat emptor" unnecessary?

Case 9-3. Three salespeople are on the selling floor on a very slow day. Two of them are standing near the cash stand chatting about their plans for the weekend. One is on the floor reading hangtags and inspecting the garments on the racks.

1. Which is the more valuable salesperson to the company? Why?
2. How can labels and hangtags assist the salesperson? Is that why they are placed there in the first place? Is it right or wrong to remove hangtags before they are placed in stock?
3. Some stores do remove hangtags before placing them in stock. If they do, how can the salesperson still learn a great deal about a garment's fabric and care instructions?

Chapter 10

Fashion management

Objectives

When you have read this chapter, you should be able to

1. Explain how the opportunity for fashion merchandising management could become a reality to you early in your fashion career
2. List the functions that fashion merchandising managers perform
3. Discuss some of the theories that have contributed to the status of management today
4. Describe the characteristics and attitudes the fashion manager needs to develop
5. Explain why it is important for a fashion manager to understand the importance of human needs
6. Outline some simple steps to good fashion management
7. Cite instances where management decisions were crucial to the successful development of Sears, Roebuck and Company

About a century ago, the United States were only thirty-eight in number, the total population was only 58 million people, and 65 percent of them still lived in rural areas. Only a few cities had as many as 200,000 residents.

In 1886, a Chicago jewelry company erroneously shipped some gold-filled watches to a jeweler in the little Minnesota town of North Redwood. Thus started a chain of events that led to the founding of Sears.

Richard W. Sears, at age 16, had been left fatherless. He learned telegraphy and began a series of railroad jobs, eventually becoming

FIG. 10-1.   Richard W. Sears (1863–1914), founder and first president of Sears, Roebuck and Co.
(Courtesy, Sears, Roebuck and Co.)

agent of the Minneapolis and St. Louis Railway station in North Red-wood, Minnesota.

When the jeweler in Redwood received the watches from the Chicago jewelry company, he had no use for them, so he sold them to Sears, who sold them at a profit to other station agents up and down the line. Sears ordered more watches, and was soon in business for himself in Minneapolis as the head of the R. W. Sears Watch Com-pany. He had started an enterprise that was destined to become one of the most dramatic success stories in American business.

How did Richard Sears get into the mail-order business?

As the watch business grew, so did the problems. Some watches didn't work, and customers wanted them repaired. Thus, after moving his business to Chicago, Sears inserted a classified ad in the Chicago Daily News:

WANTED: Watchmaker with reference who can furnish tools. State age, experience, and salary required. Address T39, Daily News.

Indiana-born Alvah C. Roebuck answered the ad on April 1, 1887 and two days later was hired. Thus began the association of the two young men, both still in their twenties. In 1893 the corporate name of the firm became Sears, Roebuck and Co.

Although the earliest catalogs featured only watches, by 1895 the new firm was producing a 507-page catalog with many other items: shoes, women's garments and millinery, wagons, fishing tackle, stoves, furniture, china, musical instruments, saddles, firearms, buggies, bicycles, baby carriages, and glassware in addition to watches and jewelry.

Sears was reorganized in 1895, when Julius Rosenwald bought into the company. During this time Roebuck, suffering from poor health, resigned, although he still lent his name to the firm. While Sears was talented in selling, advertising, and merchandising, it was Rosenwald who brought good organization to the company. He devel-oped the company so it could handle orders on an economical and efficient basis, and in 1903 became treasurer as well as vice-president. In 1906, needing additional capital, Sears and Rosenwald began to sell common and preferred stock on the open market. The company has been publicly owned ever since.

Did Sears have any early problems?

Sears' business expanded fast. By the turn of the century addi-tional buildings were built or leased in various sections of Chicago. Meanwhile, construction was started on a new 40-acre, $5 million, mail-order plant and office building on Chicago's West Side. When it opened in 1906, the mail-order plant was the largest business building in the world. Today it is still one of the largest, with more than 3 million square feet of floor space.

The Sears Chicago mail-order plant—now called a catalog mer-

FIG. 10-2. Alvah C. Roebuck (1868–1948), co-founder of Sears, Roebuck and Co. (Courtesy, Sears, Roebuck and Co.)

chandise distribution center—still occupies its original site on Chicago's West Side.

In 1906, Richard Sears made the first move to establish the company in a branch location when he opened an office in Dallas, Texas. Six years later, the branch office blossomed into the Dallas mail-order plant, offering the Southwest all the blessings of complete mail-order facilities: lower freight rates, faster delivery, reduced damage to merchandise.

Why did Sears establish branch mail-order houses?

At the start of the Dallas venture, Richard Sears hadn't foreseen a giant mail-order plant in Texas. But there's no doubt he generally favored such installations. He wrote:

> If with this trial we can get any success, the next place will get the kind of preparation that will insure success, and encourage us to cover the United States rapidly with ten or more branches. . . .[1]

Sears came amazingly close to guessing the eventual total of catalog merchandise distribution centers. Today, there are 14 in Chicago and Elk Grove Village, Ill.; Dallas; Seattle; Philadelphia; Kansas City; Boston; Minneapolis; Atlanta; Memphis; Los Angeles; Greensboro, North Carolina; Columbus, Ohio; and Jacksonville, Florida.

[1] Sears, Roebuck and Co., *Merchant to the Millions* (Chicago, 1974), p. 7.

Building mail-order plants was one thing. Making them operate efficiently was something else. Around the turn of the century a customer complained:

Did Sears and Roebuck ever make any mistakes?

> For heaven's sake, quit sending me sewing machines. Every time I go to the station, I find another one there. You have shipped me five already. [1]

Sears mail-order executives knew of these problems, and were as unhappy as the customers about them. Gradually after much experimenting, they introduced a time-schedule system, under which each order, as it arrived, was given a time to be shipped. Then, no matter what happened, the order had to be in the appropriate bin in the merchandise-assembly room at the assigned time. It traveled to the room by an intricate system of belts and chutes. The time scheduling brought order to the mail-order business and enabled the Chicago plant to handle many times the business it had handled before the system was introduced. The system became a sort of "seventh wonder" of the business world. Henry Ford is reported to have visited the Chicago plant to study the assembly-line technique.

Assembly lines *in* retailing?

While some executives were installing the schedule system, others were busy at other projects. Fanciful catalog writing started by Richard Sears became far less fanciful. Not only did the catalog copy improve, but some products—such as patent medicines—were dropped. The 1911 catalog offered such items as blood purifiers and liver and kidney remedies—"pink pills for pale people." The 1912 catalog devoted one less page to patent medicines than the 1911 catalog, and added: "The modern tendency is to put less faith in drugs and more in correct living as the best means of helping nature resist disease." The 1913 catalog came out solidly against home remedies under the banner line: "Why We Have Discontinued Patent Medicines."

The improvement in the quality of Sears goods goes hand in hand with the story of the Sears laboratory. As early as 1905 some Sears men were insisting not only on accurate catalog descriptions but on quality merchandise as well. In 1911, when the laboratory opened, the campaign for high-quality merchandise got a real push. With a laboratory, buyers no longer had to guess about quality. They could have tests. In time the laboratory was to be called the "watchdog of the catalog." It spot-tested merchandise that mail-order plants were shipping, started scientific comparisons between Sears and competitors' products, and was to help develop new products. Today, the Sears laboratory is one of the most highly valued and indispensable departments in Sears.

Why do stores have labs?

By 1925, the whole face of the country was changing. Modern roads and modern cars made it possible for Sears rural customers to hop in the tin lizzie and chug off to the nearest town. No longer was the catalog their only choice for a wide range of merchandise. Chain

[1] Sears, Roebuck and Co., *Merchant to the Millions* (Chicago, 1974), p. 8.

stores were beginning to blanket the country, and they cut into the Sears mail-order business. In 1914 there were about 24,000 chain stores. Fifteen years later there were more than 150,000.

When did lots of people start moving to the cities?

American cities were growing up, and Sears rural customers were abandoning the farm for the factory. In 1900, rural population still outnumbered urban population. By 1920 the situation was reversed, and the trend has been increasing that way through today.

Why was Wood chosen for the Hall of Fame among merchants?

Robert E. Wood was the father of the Sears retail expansion. City dwellers, Wood reasoned, weren't good catalog customers. They shopped in city stores. Valid though his arguments were, Wood had no easy time getting Sears established as a retail chain, even though Sears' first retail store, opened in 1925, was an immediate success. What to sell in the new stores, where to locate stores, how large the stores should be, how to staff them—these were the management decisions Wood had to make. He was finally successful in getting his idea accepted, and the retail operation grew—to 192 stores in 1928, 324 stores in 1929, 400 stores in 1933. During one twelve-month period in the late '20s, Sears stores opened on the average of one every other business day!

Expansion during a depression?

Despite the Depression, Sears continued to open stores during the '30s. When war broke out in 1941, more than 600 stores were operating. World War II called a halt to the Sears retail expansion, but after the war, Wood began a great postwar expansion program, and today there are more than 850 stores and nearly 3,000 other selling facilities.

In 1931 Sears retail sales topped mail-order sales for the first time. Stores accounted for 53.4 percent of total sales of more than $180 million. Today sales originating in retail stores account for more than 80 percent of total volume, including sales at catalog desks in retail stores.

Many of the basic decisions Robert E. Wood made concerning how the stores should operate proved to be right. He located the larger stores away from the crowded downtown shopping districts, predicting the age of suburbia and the motorist-shopper and located stores in outlying districts with plenty of free parking. Not only did Wood decide not to go into business downtown, he also decided not to compete directly, but to supplement the merchandise carried by downtown department stores. Today, Sears' large stores carry complete assortments of merchandise—both hard and soft lines.

HARD LINES
SOFT LINES

Gradually a comprehensive code of retail operating techniques was worked out, enabling store managers to concentrate most of their time on two essentials: selling and proper ordering. The new techniques were as vital to retail as the time schedule was to mail order.

Another milestone in retail history was passed in 1932 when Sears established the store planning and display department. Before this time, merchandise had been fitted into buildings, but now, more and more, buildings were built around merchandise.

The first store to be built from the inside out was the Glendale, California store, opened in 1935. The new store planning and display department concerned itself with all elements of the store: the proper tables, the proper fixtures, the proper space for the different departments, the flow of customers from one part of the store to another—even the width of the aisles. The store shell was built around the selling floor plan. Today all Sears stores are planned from the inside out.

How can you build a store from the inside out?

Changes occurred in the merchandising approach of the catalog—with catalog sales desks and offices and with telephone sales offices. The catalog, for years the "farmer's friend," became the city dweller's friend too. It was urbanized. Most of the catalog business no longer comes from mail orders (less than 5 percent in fact)—so the name was changed to "catalog merchandise distribution," as it is known today.

Sears, now the world's largest retailer of general merchandise, distributes broad lines of its own brand of goods through some 3,700 selling locations. Net sales for 1976 approached $15 billion. The company's headquarters and most of its buying offices are located in Chicago's new Sears Tower, completed in 1974. It owns a 41 percent equity interest in Simpsons–Sears Limited, which conducts a retail and catalog order business in Canada. It also conducts retail operations in Brazil, Colombia, Mexico, Peru, Venezuela, Costa Rica, Panama, El Salvador, Puerto Rico, Nicaragua, Honduras, Guatemala and Spain. In addition, Sears merchandise is sold in a number of European and Far Eastern countries through arrangements with other retailers.

Are there any Sears stores outside the U.S.?

Today, Sears is a vast organization doing business across the length and breadth of the United States and overseas. The present Sears organization—started shortly before the war, and completed after the war—divides the company into a Chicago headquarters organization, five territorial organizations headed by executive vice-presidents, and "zone" and "group" organizations in each territory.

The headquarters organization is the company's "banker, landlord, supplier of professional and technical skills, and, in the office of the chairman, the final authority to all company management." Store, catalog center, group, and zone managers report to the territorial vice-presidents. The territorial vice-presidents, in turn, report directly to the senior executive vice-president—field.

But there is one job—buying—that headquarters alone handles. To keep the advantages of mass purchasing, individual stores and catalog merchandise distribution centers do not as a rule buy their own goods. They buy merchandise developed to Sears specifications and made available to them by headquarters.

Why does Sears believe in centralized buying?

Sears catalogs are still big business—big in sales volume, producing more than $3 billion, and big in cost, which runs into many millions. Except for women's fashions and related lines, which are handled in New York, all the work of preparing the catalogs is done

Are catalogs becoming extinct?

FIG. 10-3. The 110-story Sears Towers in Chicago is the tallest and the largest private office building in the world. Owned and developed by Sears, Roebuck and Co., it rises 1,454 feet above the ground. The 103rd floor Skydeck is 1,353 feet above ground—the highest observatory in the United States. Served by two express elevators traveling 1,800 feet per minute, the ride to the top takes less than one minute. (Courtesy, Sears, Roebuck and Co.)

in Chicago. There are two general catalogs each year—one for spring–summer, the other for the fall–winter selling season. Each general catalog contains more than 1,400 pages and weighs about five pounds. In addition, every year Sears issues summer and winter seasonal catalogs of more than 200 pages each and a Christmas gift book of more than 500 pages. The seasonal catalogs are designed to stimulate sales and to supplement merchandise assortments in the big catalogs.

FIG. 10-4. Point—of—purchase displays such as this create customer interest and buying action.

(Courtesy, Sears, Roebuck and Co.)

Sears customers are spread from coast to coast. Their merchandise wants reflect the climate and distinctive living modes of their home areas. Floridians and Southern Californians may be thinking of barbecue sets when Minnesotans are thinking of snow tires, and so on.

Because of the varied tastes of customers, and also because of the varied climate of the United States, Sears issues each of its five major catalogs in several different editions. Once the presses start rolling, approximately 300 million catalogs pour out each year.

Why more than one catalog style?

Eddy Gilmore, former chief of the Moscow bureau of the Associated Press, once made an interesting comment on Richard Sears' "wish book." "Two innocent articles of American life—the Sears, Roebuck catalog and the phonograph record—are the most powerful pieces of foreign propaganda in Russia," said Gilmore. "The catalog comes first."

**FASHION
MANAGEMENT**

Of all the information we focus on in this part of the book, probably this chapter on management will be the most valuable to you from the standpoint of fashion advancement. You become capable of performing your job more effectively when you understand the functions and objectives of management. But most of all, you will also be ready to assume more management responsibilities in your job.

The critical shortage of qualified people for management in all areas of business is well-known. Actually, there are many businesses that would like to expand their operations into new territories, but they are unable to do so because they lack the qualified, knowledgeable people to manage the new business once it has opened. No business can operate in the black very long without good management. Businesses cannot run themselves; they must be managed.

Fashion businesses offer many opportunities for young people to assume more supervisory authority. But the most exciting thing is that they will be your opportunities much sooner than you might have thought possible.

What Do Fashion Managers Do?

FASHION MANAGER

Fashion managers do the same things that any other business manager does. The only difference between a fashion manager and a supermarket manager, for example, lies in the differences of the merchandise with which they work.

All managers need to get work accomplished systematically through the efforts of other people because they cannot do all the required work by themselves. Regardless of the level of management— from the top executives, through middle management, to the supervisory level—all are trying to get work accomplished quickly and efficiently through the people they manage. They must direct the efforts and activities of their people to accomplish the objectives of the business.

Management is an exciting area in fashion. It puts you on the inside of what is going on in the business—where the real action is. As a fashion manager, you will need to plan what you want to accomplish, organize your plans so they can be carried out effectively, staff your store with people to help you, direct them so they accomplish the plans you have, and control them so that all their activities lead to the primary goal of your fashion business. There are methods for accomplishing all these things, and we will discuss them presently; these methods will help you do a better job as a fashion manager.

The Principles of Good Management

To be a good fashion manager, it is necessary to know the principles of good management. For this, we will look at the fourteen principles that Henri Fayol developed. His first management papers appeared in 1916 in French, and they were not freely translated and used in English until much later. You can see that the concept of management as a science in itself is of comparatively recent origin; and while it is widely accepted in modern business, there are still many managers today who do not fully understand how to manage.

Fayol showed a clear understanding of the basic problems of business management. He also showed an extraordinary insight into the universality of management activities from business to industry to other organizations—religion, politics, military, and others.

His fourteen principles are as valid today as they were in 1916, and the fashion manager should know and use them. We will discuss each principle briefly. Later it will be worth your while to take some management courses.

1. *Division of Work.* To accomplish a task efficiently, it is necessary to divide the work into specific responsibilities, assigning each to the individual members of the team.
2. *Responsibility and Authority.* Responsibility is the obligation you have to accomplish the assignments which you have the authority to carry out. If you are given the responsibility to accomplish something, then you must have the authority to accomplish it in the best way possible.
3. *Discipline.* This factor involves orderly behavior among associates in carrying out their responsibilities to their jobs; it may be positive or negative. Associates are normally expected to conduct themselves properly and effectively at all times on the job. They can be motivated to do a superior job by a self-disciplined manager whom they respect. It is the manager's responsibility to see that discipline remains at an acceptable level.
4. *Unity of Command.* Employees should receive their directions and assignment from one person, and one person only.
5. *Unity of Direction.* All activities within a business firm should be harmoniously agreeable. Then the business can move in one direction, act as an integrated whole, and be assured of singleness (and consistency) of purpose.

6. *Subordination of the Individual.* The individual must subordinate (or submerge) his activities into the general interests of the firm and the other people within the firm. Individual differences, if they exist, must be reconciled by the manager.

7. *Remuneration.* Salaries should be fair and equitable, satisfactory to the employees. They should be clearly discussed with each employee so that there is no misunderstanding.

8. *Centralization.* This refers to the concentration of all management decision–making and authority in the central headquarters of a firm. As businesses grow in size and spread into far–reaching areas, there is a tendency now to decentralize decision-making to area managers within their own geographic areas.

9. *Scalar Chain.* The "chain of authority" in an organization goes from top to bottom. Fayol believed that it should be as short a "chain" as possible.

10. *Order.* This applies to good organization. Everybody and everything should have a clear place in the business arrangement.

Did Fayol cover most of
the important points?

11. *Equity.* People should be treated fairly. When they are treated kindly and with justice, they will respond by being loyal and devoted to their firm. Equity is a responsibility of managers.

12. *Stability of Tenure.* The good manager has very little turnover among the personnel in his department. Turnover is not only costly from a training investment standpoint, but it is hard on morale among people.

13. *Initiative.* The good manager should give employees an opportunity to exercise iniative, originality, and creativeness in order to increase their satisfaction on the job.

14. *Esprit de corps.* Teamwork and communication are necessary to accomplish unity of command. People must work together harmoniously and purposefully. They must be informed about the purposes of what they are doing. There must be good communication.

Fayol himself admitted that these were not all of the management principles that were important, but he listed these because he believed they were the major ones.

There are other more recent management writers whose books will be a source of much information to you. You will find them interesting and enlightening. You will also notice that most of their theories are an extension of Fayol's principles:

Frederick W. Taylor,[1] whose motion and time studies contributed significantly to methods of work.

Douglas McGregor,[2] for his emphasis on the human side of management—allowing employees opportunities to express their ideas

[1] Frederick W. Taylor, *The Principles of Scientific Management* (New York: Harper & Brothers, 1911).

[2] Douglas McGregor, *The Human Side of Enterprise* (New York: McGraw-Hill, 1960).

about how decisions should be made. When they do this, they are more aware of the problems and appreciative of the solutions that are necessary.

Chester I. Barnard,[1] who strongly believes in democratic management.

Peter Drucker,[2] who emphasized the importance of setting objectives that are measurable.

Robert Townsend,[3] who says it is easy to recognize the good leader because those who work for that person turn in superior performances on their jobs.

The Functions of the Fashion Manager

Early in the chapter we said that fashion managers must plan, organize, staff, direct, and control. These are the functions that must be coordinated so the goals and objectives of the fashion business can be achieved. Everyone in the fashion business—indeed, in any business—should clearly understand what the goals really are. Good communication is of utmost importance in achieving good coordination in the business. Group meetings should be held to discuss what needs to be done. Some participation should be encouraged on the part of the members of the group. But remember that participation in the decision making does not mean that the ultimate decision will necessarily come from the group—the final decision is the manager's responsibility, after due consideration has been given to suggestions offered by the group.

Therefore, to manage a fashion business appropriately, the fashion manager must:

1. *Plan* the objectives to be accomplished.
2. Develop the procedures and *organize* them so they can be achieved.
3. *Staff* the fashion business by selecting and training the people who will do the necessary work.
4. *Direct* and guide the group selected so members work efficiently as a team.
5. Finally, measure and *control* the results the group accomplishes.

To help you more clearly understand these fashion management functions, we will discuss each more fully.

[1] Chester I. Barnard, *The Functions of the Executive* (Cambridge, Mass.: Harvard University Press, 1938).

[2] Peter Drucker, *The Practice of Management* (New York: Harper & Row Publishers, Incorporated, 1954).

[3] Robert Townsend, *Up the Organization* (Greenwich, Conn.: Fawcett Publications, Inc., 1971).

PLANNING THE OBJECTIVES

FASHION
MANAGEMENT
PLANNING

Although the exact future cannot be predicted, we must plan for it in order to be sure that what happens is not left to chance. Planning in a business is not very different from planning in our personal lives. We simply decide in advance what will need to be done, how to do it, when to do it, and perhaps who will do it.

Planning is useful only if the objectives for the future are selected carefully. In business, certainly one of the main objectives for everyone is to make a profit. Unless you make a profit you won't be in business very long. Profit determines whether or not the fashion business is meeting the needs of its customers at reasonable costs while in competition with other fashion firms. So the objective is to stretch beyond what you have done in the past but at the same time be sure the goal is realistic enough to be attainable. Fashion businesses therefore often plan to increase their gross sales 5 or 10 percent above last year's gross sales.

It is not enough to just plan to increase sales this year over last, but you must also plan the policies, procedures, and budgets necessary to do it. Usually, fashion merchandisers plan six months in advance, and actually decide on the exact amount of sales they hope can be achieved by the end of the six-month period. Once the sales figure has been determined, they need to plan what garments they will need to buy in order to reach the sales figure—for example, how much stock they will need at the beginning of each month. They must also decide when they want their stock of fashion apparel to be at a peak so they will be able to offer good selections and assortments to the customers when they are most likely to want them. Once the plans for the next few months have been set, it is necessary to get organized to accomplish the plans.

DEVELOPING AND ORGANIZING THE PROCEDURES

FASHION
MANAGEMENT
ORGANIZING

You are already well aware of how important it is to get organized, and probably also aware that, easy as it sounds, it is not really that simple.

The fashion manager begins by grouping the planned activities together in an orderly manner. Conflicts among individuals about their work requirements are avoided when the manager carefully explains what each employee will do so that teamwork can develop. Through good organizing, positive employee relations develop, and the good morale among employees that follows is probably one of the greatest contributing factors to the success of the business. It is those who work for you (assuming you are a manager) who influence your fashion sales and services to your customers.

An organization chart can be used appropriately to plot the lines of authority in your fashion business and to clarify the job assignment for each person in it. Accurate job descriptions also assist in clarifying authority and responsibility.

Does it help to have an organization chart?

With the help of your organization chart, a clear understanding of how you will proceed, and the number of people you will need to assist you, it is time to begin staffing your fashion business.

STAFFING A FASHION BUSINESS

This function is probably pretty well understood already, because you know it involves hiring the right people to get the job done that you want done. It is necessary to recruit competent fashion employees and select the most capable people you can. Then it is important to train them well. Staffing also involves promoting your competent people into positions of more responsibility as they warrant it.

FASHION MANAGEMENT STAFFING

In a smaller fashion business, staffing is the responsibility of the manager of the store. In a larger business, there will be a personnel division that is responsible for recruitment and selection with the fashion department manager's approval. Personnel departments usually give basic store training to the new people for a day or two, maybe as long as a week, so they will know about the company history, its policies, and what the rules and regulations are. The new employees are taught how to operate the store's cash registers and the approved record-keeping procedures for sales. At that point, the new employees report to the assigned fashion department, and further training then becomes the responsibility of the department manager. After a period of time, it is necessary to hold appraisal reviews with the new person so he or she will understand how they are getting along on the job. This evaluation is very important to employees because it will help them understand areas where they need to make improvements, what they are doing that is considered very helpful, and suggestions of ways in which they can expand their responsibilities. Everyone likes to know how he/she is doing from time to time and especially when individual efforts are being recognized and appreciated.

DIRECTING AND GUIDING THE TEAM

This is one of the most important functions that a fashion manager performs, because it involves motivating the fashion salespeople to do the best they can. To motivate them, you need to understand the best way of appealing to their basic human needs. Everyone has physical needs, social needs, and emotional needs. Some needs are very simple and easily satisfied, while others are more complex. Hunger is a simple physical need, for example, and is easily satisfied by eating. But it isn't so simple if you don't have the money to buy the food you

FASHION MANAGEMENT DIRECTING

BASIC HUMAN NEEDS

want to satisfy the need. So certainly it's a basic reason for working in a fashion job or anywhere else.

There are many other reasons and needs that are experienced in a fashion merchandising job once the basic needs are satisfied. For example, there is a need to achieve the esteem of co-workers for doing a good job. This is an *emotional need* and is closely associated with the need to do the best job possible. When you do your best you have the satisfaction of feeling fulfilled and self-actualized.

To properly motivate your fashion employees, it will help if you understand their levels of needs. Dr. Abraham Maslow developed the order of human needs in the following order of importance:

MASLOW'S HIERARCHY OF NEEDS

1. Basic physiological needs
2. Need for safety and security
3. Need for affection and social status
4. Need for esteem
5. Need for self-realization (actualization)

Physiological needs must be satisfied first; then comes the desire for safety, and so on. Many needs may be acting simultaneously, so a decision must be made about which to satisfy first. It is helpful to visualize the priority of needs and the way they rank in our lives by using a stair-step presentation (see Figure 10-5).

1. Basic Physiological Needs. These physiological needs are our needs for survival. They consist of needs that must be satisfied first—those for food, liquid, oxygen, comfortable body temperature. When we are not hungry or thirsty, then other needs become prominent.
2. Safety. Freedom from fear in our daily lives; routines that avoid sudden changes that would cause confusion; job security; police protection from aggressive acts of other people—all these are safety needs.
3. Affection. This need involves our desire for friends and the general feeling of belonging to a group. It also is a need for love and praise.
4. Esteem. This need involves our desire for the respect of other people, their admiration for us, and their opinion of us. We constantly evaluate ourselves and our abilities by our own recognition of our abilities, and also through the attention and appreciation we receive from other people.
5. Self-realization (actualization). Maslow ranks this need as being at the highest level because it follows the satisfaction of all others. When we are satisfied with our life as we have lived it and the goals we have accomplished, then we experience successful self-realization of our needs. We have actualized our highest desires. We have become what we could become.

5. SELF-ACTUALIZATION

Need to make a genuine contribution to our job, our profession, to civilization, or to our fellow human beings.

Fulfillment.

Becoming all that we are capable of becoming.

Inner nature for potential.

Causes people to choose jobs which they like.

Satisfaction from accomplishing a task.

Challenging work.

Creativeness.

4. SELF-ESTEEM

Need to feel a genuine pride in our own importance and worthiness. Need to feel "We are really SOMEBODY." Need to feel others agree that we are worthy. Human dignity Successful work experience brings self-esteem. Managers who take time to compliment their associates for a good accomplishment satisfy this need.

3. SOCIAL & STATUS NEEDS

Need for:
Belonging to a group
Affection
Love
Friendliness
Social activity
May be competitive—"to have what the Joneses have."
Note: Mostly met off the job, but since 1/3 of the day is usually spent at work, some satisfaction can be met there. Liking those you work with helps satisfy this need. Enjoying conversation with others at coffee breaks or lunch.

2. SAFETY and SECURITY

Need assurance that our basic needs will be satisfied for a reasonable length of time, with less effort and worry. A guarantee for tomorrow.
Satisfied by:
Pensions
Personal Body Security
Economic Social Security
Savings Accounts

1. BASIC PHYSIOLOGICAL NEEDS

Survival Needs.
Life Preservation.
Need food, water, sleep, air to breathe, right body temperature

LIMITED NEEDS

Usually satisfied through economic behavior.

HIGHER ORDER NEEDS

(Dominant in advanced civilizations)
Cannot be satisfied through money alone.

FIG. 10-5. Maslow's Order of Priority of Human Needs.[1] Data (for diagram) based on Hierarchy of Needs in "A Theory of Human Motivation" in *Motivation and Personality*, 2nd Edition by Abraham H. Maslow Copyright © 1970 by Abraham H. Maslow. By permission of Harper & Row, Publishers, Inc.

Self-realization varies from person to person because of individual capabilities. But everyone can achieve his potential, within reasonable limitations. Having achieved one level isn't neces-

[1] Abraham H. Maslow, *Motivation and Personality*, 2nd ed. (New York: Harper & Row, 1970).

241

sarily a stopping place, because we usually set a higher level for accomplishment.

Basic physiological needs must be satisfied first, as Maslow's theory suggests. Once we are not hungry, we can aspire to achieve satisfaction for a succession of other needs at a higher level.

Needs may take precedence over one another, also. If we are exceedingly hungry, it is our first need, satisfaction. But if a fire breaks out in the building, our need for safety would precede our need to eat.

Likewise, our need level affects our aspirations for achievement. We continue to aspire to satisfy our higher-level needs in relation to our ability to do so.

We should be continually aware of how to identify the needs of the people under our management and attempt to satisfy them. For example, the basic physiological needs can be satisfied for the most part through the salary payments. Additional satisfaction could be provided by vending machines, air-conditioning, clean store environment.

Safety needs can be satisfied by the worker himself if he knows that he is doing a good job and meeting the job performance level that management expects. Steady employment assurance also satisfies this need.

Need for affection and recognition can be satisfied if the manager will take time to praise the employee for the activities that he does especially well. *Praise before criticism* is a well-known maxim in management.

Esteem needs are met through the recognition that the employee receives for successful work accomplishment by management and co-workers. Since employees are always concerned about how they are doing in relation to their co-workers, it is the manager's responsibility to encourage them in all areas in which they need improvement. Under no circumstances should a manager criticize an employee in front of his co-workers; on the other hand, every opportunity should be made to reinforce the employee's sense of self-esteem through praise that is honest and truly warranted.

The last and highest need requirement, self-realization, probably is best satisfied when the employee feels fulfilled by the job he is doing, and truly enjoys each day's work. The good manager can help an employee reach his job status by showing concern for the employee's welfare and satisfaction of the needs that are prior to this highest need. True motivation can be achieved by helping an employee *want* to reach a higher level of self-realization, a higher goal level, and an efficient learning level.

Fashion managers also need to be aware of the correct way in which to communicate with their people. They must be able to speak or write in a clear and understandable way. They must not assume that they are understood, nor must they ever assume that things are

Is any one need important all the time?

Why must a manager know what employees need?

Is it hard to keep employees satisfied?

Can our jobs satisfy some or all of our needs?

known implicitly. Whether instructions should be spoken or written depends on which would be the most effective presentation. Oral communication is speedy and questions can be asked and answered if need be. On the other hand, the written communication can be retained for reference in the future. Instructions may be given orally, but it is probably a good practice to write them down unless they are of minor consequence.

Should instructions be oral or written?

Styles of leadership (and the fashion manager *must* lead) are of three kinds: *autocratic, democratic,* and *laissez-faire.* The fashion manager who leads and directs his associates in the autocratic style relies entirely on his authority to command people to do as he says. The democratic leader solicits the participation of those who are affected and often acts on their advice. The laissez-faire leader gives a free choice to employees to do as they wish, and exercises no decision making whatsoever. Since a fashion manager *must* lead, his choice of leadership style will be determined somewhat by the situation that demands the leadership, but it is important that he/she remain close to the fashion employees and secure their participation as often as possible in making a final decision. People actually expect to be led and they work with more confidence and enthusiasm for the fashion manager they admire.

Is a fashion manager a leader?

AUTOCRATIC

DEMOCRATIC

LAISSEZ-FAIRE

The last function of management that a fashion manager must do is equally as important as the others and it involves controlling the fashion employees.

MEASURING AND CONTROLLING THE RESULTS

In the control function, the fashion manager must measure the progress and accomplishment of employees. If there is any deviation from standards, corrective action must be taken.

FASHION MANAGEMENT CONTROLLING

This can be a very complex problem, especially if there is any vagueness in the measurement of results. Usually, if the fashion department is reaching the desired results at a reasonable cost and without too many serious errors, then a general appraisal of success may be assumed.

It is best that controls be as objective as possible. They should be clear and positive so that employees can be told in definite terms why they are or are not doing a good job. For this reason, budgeting is used by almost all fashion managers. Budgeting involves setting plans for a given future period in numerical terms. Sales quotas for a future period are often used. At the end of the period, it is clear to the fashion employees whether these quotas have been met or not.

Although budgeting is important and useful, personal observation of fashion salespeople is still one of the most reliable measures for control that there is.

Fashion Management: The Golden Rule

As complicated as the management functions may appear to you at this point, we must not close this chapter without assuring you that fashion management is really a natural and simple process.

In its easier form, good management is simply, "Do unto others as you would have them do unto you," a maxim you will recognize instantly.

Our world divides itself naturally into leaders and followers. Each person must make his own contribution in a simple and natural way. This certainly doesn't mean we should work any less hard, but it does mean that activity is of value only in terms of attainment. The success of any business organization depends on having an adequate number of people in the right jobs at the right time, all producing at their highest capacity. Management is the development of people and not the direction of things.

Thus, good employee relations within a business organization are the most important contributing factor to a sound and successful business. To build sound employee relations you have but to take into consideration the simple motives and desires of human beings. A few of their natural interests should be carefully pointed out to you, because when you become a manager, you will quickly recognize that each of these interests applies to fashion merchandising management.

Why should an applicant and the new employee be treated in a friendly way?

1. Treat new applicants courteously and make them feel at ease. The atmosphere of the employment office determines the prospective employee's important first impression of the business. Morale begins at this point.

2. Welcome the new employee through simple induction procedures and orientation training which make him feel he is valuable to your company.

3. Give the new employee simple and intelligent instruction in what he is expected to do, how it can be done, and what constitutes a job well done. Then evaluation can be keyed to simple standards of performance in quantity, quality, time, and cost.

4. Be sure the new employee gets capable supervision and continues to get training so that morale remains high. This is simple to practice and the dividends are big.

5. See to it that new employees are recognized for their importance in your business. The management that recognizes that each individual on the payroll has intelligence, ability, and something to contribute to the company's operation—no matter how small—will satisfy a basic desire in that individual.

6. Be sure employees see their daily work as a service to others. This too concerns a natural human need. Help employees to see the company's objectives, policies, accomplishments, manage-

ment philosophy, and the part they play in the development of the company.

7. Give employees realistic recognition for a job well done. Give promotions when abilities and merits justify them.

8. Give special recognition to inspire greater effort in employees. Most people will work hard and long for such incentives as a pat on the back or public acknowledgment of management appreciation. Make special awards, give bonuses or prizes in a fairly administered way to increase the human desire to produce more when more recognition is given.

How can you get employees to do better all the time?

9. Since every human being likes to work in an organization in which there is universal confidence in the ability and fairness of top management, develop employee confidence through fair and honest management policies. Offer management that is sincere and open in all its negotiations—frank and aboveboard at all times. Personal contacts that allow management and employees to know each other as personalities is a simple means to this end.

10. Emphasize the importance of being healthy and sound in mind and body—take an interest in employees. No one can work well if he/she is ill. Offer as many benefits as possible—paid vacations, medical examinations, hospitalization plans, safety programs, credit unions, employee counseling. All these improve morale and production.

11. Satisfy the basic instinct in all of us for security. If a person is worried about his job or about the welfare of those dependent upon him, he cannot produce effectively. While we all know that our earning capacity will diminish eventually, the fear of want in old age is a constant worry. So offer annuity plans, insurance programs, opportunities for savings, and job stability to counteract this fear.

12. If it becomes necessary to terminate an employee, be sure that he has a full understanding of the reasons for termination. A pink slip attached to a time card is not the way to effect a correct termination. An exit interview must be properly conducted and timed.

Simple Steps to Follow in Fashion Management

Here we present a few simple steps which, if followed carefully and with reasonable attention to sequence, will assure adequate management application and improve human performance. They work equally well with old or new employees.

1. Develop a simple outline of the functions and operations to be performed by the person involved. Be sure it is an understandable statement of what the employee is to do, what authority he has in doing it, and what his relationships with other people are.

2. Develop a simple statement of results that are considered satisfactory. While this may seem almost impossible at first for some activities, a sincere discussion of expected results will often produce very definite and acceptable objectives.

3. Check actual performance against the standards that have been set at regular intervals.

4. Make a list of corrective actions necessary to improve performance where such improvement is needed. No employee can develop into a better worker unless he continuously increases his skill, gains knowledge, changes old habits, and assumes constructive attitudes. The manager should know where improvement is needed.

5. Select the best sources from which the person involved can obtain help and information. Perhaps his best source is his immediate supervisor or other individuals in the organization, or perhaps people outside the business could be brought in to help. The most advantageous should be selected.

6. Set aside *in advance* a time to supply the help and information that is needed. If time isn't set aside in advance, then time will never be found without interrupting the normal function of the business.

7. Discuss with mutual agreement what constitutes a fair day's pay for a fair day's work, as well as what nonfinancial incentives are worth working for. With a firm base of fairly administered financial rewards, a climate can be developed that will make people want to stay with you.

No specific system of carrying out these recommendations is needed. Method is relatively unimportant if a continuous attempt is made by intelligent people to do what is suggested.

If people in a business organization received as much attention as material items, and if attention were paid in a conscious, orderly way rather than in haphazard and spasmodic bursts of enthusiasm, the results would be astounding.

Conclusion

The management experience can be very pleasant and natural. It should be approached simply. Employees react quickly and favorably to understanding, fairness, and consideration.

The greatest single reward any manager or supervisor can receive is to have those who have been under his/her direction say that they are better workers, better citizens, and better producers because of his/her leadership. Such an attitude builds morale and loyalty, and these will accomplish the positive, constructive behaviors that make a business a success.

1. Define or identify the following:
   a. Retail assembly lines
   b. Hard lines
   c. Soft lines
   d. Planning a store from the inside out
   e. Mass purchasing
   f. Fashion manager
   g. Henri Fayol
   h. Fashion management planning
   i. Fashion management organizing
   j. Fashion management staffing
   k. Fashion management directing
   l. Fashion management controlling
   m. Basic human needs
   n. Dr. Abraham Maslow
   o. Autocratic fashion management
   p. Democratic fashion management
   q. Laissez-faire fashion management
2. Think of someone who is in management—someone for whom you have worked would be best. If that person was a good "boss," why did you like to work for him or her? If not, what might he or she have done that would have been better?
3. Do all managers perform essentially the same activities? For example, would the manager of a city government differ from a fashion manager in what he does to manage associates? Support your answer.
4. Now that you know Maslow's order of priority of human needs, identify the need levels which you experience almost daily. How do you satisfy them?
5. How will you know when you begin to approach the high level of self-realization or self-actualization? Will you desire to seek a higher level perhaps?
6. "A MANAGER MUST LEAD." Do you agree?
7. What is the very simplest management principle that you can follow?
8. If you should become a fashion manager, what kind of a manager do you hope you can be?

1. If you are working in a fashion business, analyze the style of leadership that your manager uses. What are your manager's strongest points, and how are they exhibited? Does your manager have any weak characteristics in management style? (If you are not working in a fashion business, you may still accomplish this activity by visiting with the manager of a favorite fashion store of yours.)
2. Talk with the manager of a small fashion specialty store about the activities he or she performs in addition to the functions of planning,

organizing, staffing, directing, and controlling. No doubt that person will do all the buying for the store. What else does he/she have to do?

3. Ask several managers how and why they enjoy being managers. Also ask them what experience and training they had before they entered management.

Case Problems

Case 10-1. Barbara has had an unhappy and frustrating first day on her new fashion job. She has had no formal training on cash register operation because it is such a busy season of the year, and she was needed on the sales floor just as soon as she reported to work. If she makes a sale, she is expected to ask someone else to operate the cash register for her. She has done her best, but everything is so unfamiliar to her that all day she feels that she is really nothing more than a big bother to everybody because she has had to ask so many questions. She can't wait for this day to end.

1. Analyze the type of indoctrination and training that Barbara received the first day. What could have been improved?
2. Even if Barbara had had former experience in a fashion store, should she have received specific instructions about how her new store operated?
3. Do you know anyone who has ever had a similar experience? Did that person stay with the company very long? Why? Is management part of this problem?

Case 10-2. The manager of a branch specialty fashion store in a large mall was complaining to a friend of his, as they had coffee one morning, "Business has just been terrible! I don't know what to do. My salespeople act like they're doing a customer a great favor if they wait on them. I tell them to get out and *sell, sell, sell*—but they don't pay any attention. I lost two salespeople last week—they said they had to have more money. I pay more than they're worth as it is. And they're always unhappy—keep complaining about the lines I carry, or something else like the colors don't match, or we don't carry enough size 8's—I dunno—it's always something. They just don't make any effort to trade up or do any suggestive selling—they just don't want to work! You don't seem to be having any trouble, Bill—what's your secret? Didn't you tell me that your sales this year were above last year's?"

1. Do you think there is anything wrong with the manager's attitude toward his salespeople? How would you suggest that he correct it?
2. What do you suppose that Bill is doing in his store that the manager of the other store is not doing?
3. If you were a management consultant, what recommendations would you make?

Case 10-3. You have just been named department manager of your sportswear department. You feel qualified for the job and are anxious to do the best possible job of management because this is your first attempt to manage a department. You have seven full-time salespeople and four part-time salespeople. Your assistant manager is older than you by about ten years. You have always been good team workers in the past and have worked together pleasantly. However, you sense that being assigned assistant manager is a big disappointment to your friend, and you feel that you will have difficulty with this person. It isn't anything obvious—just a feeling that your former relationship may not last into your new job status. On Monday morning, you will hold your first sales meeting, and you must plan what you are going to say to your salespeople, as well as announce plans for department changes you may wish to make, if any.

1. First—how are you going to handle your relationship with your assistant manager? Would it be wise to discuss the situation together?
2. What would you plan to say and do at your Monday-morning meeting?

Case 10-4. You are the manager of the "better shoes" department, have a good staff, and everything has been going well. However, a new woman you have hired begins arriving a few minutes late each day. If she isn't late, she comes rushing in just as the bell rings. You have noticed that she is also taking longer than is allowed for lunch, but she makes excuses for this. The other day, she was out of the department on several occasions when business was slow—visiting here and there in the adjoining departments. You have begun to notice a look on the faces of the other salespeople, and you realize that they are waiting and watching to see what is going to happen. You sense that they think you are too lenient with the new woman because you like her very much. The time has come to do something about morale in the department.

1. What must you do? How will you do it?
2. Role-play this incident in class. Show the right way and the wrong way to correct the new woman's infraction of rules and regulations.

Case 10-5. You manage a specialty store (either men's or women's —your choice) and you will soon have a vacancy for an assistant manager. You would like to promote one of your good salespeople to the job—actually you have two under consideration. Both have good sales records, have worked for you for over two years, are well liked by their fellow employees and customers, and are genuinely motivated workers.

The first worker is five years older than the other, quite happy in disposition, is outgoing and friendly to everyone, needs more salary because of family responsibilities which the assistant's wage would satisfy, but has never indicated to you that advancement is a concern. The second person indicated to you when he was hired that advancement would be important as ability warranted. He has been attending college to earn a degree in merchandising management, is more quiet and reserved in manner than the other person, but friendly and cooperative.

The two are so similar that you are having great difficulty in making a decision about which to recommend for the promotion. You have discussed it with your divisional manager and the personnel director. The divisional manager suggests that you prepare an objective list of qualities that can be rated and compare the two individuals on this basis—then promote the one who rates highest.

1. What qualities would you list that could be measured objectively? What problems will you encounter in preparing your rating list?

Chapter 11

Basic fashion merchandising mathematics

Objectives

When you have read this chapter, you should be able to

1. Describe and explain the importance of the use of an electronic data processing system in the fashion retail business
2. Compute some of the common retail arithmetic requirements, such as percentage comparisons, retail pricing dollar markup, and retail pricing using cost
3. Explain the importance of the physical inventory and how it is used
4. State why stockturn is of such consequence in the fashion business particularly
5. Explain how an economic-history decision on the part of the president of Montgomery Ward held the company back at a time when it should have been expanding

MONTGOMERY WARD

Montgomery Ward, the nation's first mail-order merchandiser, celebrated its 100th anniversary in 1972, and thus entered its second century rededicated to the principles of its founder, Aaron Montgomery Ward. First in American business to establish the policy "satisfaction guaranteed or your money back" for customers throughout the nation, Montgomery Ward's promise is still the cornerstone of consumer protection.

The Grolier Club, a New York society of book-lovers, evaluated the industry originated in 1872 by Aaron Montgomery Ward, saying: "No idea ever mushroomed so far from so small a beginning, or had so profound an influence on the economics of a continent, as the concept, original to America, of direct selling by mail for cash. Aaron Montgomery Ward conceived the idea in 1869, was wiped out in the Chicago fire, but started Montgomery Ward & Co" (quoted in the Latham book cited below).[1]

How did this catalog influence American living standards?

In 1946, the Grolier Club included a copy of the Montgomery Ward catalog among its collection of 100 American books chosen for their influence on American life. "The mail order catalogue has been perhaps the greatest single influence in increasing the standard of American middle-class living. It brought the benefit of wholesale prices to city and hamlet, to the cross-roads and the prairies; it inculcated cash payment as against crippling credit; it urged millions of housewives to bring into their homes and place upon their backs and in their shelves and on their floors creature comforts which otherwise they could never have hoped for; and above all, it substituted sound quality for shoddy. . . ."[2]

Why did Ward think he could sell goods by mail?

After the Civil War, in 1866, young Montgomery Ward went to Chicago, the rail and shipping center for the growing Midwest. While working for a wholesaling firm and traveling to country stores by horse and buggy, he conceived the idea of selling direct to country people by mail. Through a mail-order store that would distribute a catalog listing goods with descriptions and prices, the country people could order goods by mail and the store could ship their purchases (cash on delivery) to the nearest railroad station. By 1871, Ward had finally saved enough money to buy a small amount of goods at wholesales prices to inaugurate his idea. He was never to sell that merchandise, however, because the devastating Chicago fire destroyed all of his merchandise, as it also destroyed the property of thousands of others. But Ward, like the city of Chicago, "dusted himself off and

---

[1] Frank B. Latham, *1872–1972, A Century of Serving Consumers* (Chicago: Montgomery Ward, 1972) p. 2.
[2] Latham, p. 2.

FIG. 11-1. Aaron Montgomery Ward (1844–1913) originated direct selling by mail for cash. (Courtesy, Montgomery Ward, Chicago)

went back to work," and by August of 1872, with a total capital of $1,600, he rented a small shipping room and sent out his first one-page price list to the country people of Iowa, Illinois, Indiana, Kansas, and Missouri.

During these difficult times, one of the people who had a profound influence on Ward and his mail–order idea was his close personal friend and partner, George R. Thorne. He and Ward married sisters. Thorne had five sons, all of whom subsequently entered the business. One of them, Charles H. Thorne, became president and chairman of the board. George R.'s great grandson, Charles H. Thorne, II, today holds a position in the company's public relations department.

Most of the items on Ward's first price list were priced at $1. Item No. 1 was "12 yards best quality prints, $1.00." Other one-dollar offerings were red flannel, hoop skirts, bustles, paper collars, cotton hose, wool socks, boys' winter caps, shawls, and "1 ostrich plume and 3 bunches fine French flowers."

Business did not flourish after this price list went out, because the Panic of 1873 had caused Wards potential customers, the farmers, to suffer extremely low crop prices. They were also somewhat suspicious of Ward because they did not know him, and he was a name far away in the big city.

Why did customers not trust Ward at the beginning?

But business did gradually improve, and the Montgomery Ward

business quarters were enlarged. Catalog No. 10 contained four pages with 394 items.

It was Catalog 13, Spring-Summer 1875, that contained the earliest and strongest Ward pledge of consumer protection:

> *We guarantee all of our goods. If any of them are not satisfactory after due inspection, we will take them back, pay all expenses, and refund the money paid for them. When in the city please call and see us.*

CAVEAT EMPTOR

This was a startling statement appearing when the warning "caveat emptor" existed in business everywhere. It produced a booming business and the company enlarged again.

Ward wrote all the early catalog copy, and he carefully examined products before he made any promises to the customers. He worked long hours, but he found time to go to one of the packing floors and

How did Ward help his employees enjoy their work?

SURVIVAL OF THE FITTEST

organize a dance for the employees at lunchtime. Employee relations within Wards have always been exceptionally good. Company employees have always enjoyed many benefits and good working conditions, contrary to the general rules of "the survival of the fittest" during early times. Ward's has provided vacations with pay, overtime pay, medical benefits, and many other thoughtful considerations for employees' welfare.

What did the early Midwest settlers need?

Living conditions during the late 1800s in the Midwestern prairies were harsh for the people struggling to get started there. Undoubtedly, the Ward catalog helped them, not only to pass the lonely hours, but also to supply them with their many needs as homesteaders, as well. Windmills, pumps, feed-cutters, corn-shellers, and other farm equipment; cast-iron stoves for heat and cooking; and kerosene lamps for light were all featured items in the catalogs.

By 1887 a half-million dollars' worth of stock was being handled, and by 1890, orders swamped the company's facilities, so further expansion was made. Wards celebrated its twenty-fifth anniversary in 1894 with record-breaking sales and profits, and a special "Catalogue

WISH BOOK

and Buyers' Guide." Not only was the catalog really a "wish book," satisfying many dreams, but it had become a sort of textbook, combining arithmetic, dictionary, and geography. Teachers made good use of it in the country schools. When an object was mentioned that the youngsters had never seen, out would come the "big book." The students would go through the pages, and there was the item!

Business continued to increase from all over the United States, so Wards opened mail-order houses in Oakland, California; Baltimore, Maryland; Fort Worth, Texas; Albany, New York; and Denver, Colorado.

In 1913, Mr. Ward died at the age of 70, and the nation lost one

FIG. 11-2. A reproduction of the tiny 1875 catalog. Historically, it is notable because it marks the first time a business adopted a "Satisfaction Guaranteed or Your Money Back" policy.

(Courtesy, Montgomery Ward, Chicago)

of its greatest merchants. His direct-selling-by-mail-for-cash idea had profoundly influenced business practices and living conditions everywhere in the United States.

When mail-order business slowed because there were fewer people living in rural areas, and those could easily drive their cars into the cities, Wards expanded into opening many new retailing stores.

During the great Depression years, Sewell Avery became chairman of the board, chief executive officer, and general manager. He

Did Mr. Ward affect business for all time?

255

FIG. 11-3. Montgomery Ward corporate headquarters, Chicago.
(Courtesy, Montgomery Ward, Chicago)

guided Wards through a particularly difficult time; by 1933 sales had moved up, and continued to do so through World War II.

When the war ended, all American businesses were faced with deciding what to do about expansion after the war. Avery decided that the risks were too great for expansion and that depression would surely engulf the country as it had always done after a great war. This later proved to be the wrong decision. History did not repeat itself, and the companies that expanded their operations were in better condition than those that did not. Avery's decision caused Wards several lost financial years.

However, when he resigned, modernization of the stores was begun again, and retail expansion resumed. Ward's own private brands replaced many national brands of goods and Wards entered its "turn-around years" in the 1960s. Capable and experienced merchandisers were hired, manufacturers who could schedule production runs to supply and resupply merchandise were carefully selected, products were carefully analyzed for quality to be sure they met company specifications, credit was introduced, and electronic data processing was installed.

So, after years of internal struggle, the modern Wards emerged. In 1968, it merged with Container Corporation of America to become Marcor, and the first year ended with higher sales for each company.

By the end of 1971, Wards was serving 30 million customers from 21.5 million square feet of space, through 2,100 outlets (retail stores, catalog stores, and catalog agencies).

*Do people still buy
from the catalog?*

The catalog remains important and continues to produce almost a quarter of Wards total sales volume. The company's future in catalog merchandising remains bright. Computer technology applied to the catalog has established accurate inventory requirements and automatic replenishment.

During the year-long celebration of Montgomery Ward's 100th anniversary, "Century 2," scores of new products were introduced, Aaron Montgomery Ward was inducted into the Chicago Merchandise Mart's Hall of Fame, and a commemorative U.S. postage stamp was issued in his honor.

Montgomery Ward became a part of the Mobil Corporation in 1976 and today is a fast-moving, growing organization still committed to the improvement of the lifestyles of American families.

*Is there fashion
interest at Ward's?*

Fashion emphasis began throughout Wards when Rita Perna joined the company as fashion coordinator in the New York buying office. She became an assistant vice-president and fashion coordinator in 1971, and is the first woman vice-president in the company history. She is a past national president of the Fashion Group, Inc., U.S., an international professional association of women executives representing every phase of fashion manufacturing, marketing, retailing, communication, and education. There are over 5,000 members in thirty-two regional groups in cities of the United States, Australia, Canada, England, France, Mexico, and Japan. The Fashion Group serves as an international clearinghouse for the exchange of information on tastes, trends, and developments in fashion.

When the current chairman and chief executive officer of Wards, Edward S. Donnell, made a speech at the company's 100th anniversary celebration banquet to 1,000 store and merchandise managers, he said:

> The challenges and opportunities of the 70's and beyond are greater than ever for all retailers. Yet, even as we move ahead into the 70's, with all its anticipated improvements in services, we daily will reaffirm Montgomery Ward's 100-year-old credo of "Satisfaction Guaranteed" as the best of all possible protections for all consumers.

FIG. 11-4. Rita Perna, fashion coordinator and vice-president of Montgomery Ward since 1971, is the first woman vice-president in the company's history.
(Courtesy, Montgomery Ward, Chicago)

Regardless of size, all fashion businesses are involved in the control function of maintaining accurate records of their operations.

OPERATING EXPENSES

COST OF GOODS SOLD

What is EDP?

Fashion decisions are based on operating expenses, inventory levels, sales records, earnings, cost of goods sold, and many other factors. As competition continues to increase, the need for accuracy and current, up-to-date factual information makes it necessary for more and more businesses to convert their record keeping to EDP (electronic data processing). The electronic computer is the most sophisticated and fastest method available to fashion management to provide its businesses with a chance to be competitive. It provides business ways in which to secure faster, less expensive, and more efficient methods of processing the burden of paper-work. The computer revolution has been called the second Industrial Revolution

FIG. 11-5. Colorful styles as displayed and merchandised for the fashion-conscious junior customers at Montgomery Ward is evidence of their emphasis on fashion after their turnaround years.
(Courtesy, Montgomery Ward, Chicago)

by many. An example of what this kind of processing has done for Miller & Paine (Lincoln, Nebraska) will be included for your information.

It is not the purpose of this chapter to replace a thorough course in the mathematics of merchandising, but rather to help you see what records must be kept, why they are needed, and how they are used.

It should introduce you to some of the kinds of math you will need to understand in the early part of your training on a fashion job.

Electronic Data Processing in a Fashion Business

All of us have felt the impact of electronic computers in our lives. They calculate our telephone and electric bills; in fact, we see evidence of their use in most of the bills, statements, and receipts we receive.

Why is EDP being used more and more in business?

Electronic computers are being used more and more by both large and small fashion businesses to assist them in keeping a competitive edge. They increase the timeliness of information and represent the fastest method of record keeping available. Computer printouts guide fashion executives in making decisions about inventory, buying and planning for the future, and controlling operating expenses.

The first retailer to implement the entire National Cash Register 280 Retail System in all its stores was Miller & Paine of Lincoln, Nebraska. More than 100 terminals were installed at their downtown and suburban stores, and all point-of-sale terminals were equipped with wand readers to capture sales information instantly. The wands substantially improve customer service because of extensive use of a unique color-bar code. Their green, white, and black color bars, which are read electronically, are utilized on employee name tags, customer credit cards, and on merchandise tags.

POINT-OF-SALE TERMINALS

How is EDP actually used?
What can a color-bar code tell?

For reporting purposes, Miller & Paine is organized into 60 departments and 900 classifications. The ready-to-wear department consists of popular-priced dresses, coats and suits, better clothing, and lingerie and foundations. Further information in the ready-to-wear classifications identifies season, style, vendor, size, and color. The color-bar code tags for all merchandise are created on tag printers which encode up to fifty-six characters of information in the series of color bars. Built-in logic of the tag printer automatically applies six different checks to make sure all characters are encoded correctly. Besides those referring to price, there are characters to identify merchandise by department, class, and other information.

Are terminals like cash registers?

DAILY BEST-SELLER REPORT

The detailed information captured at the point of sale is recorded on magnetic tape by data collectors and is processed daily to provide timely, up-to-date reports for management and buyers. The terminals improve the accuracy of the sales information on which merchandisers base their buying. The buyers receive not only a daily best-seller report, but a weekly and monthly stock status report as well. With this report buyers can easily determine reorders for particular colors or styles. The weekly stock status report summarizes merchandise activity at the unit control level for the week. The monthly stock status report gives a complete accounting of all merchandise, shows sales

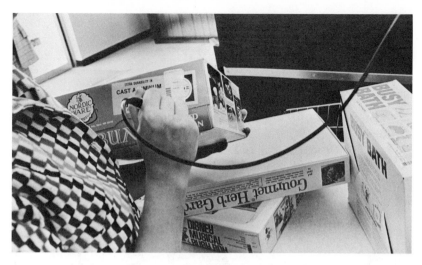

FIG. 11-6. Using an electronic wand, the cashier reads product and pricing information directly into the NCR 280 terminal, eliminating the need for her to enter it through the keyboard. This has speeded traffic through the checkouts so much that even on a busy Saturday this store keeps only two of the four checkout stands open.

(Courtesy, The National Cash Register Company, Dayton, Ohio.)

for the current month and the previous six months, and provides information on new receipts and stock on hand. A terminal in the receiving department gives information on all receipts and vendor returns.

VENDOR RETURNS

While the system is improving the accuracy of inventory information for buyers, the terminals are also making procedures easier for the credit department. The computer is programmed to print such phrases as "dress," "blouse," "skirt," "white shirt," etc., and this permits a company to eliminate the mailing of charge slips. In stores that do not have this kind of a system, there is a tremendous amount of manual work because individual slips have to be filed alphabetically behind a customer's name. Hand-stuffing of charge slips with statements is another time-consuming practice, and the possibility of error is a source of trouble for credit departments. Elimination of charge slips allows more opportunity for promotional messages to accompany customer statements for the same amount of postage formerly required just to mail the statement and copies of the sales slips.

Can you still use credit with EDP?

When such a new system is installed, employees throughout a store must receive instruction for a smooth conversion to the new electronic system. Everyone has experienced some problem with computer statements, no doubt. Unless employees are thoroughly and competently trained, an electronic system can cause great problems.

Does it take a long time to learn EDP systems?

Immediately before the public debut of the new terminal system at Miller & Paine, management held a private sale on a Sunday afternoon

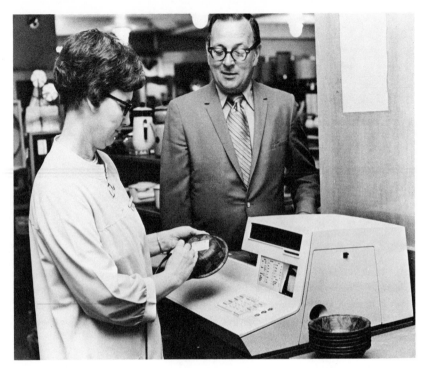

FIG. 11-7. The installation of NCR 280 retail terminals in the housewares department enables personnel to capture unit-level information instead of mere department number and classification code.

(Courtesy, The National Cash Register Company, Dayton, Ohio.)

when the store was normally closed, during which the employee discount was increased to 25 percent. They also programmed the terminals to calculate the sale discount rate and sales-tax calculations. Salespeople, who had already received training in the new system, were thus given an opportunity to demonstrate their ability in using the new system before customers were introduced to it.

OUT-OF-STOCK
SITUATION

Is this the way to eliminate being out of some of things that customers want?

Not only does such a system provide quick and unobtrusive credit authorization, but also—from the shopper's standpoint—out-of-stock situations are sharply reduced. The system provides instant reports of sales data; managers can keep abreast of sales trends literally hour by hour and can have information down to the unit level at any time they request it. Older methods did not allow sales in such detail because only gross figures were available, and they are hardly a true barometer of daily business.

How does EDP help salespeople?

Electronic terminals guide salespeople through each sale and eliminate the costly errors on sales slips which cost most retailers dearly. But inventory control by manual methods at peak periods—when buyers most need adequate unit sales information—is probably

FIG. 11-8. Salespeople are free to practice on the terminals at any time. The instructor is always available to answer any questions.

(Courtesy, The National Cash Register Company, Dayton, Ohio.)

the major problem for most companies. Therefore, capturing information at the point of sale and processing the information quickly is the great advantage automated systems provide. Wand reading improves the accuracy of the information and speeds the cashier operations. With a single pass over the merchandise tag, the information is entered into the terminal, which displays the price, adds it to the customer's bill, computes sales tax, and prints out the sales slip at the end of the transaction.

It is readily understandable why the electronic methods are being adopted by more and more fashion businesses, because speed is actually the middle name of the fashion business.

We have illustrated only one of many electronic systems available to fashion retailing. Such systems are being adopted at the apparel and fabric manufacturing levels also. Students entering the automated world of fashion business would be well advised to recognize the impact of the computer on business and avail themselves of the opportunity to learn more about computers as a part of their business education. Computers are an integral part of the fashion business now, and the trend is destined to become the foundation of

Is NCR the only system available?

the fashion business in future years. Students should learn what the computer is, what it can do, and how it can serve the fashion business better in the decades ahead.

The vast amount of data available from the computer is rapidly changing retailing. The planning, pricing, and inventory control of merchandise have all become exceedingly complex. It isn't the purpose of this chapter to go into all the aspects of this merchandise planning and the factors that are involved in the elements of profit. These should be reserved for an advance course in fashion merchandising and buying. However, there are several basic formulas and terminology with which you will soon need to deal in your fashion job, so these will be discussed and explained briefly.

I'm just a beginner. Why do I need some retailing math?

Comparison With Last Year's Records

"LAST-YEAR-ITIS"

It is quite common to make comparisons with the records of the last year. If you hear, "Did we beat last year today?" or "How does this year compare to last?" how do you come up with accurate answers?

How are we doing? Are we improving or not?

An increase or decrease is usually expressed in percentages, rather than in dollars and cents, because percentages are easier to compare.

PERCENTAGE
INCREASES OR
DECREASES

FORMULA 1. To find the percentage of increase or decrease, find the difference between the original amount (last year, for example) and the current amount (this year) by subtracting the amounts. Then divide the difference by the original amount (last year's figure).

Example:

To find the increase in sales this year over last year:

Current year's sales	$125,000
Last year's sales	−100,000
Difference	$ 25,000

$$
\begin{array}{r}
.25 = 25\% \text{ increase} \\
\$100,000. \overline{)\$25,000.00} \text{ (The difference)} \\
20\,000\,00 \\
\hline
5\,000\,00 \\
5\,000\,00 \\
\hline
00
\end{array}
$$

(Original amount)

Example:

Or, if expenses this month were $2,000 and last month they were $2,500, how much were they lessened this month?

Last month's expenses	$2,500.
This month's expenses	2,000.
Difference	$ 500.

.20 = 20% decrease in expenses this month

$2,500. $\overline{\smash{)}\$500.00}$
      500 00
          $\overline{00}$

Or you may want to use percentages in other ways, also.

Example:

If a dress was reduced from $80 to $60, what was the percentage of markdown?

Original amount	$ 80.00
Reduced to	− 60.00
Difference	$ 20.00

          .25
$80.00 $\overline{\smash{)}\$20.00\ 00}$
      16 00 00
       $\overline{4\ 00\ 00}$
       4 00 00
        $\overline{00}$

The percentage of markdown on the dress was 25%.

Example:

If an apparel manufacturer increased his production from 4,000 dresses to 5,000 dresses, what was the percent of increase in production?

  5,000
− 4,000
 $\overline{1,000\ \text{(difference)}}$

         .25
4,000 $\overline{\smash{)}1,000.00}$
    800 00
    $\overline{200\ 00}$
    200 00
      $\overline{00}$

Production was increased 25%.

Price Lines

Establishing price lines is a standard retail practice. Price lines refer to the specific retail prices of the merchandise carried in the store. For example, dresses might be offered for sale in the price lines of $25, $35, or $45. (Many retail stores have ceased using the psychological pricing system of using odd cents in their prices, because they do not deceive customers, and they are more difficult to handle arithmetically. So, instead of price lines of $24.99, 34.99, or $44.99, they use the actual round figures for which the prices stand.)

Price lining assists customers in choosing garments, makes it easier to sell, and simplifies display of the garments. When buyers go to market, they must buy garments that can be sold profitably at the established price lines in their departments, so they must consider the costs and markups of the garments, as well as style, quality, fabric, and other considerations.

Price range refers to the difference in prices between the lowest price line and the highest price line. The price range in a blouse department might be from $5 to $20.

Markup

Markup is the difference between the cost price of merchandise and its retail price.

If the retail price is	$ 20.00
the cost price is	12.00
the $ *markup* is	$ 8.00

Markup for successful retailing must not only cover the cost of the garment, but the costs or expenses involved in selling it and a reasonable profit for the efforts and capital involved. Usually it isn't expressed as a dollar markup but rather as a percentage.

FORMULA 2.

$$\text{Markup percentage} = \frac{\text{Dollar markup}}{\text{Dollar retail}}$$

Example:

Using the figures above, if the buyer purchases a blouse for $12 and plans to sell it for $20, what is the retail markup percent?

Solution:

We found that the dollar markup in the above calculation was $8.00.

Therefore, the markup % = $\dfrac{\$\ 8.00\ \text{(Dollar markup)} =}{\$20.00\ \text{(Retail price)}}$

$$.40 = 40\% \text{ (Markup percentage)}$$

$20.00 $\overline{)\$8.00\ 00}$
  8 00 0
  ————
   00

The markup percentage on the blouse is 40%; or, you may also say:

The markup is 40% of the retail price of the blouse.
Therefore: COST + MARKUP = RETAIL
Expressed in percentages it would be:
$$60\% + 40\% = 100\%$$

Suppose you know the cost of the blouse is $12.00 and that you wish to achieve a 40% markup, how do you decide what retail price to put on it?

Remember: Cost + Markup = Retail
$$\$12.00 + \quad 40\% \quad = 100\%$$

FORMULA 3.

$$\text{Retail} = \frac{\text{Cost}}{100\% - \text{Markup }\%}$$

or

Solution:

$$\text{Retail} = \frac{\$12.00}{100\% - 40\%} = \frac{\$12.00}{.60} = \$20.00$$

$$\begin{array}{r} \$20.00 \\ .60\overline{\smash{\big)}\$12.00\ 00} \end{array}$$

When a buyer goes into the market to select garments for a new season, there is a price line to consider. When the buyers know, for example, that they must select garments for their $25 price line, and that they want to achieve a 40 percent markup, what cost garments must be located and bought?

FORMULA 4.

$$\text{Cost} = \text{Retail} \times (100\% - 40\%)$$

Solution:

$$\begin{array}{r} \text{Cost} = \$25.00 \times .60 \\ \$\ 25.00 \\ \times\ .60 \\ \hline \$\ 15.00 \end{array}$$

To achieve a 40 percent markup for a $25 price line, the cost of the garments bought in the market must not exceed $15.

Markup tables are available for buyers to help them quickly determine different percentage markups and retail prices at varying costs. Such a markup table is shown in Table 11-1.

I might be slow in figuring markup—is there an easier way?

Taking Inventory

Inventory may be taken once a year, usually at the end of January, or twice a year, at the end of January and again at the end of July. These

Why are they taking inventory?

TABLE 11-1.   Markup Table

cost	25%	33⅓%	40%	45%	50%
		% profit at retail selling price			
2.25	3.00	3.38	3.75	4.09	4.50
2.75	3.67	4.13	4.59	5.00	5.50
2.87½	3.83	4.31	4.80	5.22	5.75
3.25	4.33	4.87	5.41	5.90	6.50
3.75	5.00	5.62	6.25	6.80	7.50
4.75	6.33	7.12	7.91	8.62	9.50
5.75	7.66	8.62	9.57	10.45	11.50
6.75	9.02	10.10	11.29	12.26	13.50
7.75	10.33	11.62	12.91	14.08	15.50
8.75	11.66	13.12	14.57	15.80	17.50
9.75	13.00	14.62	16.25	17.72	19.50
10.75	14.33	16.12	17.91	19.54	21.50
11.75	15.66	17.62	19.57	21.36	23.50
12.75	17.00	19.12	21.25	23.16	25.50
13.75	18.33	20.62	22.91	25.00	27.50
14.75	19.66	22.12	24.57	26.80	29.50
15.75	21.00	23.62	26.25	28.60	31.50
16.75	22.33	25.13	27.91	30.40	33.50
18.75	25.00	28.12	31.25	34.00	37.50
19.75	26.33	29.63	32.91	36.00	39.50
22.75	30.33	34.13	37.91	41.40	45.50
24.75	33.00	37.13	41.25	45.00	49.50
26.75	35.66	40.13	44.57	48.60	53.50
29.75	39.66	44.63	49.57	54.00	59.50
32.75	43.66	49.13	54.57	59.40	65.50
35.75	47.66	53.62	59.57	64.60	71.50
37.75	50.33	56.63	62.91	68.60	75.50
39.75	53.00	59.63	66.25	72.20	79.50
49.75	66.33	74.63	82.91	90.40	99.50
59.75	79.66	89.63	99.57	108.60	119.50
69.75	93.00	109.63	116.25	126.80	139.50
79.75	106.33	119.63	132.91	145.00	159.50
89.75	119.66	134.63	149.57	163.00	179.50

are the ending periods of fall-winter and spring-summer fashion seasons. Some fashion stores take an inventory once a month, or some take a complete inventory every week.

To take inventory means that an actual count of the fashion garments in the store is made. It is a physical count of material things, and therefore is called the *physical inventory*. Everything is counted —floor merchandise, stockroom supplies and, under-counter items.

There are several reasons for taking inventory:

1. To compare the amount of fashion merchandise you actually have with what your books and records indicate you should have.
2. To prepare financial statements that will indicate to you if you have a profit or loss for the period.

3. To locate older stock that should be put on clearance status. Fashion items become outdated rapidly, so a careful check should be made frequently.
4. To make sales personnel more aware of the older stock that should have extra sales emphasis.

HOW IS INVENTORY TAKEN?

Inventory must be taken accurately and thoroughly. A store or department should be sectioned into specific areas and assigned to individuals. Inventory sheets with full instructions should be given to each person involved in the physical counting. These tally sheets carry spaces for garment description, classification, quantity, retail or cost price of each, and the extensions for totals.

Most stores close for a day of inventory taking, or make the count on a holiday. To try to take inventory during a regular sales day can lead to inaccuracies if an item is sold after it has already been tallied and the salesperson forgets to remove it from the inventory list.

Inventories can be taken at cost or retail prices of the goods. It is more accurate, most retailers believe, to take the retail inventory.

Cost Codes

Reading cost codes on hangtags is sometimes difficult for people who are not used to dealing with them. Examples of cost codes frequently used are:

1. A word or phrase composed of ten different letters. MONEY TALKS, and MAKE PROFIT are common ones.

M O N E Y   T A L K S
1 2 3 4 5   6 7 8 9 0

A cost of $12.50 would be coded MOYS on a sales ticket.
To avoid repeating the same letter in a cost code an "X" may be used. A cost of $11.00 would then be written MXSX.
2. Sometimes the cost price is hidden in a series of numbers which appear to be a serial number. Thus a cost price of $8.50 might appear as 7585001, the first two numbers referring to the year of purchase and the last two numbers indicating the month of purchase.

You can see that taking inventory by cost figures using a cost code could have some inaccuracies, especially when some employees are not accustomed to working with them; consequently it is becoming more common to simply take an inventory of the retail selling price of each garment. Then the costs are applied in the general offices.

When the inventory counts are completed, the reports are ana-

*What is a stock
shortage? How is it
discovered?*

lyzed. A comparison is made between the book value and the actual count of the merchandise on the sales floor. As you may remember from Chapter Six, if the two totals do not agree, then there is a merchandise shortage or overage. If there is less merchandise on the selling floor and in stock than the books show, there is a stock shortage. The reasons for a stock shortage, a major problem in retail these days, are: (1) loss of goods from shoplifting or theft, and (2) paper errors made either in the offices or in the physical inventory count. Sometimes a recount of inventory is made if the shortage is very large. Stock overages occur less frequently and usually result from paper errors.

Stockturn

*Why do they keep
telling me to try and sell
more fashions?*
STOCKTURN

Because more profits are the result of greater stockturns, this is an important consideration. Stockturns refer to the number of times that you sell out a stock of items and continue to do so.

> **FORMULA 5.** To compute stockturn, divide the *net sales* during a given period by the *average retail stock value* of that period.

$$\text{Retail stock turnover} = \frac{\text{Net sales}}{\text{Average retail stock}}$$

If net sales were $10,000 and average retail stocks were $2,000,

$$\frac{\$10,000}{\$\,2,000} = 5 \text{ stockturns at retail for the period}$$

A comparison of two different stockturn figures will show you how profits are affected. Suppose you carry an average inventory of $100,000 and turn it two times. Your sales will be $200,000, and if your profit is 10%, you'll have a profit of $20,000. If you turned the stock four times, your sales would be $400,000 and your profit would be $40,000.

But where do you get your average retail stock figure? This is sometimes figured by averaging the beginning-of-the-year-stock total with the end-of-the-year stock total, thus:

February 1, 1980, beginning stock   = $2,300
January 31, 1981, ending stock   =   1,700
                              2 $\overline{\smash{)}\ \$4,000}$ = $2,000 average stock

This method is not considered to be sufficiently accurate because it doesn't truly reflect the amount of stock at all times, particularly in peak stock periods.

So, stocks are sometimes averaged on three or four stock periods, such as beginning, second quarter, third quarter, and ending stock. This may give you a better picture of the average retail stock on hand.

But the preferred method of averaging retail stock is to average all the stock figures for the beginning of each month plus the ending stock for the year. The beginning stock for each month is tabulated and the ending stock for the year is included, and the total is averaged by 13.

Fast stockturn is accomplished by increasing your sales volume. Not only does it increase your profits—it also allows you to bring in new fashion garments more frequently to keep your customers interested, and eliminates expenses and markdowns. It should be one of the chief objectives of a fashion department. Therefore, you will hear "let's sell more merchandise and get stock turnover" quite often on the fashion job. When you do, you will know why it is of such importance to everyone in the store.

Financial Reporting

Perhaps the best way to illustrate the importance of accurate records in business is to show an example of the kinds of reporting that all large businesses publish annually. This is public information about the financial condition of the companies and is available to the general public.

In their 1976 annual report, a leading fashion department store in the Washington D.C. metropolitan area, Woodward & Lothrop, Inc. reported the largest sales and earnings in their history for the year ending January 29, 1977.

TABLE 11–2.   Woodward & Lothrop Statement of Earnings

(in thousands except for per share data)	1976	1975
Net Sales (including leased department sales)	$241,389	$218,468
Costs and Expenses		
Cost of merchandise sold including buying and occupancy costs	166,229	152,939
Selling, general and administrative expenses	48,897	42,498
Interest expense	3,627	2,910
	218,753	198,347
Earnings Before Income Taxes	22,636	20,121
Provision For Income Taxes	10,900	10,320
Net Earnings	$ 11,736	$ 9,801
Net Earnings Per Common Share	$4.89	$4.10

Woodward & Lothrop, Incorporated, 1976 Annual Report.

"Woodies," as this store is known to its customers, operates a 738,000 sq. ft. store in downtown Washington D.C., which accounts for approximately 20 percent of sales. The Metro subway system opened its doors into Woodward & Lothrop in 1976, making it the only downtown store accessible via subway. There are also twelve suburban locations, with another opening in 1978.

Inspired by the approach of the store's 100th birthday in 1980, plans have been initiated to add new dimensions to every aspect of the organization. In merchandising using the "lifestyle approach" they are making great strides in their fashion objectives—to carry contemporary trends and traditional classics for today's fashion conscious consumer. A special program—"Total Involvement"—is underway with one key objective: gracious customer service. It is a complete program of visual and tangible elements—monthly personnel and training seminars as well as more frequent, less formal meetings to communicate important happenings to the selling staff. Fashion directors highlight the latest fashions arriving in the store, what they're advertising, how to sell it, and most important, how to assist customers so they will want to return.

Woodward & Lothrop ranks as one of America's premier department stores and will continue to hold that position.

Conclusion

In this chapter we have emphasized the impact that electronic data processing is having on business, why it is of so much help to business, and what some of the terminology and formulas are that you will need to understand on any fashion job. Finally, we closed the chapter with an illustration of the business reporting that is customary for large companies.

The purpose of presenting these basic fashion mathematics was to make you more aware of the kinds of math you might encounter early on a fashion job. A good understanding of these basics will help you understand the more complicated problems ahead. These are fundamental on any fashion job, and you must master their use. Do not leave them until you are able to use them easily and with understanding.

Review Questions

1. Define or identify the following:
   a. EDP (electronic data processing)
   b. Operating expenses
   c. Cost of goods sold
   d. Point-of-sale terminals
   e. Daily best-seller report
   f. Vendor returns

g. Out-of-stock
h. Unit sales information
i. "Last-year-itis"
j. Percentage increases
k. Price lines
l. Price range
m. Fashion markup
n. Physical inventory
o. Cost codes
p. Merchandising shortage
q. Stockturn
r. "Wish book"

2. Find the percentage of increase in sales this month over last month, if this month's sales are $35,000 and last month's sales were $29,000. (Use Formula 1.)

3. Find the percentage of markdown on twenty coats reduced from $150 to $100.

4. What percentage of markup would a buyer achieve if the garments were purchased at market for $15 each, and marked to sell at $25?

5. If the buyer determines to sell the garments in problem 5 for $22.50, giving the customers a special price, what percentage of markup would be achieved?

6. If the buyer selects garments at a cost of $25 at market and wishes to achieve a 40 percent markup on them, what retail price would he use?

7. If you have price lines of $20, $30, and $40, and your desired markup is 40 percent, what would your buyer seek at market to stock these lines? (What cost on garments must he *not* exceed for each price line?)

8. Using the mark up table, compute the selling price for the following items:
   a. Cost of $15.75 at 33⅓% _____ (Actual)
      What retail price would you place on it?_____
   b. Cost of $79.75 at 45% _____ (Actual)
      What retail price would you place on it?_____
   c. Cost of $3.25 at 50% _____ (Actual)
      What retail price would you place on it?_____

Suggested Student Activities

1. Visit several fashion departments or stores in your area and list the price lines they place on their garments. Note whether they price garments in round figures or use odd-figure endings. Compare the stores by price lines. Especially note if any of the stores have price lines that are so near each other that it would be difficult to determine the difference in the value of the garments.

2. Visit a local stockmarket broker and secure copies of the annual

reports of several publicly owned companies that are fashion-oriented. Compare their sales figures for the year reported (current) with their last year's sales (usually reported) and note the change. If they do not show a percentage of change—either increase or decrease—figure the percentage of change for yourself.

3. Follow the stockmarket reports for the New York Stock Exchange, and read the sales volumes and current price of the stocks of several large fashion-related companies. Chart the rise and fall of these stocks over a period of several weeks. Examples of companies would be:

	ticker symbol
Sears, Roebuck and Co.	S
Hart, Schaffner & Marx	HSM
Macy, (R.H.) & Co.	MZ
Jonathan Logan	JOL
Marshall Field	MF
Federated Dept. Stores	FDS

You will find many, many more—and this activity will increase your knowledge of the large fashion companies and fashion producers in the U.S. You might ask a member of your business division for assistance if you need additional help in reading the stockmarket reports. You will also see that the fashion business is indeed very *big business* in the U.S.

Case Problems

Case 11-1. Madeline is the assistant manager of the better sportswear department of a large department store. Her manager asks her to prepare figures to help her in the preparation of a six-month merchandising plan for February through August of next year. The planned increase in sales is to be 10 percent next year, each month. Madeline agrees to do this, but she is puzzled about where to begin.

1. What figures from last year will Madeline need to figure a 10 percent increase in sales for the coming six months?
2. Assuming the following monthly sales totals for last year:

February	$26,000
March	$42,000
April	$52,000
May	$63,000
June	$59,000
July	$43,000

what should the planned increase in sales be at 10 percent this coming year? State the sales goal for each month next year.

Case 11-2. You are the manager of the sportswear department for a large chain department store. It is Friday afternoon, you are busy, and it has been a very busy week. You are looking forward to going home at 5:00 P.M. for a restful evening to do your hair, read, and just relax, because you have a sale tomorrow in your department, and you want to be ready for it. At 4:45 you receive word that you have 500 pieces of sportswear on the dock. You feel that it is needed on the floor when the store opens at 10:00 A.M. in the morning for the big sale. The items must be marked, stripped, hung, and placed on the floor. There is coding to do and you must make the record of the shipment in your markup book if the items are placed in stock. You're tired, you really wanted to go home for a quiet evening. You have a problem—you could ignore the shipment until tomorrow morning and perhaps come in about 8:00, or you could stay this evening and get the work well on the way.

1. This is not an unusual happening for a manager to face. What would you do in an actual situation like this?
2. Should you decide to go home at 5:00 P.M. and come back in the morning, what do you think the consequences would be for not getting the new merchandise on the selling floor at store opening at the beginning of the sale?
3. If you should decide to work late on Friday evening to be sure the merchandise gets to the selling floor the next morning, do you think executive management people would know? Or care?

Case 11-3. You are at market for the first time, strictly on your own, to buy junior dresses for your department for your $25 price line. It has been customary to search for garments wholesaling for $12.50 or less, on which you can achieve a 50 percent markup and fast turnover. You have visited all the resources from whom you have bought in the past, and several new ones also, but you have found the selection of dresses very limited and of poor quality, color, and style. You feel that your customers will not like them and very likely would not buy them. At a new resource, you explain your problem to the sales representative who is showing you a good-looking dress line that wholesales for $15. Since you could not achieve a 50 percent markup on these at your $25 price line, you are debating what to do. The sales representative is anxious to get the business from your store, and offers to sell you the $15 garments for $13.50, if you will take the remaining ten dozen that he has in his line. It is late in the afternoon, and the market will be closing soon. You ask the sales representative if you could let him know the first thing in the morning after you talk to your general merchandise manager. He agrees to this arrangement. In the evening, you call your general merchandise manager at home, but discover that he is out of town for the remainder of the week and cannot be reached.

1. Should you purchase ten dozen dresses at $13.50 each, and take a smaller markup than the one you had previously agreed on with your general merchandise manager?
2. Or should you stay with those that you have found that cost $12.50, and hope that with good sales promotion and floor sales effort, you can sell the garments without taking too large a markdown?
3. Role-play the explanation you will make to your general merchandise manager when you return to the store if you do decide to purchase the $13.50 garments.
4. If you stay with your decision not to exceed $12.50, explain what you must discuss with your general merchandise manager about your price lines after this market trip.

Case 11-4. You are the manager of a men's furnishings department in a store that has recently installed computer terminals with wands. All salespeople in your department have been trained to use the new terminals, and you department is doing quite well with them. However, you have one salesperson who has made repeated errors, and seems to be afraid of using the terminal. He has on several occasions asked the person who was at the cash desk to ring up his sales for him. This is causing a problem in the department, especially at busy sales periods, so you realize that something must be done.

1. What suggestions would you make to the salesperson who is having difficulty?
2. Would you terminate the salesperson if he cannot soon learn to use the terminals accurately?
3. If he is truly a good salesperson, whom you do not wish to terminate, what must you do?

Case 11-5. You have just finished taking inventory in your department. When you check your actual count of merchandise figures against those that your books show you should have, you discover a large discrepancy—over $20,000.

1. What would you do first to try to discover where the discrepancy occurred?
2. Suppose you do not find any errors in the actual physical count of merchandise on the floor. What do you think may have happened?

Chapter 12

The future of fashion merchandising

Objectives

When you have read this chapter, you should be able to

1. Mention several trends and directions for the future of which fashion merchandisers should be aware
2. Explain the impact that changes in transportation may have on the lives of fashion customers, and how these may change the locations or types of fashion business as they are conducted today
3. Support the theory that shopping centers of the future will become recreational centers and living centers, as well as shopping centers as we know them today
4. Explain why the great merchandising establishments of the past will probably be the ones that will continue to set the pattern for dealing with the customers of the future
5. Discuss how fashion merchandising companies are meeting the challenges of the future in various parts of the United States.

What's new in store design and layout?

Growth, expansion and innovation are the key words for the development of Foley's in one of the fastest growing cities in the Southwest—Houston.

Foley's was founded in 1900 by Pat and James Foley and Frank Matzinger. In 1917, Robert I. Cohen, Sr. of Galveston and his son, George S. Cohen, purchased the Foley family's interests. In 1945, Foley's became a unit of Federated Department Stores, Inc.

Under Federated, Foley's planned the present downtown store, which opened as a six and a half story building in 1947. With its windowless design, forecasting new developments of the future, this store aroused the interest and curiosity of architects and engineers throughout the United States. The store revolutionized retail operations and pioneered the mechanized handling of merchandise. An expansion program was begun in 1955 with the addition of three and one-half floors to make Foley's one of the largest stores in the South. In 1956 came the half-block addition to the parking garage and the inauguration of Houston's first self-park operation. At the same time, the store's Budget Store was expanded to cover two full blocks connected by a tunnel under the street.

The fast-paced growth of Foley's hastened the development of six branch stores, the first of which was opened in Sharpstown in 1961, followed by a store in Pasadena less than a year later. In 1966, Foley's opened its Almeda branch store, and the next year, 1967, a Foley's Northwest was opened.

In 1974 Foley's Memorial City was opened, the first of its kind anywhere. Color, light, metal, and sophistication added to the drama of this exciting department store. From a concept born in Europe, the Memorial City store opened as basically a stage of 135,000 square feet with four walls and ceiling. The stage settings were modular, flexible, movable, functional, and beautiful.

Like a mall within a mall, the store had but one aisle circling the entire facility. Every single department had an aisle presentation—every single shopping area had a convenient entrance to meet specific shopping needs. There was no one single supportive wall in the entire complex. The store was a giant room, given life through a grid ceiling 14 feet above the main floor. Electricity, plumbing, air-conditioning, and heating were all programmed through invisible black-coated "extra ceiling" space. Traditional materials gave way to the abundant use of fabrics, wood fixturing, and self-contained units for delineation of departments and shopping needs.

One Foley's executive commented that building this store was like "re-inventing the wheel.", "Everything we did," he went on, "meant testing and retesting to make sure that it would work—that it was visually up to standard as well as functional." Architects, designers, engineers, all went into the marketplace and literally designed

FIG. 12-1. Brown cascading glass dramatically highlights the three outside entrances to Foley's Greenspoint store. The 207,000 square foot, two-level facility is Foley's sixth branch store. (Courtesy, Foley's, Houston, Texas.)

not only fixturing but structurally sound prefabricated elements to give Houston the nation's first totally modular department store.

There was a flow to the organization of the entire store which made shopping an experience in light, color, and intimacy. The entire store was carpeted in a neutral, warm tweed/beige—only the single main aisle was a subdued perma-grain surface that highlighted in every case the merchandise presentation.

During the preopening tour by the store executives, an employee was found stationed in her department ironing the cloth walls. Fabric —flown, hung, fastened, sconced, and draped—plays a major role in the flexibility of the store.

In 1976 Foley's Memorial City was expanded to 264,000 square feet and the modular design concept was modified. The expansion, which affected all departments, also included the addition of a full-line furniture department and a Budget Store. These two new areas were built along the more traditional concepts of design with standard ceilings and supportive walls not found in the other departments of the store. A majority of the departments continue to be serviced by the innovative central core stock area with the exception the Budget Store.

Foley's opened its sixth branch store—Greenspoint Mall—in August, 1976. A truly unique store totaling 207,000 square feet on its two merchandising floors, Foley's Greenspoint incorporates the modular concepts introduced in the Memorial City store with the more traditional.

The focal point of this store is the two-story Escalator Pavilion. Built on the "loop plan," this store has a single main aisle on both floors. Men's, women's, children's, and junior fashions circle the first floor aisle. Each area is located at one of the four entrances for ease of shopping. Departments on both floors are built around and serviced by the central core stock area. Stock areas are fed from the dock by a conveyor system which hoists merchandise over the heads of customers through the grid ceiling fourteen feet above the main floor. The additional height and greater flexibility allowed by this ceiling structure create tremendous options for multilevel merchandising, creative displays, and a myriad of lighting effects.

A departure from time-honored notions of retailing, Foley's recent store developments reflect their continuing leadership and knack for newness in every concept of retailing. We can look forward to more design innovations of this type in retail stores of the future.

Probably there is nothing more exciting and intriguing to do than speculate about the future. As the 1900s race toward their conclusion, many people are looking ahead and planning for the next 25, 50, or 100 years—on into the twenty-first century. In the business of fashion merchandising, we must look ahead and seriously consider the trends that our society is taking today.

There are many things in fashion merchandising that foretell the directions in which we are moving. For example, we will surely see a continuation of the vast technological developments of our immediate past. We can be reasonably sure also that the changes of the future will be exceedingly complex. Our lives will be greatly affected, just as they have been in the last few years. Undoubtedly the changes will be for the better. Business has always been affected by the needs of society and responsive to the problems of people. The great merchandising establishments that interpreted customer needs the best in the past decades are the great merchandisers of today and tomorrow.

As someone has wisely said, the best way to know what the future holds is to look at what is happening in the present. Perhaps there is really no other way to begin to think about the future. Current trends that appear to be forward-thinking developments of today are proving to be successful ventures, so it is probable that many of them will be the direction that fashion merchandising will be taking.

If you look at your own community, you are already aware of the many changes that are occurring in merchandising. What is happening in your community is happening all over the world.

There are so many exciting things happening that it is only possible to look at some of the most important current trends in this chapter. You will undoubtedly be able to think of many, many more equally important.

Technological Developments

TELEVISION AND ELECTRONICS IN BUSINESS

The vitality that business has had during this country's past 200 years will surely continue. Television hookups will unquestionably affect the retail industry more in the future; business will be accomplished through television much as we use our telephones today. This development, called phonovision, will allow us to shop for fashion merchandise without having to leave our homes.

Actually, one of the most prevalent trends evident today in fashion merchandising and retail selling is the application of electronics to all phases of these operations. Up to the present time, electronics has been used in the data processing systems designed to analyze the flood of figures connected with accounts-receivable, accounts-payable, payroll, sales audits, and unit control. The increased requirements for fast, accurate reporting and the decreasing costs for the data processing hardware will make the use of these electronic tools mandatory for the medium-sized as well as the larger businesses.

While the installation of electronic equipment is a difficult transition, it has alleviated many of the errors in order writing, errors by billing clerks, and mistakes in addition. All of these errors have been a source of customer dissatisfaction with the accounts-receivable departments in most great stores in the country. Retail credit will continue, but probably because of the necessity for electronic handling of accounts, no credit will be granted to customers unless they are carrying their credit cards. Hence there doesn't appear to be any doubt that we will remain a credit-card society in the future. We do enjoy the benefits of credit.

Because of the electronic memories, retailers are doing a more precise job of marketing today than ever before. The merchants of the past knew their customer characteristics because they knew their customers personally. Not so today, when stores have grown to such size and number. The intimate customer contact has been lost in many businesses. Through the use of electronics information about customer

PHONOVISION
Will we shop by phone and see what we are buying?

Will we have more or less EDP in the future?

Will there be more or less credit in the future?

ages, habits, sizes, preferences, and buying potential, today's fashion buyers have vast amounts of stored information with which they can readily determine their buying needs.

Electronics will offer greater opportunity in the future for learning more about merchandise defects, and merchandise wearing potential as well. Already there is a great deal of information available—there will be more in the future. Perhaps the new generation of retail buyers and merchants will require a data-oriented curriculum in their training. Educational institutions are already recognizing this requirement and data processing introductory courses are required or strongly recommended as an elective in most fashion merchandising programs of training.

Will other scientific developments affect fashion?

There are vast possibilities and probabilities in electronics. For example, if electronics is continually applied to medical research, it is entirely possible that knowledge of individual growth and weight problems may lead to control of height and weight. Such a development would have a dramatic effect on the design, sizing, and construction of wearing apparel, and in turn affect what merchandise will be made available to customers for purchase to satisfy their needs.

How could a store sell by phone?

Mass use of phonovision, which we mentioned earlier, as a primary means of communication, will open up a completely new dimension in remote buying and selling, in addition to mail-order shopping. With phonovision, customers will be able to call up their favorite local or out-of-town stores and see any article that interests them as they stay comfortably situated in their homes. Perhaps stores will provide shopping guides with sample reference swatches, or perhaps sample smells, enabling shoppers to make buying decisions with the same assurance they would have in the stores themselves even though they may be from 5 to 5,000 miles away from the actual selling floor.

The possibilities and unlimited potential of phonovision will certainly change the techniques of phone sales solicitation too. Imagine how exciting it will be to be able to call a customer directly and show new products and fashion merchandise this way. If the customer makes a purchase, perhaps the plastic charge card will be inserted into a special telephone slot, the sales check will be automatically recorded at the store, the customer's account will be charged or a cash payment will be made by a simultaneous telephonic withdrawal of the amount from a bank account. This is a truly revolutionary concept.

If such innovations occur, this will mean vastly enlarged telephone shopping rooms and more telephone sales personnel. Important as visual merchandising is today, the challenge of this area tomorrow boggles the mind.

The one constant we can be sure of is that our great merchandising institutions will continually find better ways to improve customer personalized service. Electronics will make it possible for the markets of the world to be searched for the choicest and most beautiful goods.

As electronics become more and more efficient and less costly, they will enable fashion merchandisers to render even greater satisfaction to their customers. There is no question that the innovations of the future will increase the glamor and excitement of fashion merchandising.

THE INTERNATIONAL METRIC SYSTEM

Although the metric system may not actually be a technological development, it is fast coming into being as an international language and is further evidence of our shrinking world. The International Standards Organization (ISO) is continually working to reduce and resolve international differences through the application of the metric system. Some businesses are already converting to the system on a carefully planned basis. For example, General Motors has been using the metric system since 1966 for the worldwide standardization of automobile parts. When the system becomes fully operational, parts for automobiles will be interchangeable from one brand of vehicle to another kind.

INTERNATIONAL METRIC LANGUAGE

INTERNATIONAL STANDARDS ORGANIZATION
Will universal use of the metric system make world trade easier?

The metric system will greatly simplify our current system of measurement. It is like our traditional numbering system, but it is in units of ten, with which we can deal much more easily. Although the transition to such a system won't be easy, it should eventually make international trading much easier.

Won't the metric system be hard to learn?

One of the greatest fears of business today is that the changes are coming with such rapidity that "new" developments may be obsolete before they leave the planning boards. Be that as it may, only the business institutions and individuals who remain constantly aware of trends and directions will be able to survive in tomorrow's world of fashion merchandising.

TRANSPORTATION IN THE FUTURE

One of our current problems, as you are well aware, is the energy crisis in America and throughout the world. This is a vital concern of business everywhere. Its outcome will have a great influence on the future of fashion merchandising, primarily because customers must have transportation of some kind to get to fashion shopping areas. Even with developments like phonovision, there will continue to be a need and a desire on the part of consumers to pursue the age-old "recreation" of going shopping.

Most specialists in transportation problems agree that the direction we take will depend on the people and where they choose to work and live. And where people choose to work and live is just as dependent on the forms of transit that will be available to them. At this time, it appears that our system of transit for the future will have to be a balanced and integrated system combining all our current methods of transit.

Specialists believe also that there will be greater use of mass-transit means. Some predict that by the year 2000 there will have been a fivefold increase in mass transit. It will be most difficult to move Americans out of their cars, especially in areas where mass transit is not convenient and accessible. And if automobiles remain a major form of transportation, they may eventually have to be converted to some form of magnetically controlled system for more efficiency. Such methods as hooking up cars on a guideway, much as the carwash systems work today, may be developed.

City buses, long active in mass transit, will surely continue to transport many people. Large bus companies are planning on greater rush-hour ridership in the future, and the newer buses are already more attractive, with their expanded window areas that are virtually unbreakable, wider doors, and easier entry.

There are equally fascinating plans being developed for driverless vehicles that would operate on fixed, elevated guideways, or on air-cushioned, electrically driven pallets; hovertrains, monorails, minitrams, and a multiplicity of people-mover subsystems. Just as inexpensive and convenient car usage over improved highways has encouraged city sprawl in the past, it is likely that our current energy crisis may reverse this trend—rapid transportation to central-city locations may encourage a return to more urban living. With the great revitalizations that are taking place in central business areas currently, it is evident that many people who are carefully planning for the future believe that a return to the central-city areas may be imminent. Fashion merchandisers of the future must seriously consider the trends and directions that appear to be developing in transportation today and meet them flexibly and intelligently.

Shopping Centers

As you are already aware, shopping centers as we know them represent one of the most dynamic and vital developments in retailing during the last twenty to twenty-five years. They have become very important marketplaces in the United States, and they are becoming significant around the world as well.

THE GRAND BAZAAR

However, we can't really claim that shopping centers are unique to our times. We should recall one that is slightly older. It is the Grand Bazaar, located in the lovely old city of Istanbul, Turkey (once known as Constantinople), where Europe and Asia meet at the Black Sea. It is at least 500 years old, and is probably the world's largest covered shopping mall. It has over 4,000 shops which offer superb buys in leather and suede, Bursa silks and embroidery, copper lamps, colorful carpets, beautiful jewelry. It is a thrilling place to shop not only because the salespeople can speak approximately ten different languages well enough to bargain with almost any tourist-customer, but because haggling over prices is still the rule. Although the government has set a price ceiling on most of the items sold there, it is still "matching wits" with a customer that is the salesperson's major challenge.

Whether the Grand Bazaar is indeed the forerunner of modern shopping centers or not, since the 1950s they have shown strong growth and expansion. Some people believe that they have become the most dominant factor in retailing today, and predict that in the 1980s they will account for more than half of the retail sales in the country. There are retail chains that attribute as much as 80 percent of their total sales to their shopping-center branches.

Why do people like shopping centers?

The reasons shopping centers occupy such a significant position in today's retailing world are well-known to most people. Family incomes and leisure time have continued to increase; consumers seek modern, comfortable, and accessible stores in which to shop; and developers and retailers have continued to acquire greater skill and professionalism in serving the needs of their customers.

What states have the most shopping centers?

In 1973, California had nearly 2,000 shopping complexes; Texas had 1,400; New York 850; Florida 800; Pennsylvania 750; and Ohio 700; to name a few states with the greater numbers. Canada, too, has vast shopping malls—almost a thousand. Abroad, Australia has the

Are there any abroad?

largest number of shopping malls, with Puerto Rico, England, France, Germany, Sweden, Switzerland, Africa, Japan, and Denmark following in that order.[1]

At this point it would be interesting to take a quick look at some well-known shopping centers, including one in Germany.

MAIN TAUNUS CENTRE, RHINE-MAIN, GERMANY

Is a foreign shopping center any different from one in the U.S.?

This famous shopping center is the largest regional shopping center in Germany. Opened in 1964, it is located near the junctions of several busy thoroughfares leading to the cities of Frankfurt, Mainz, and Wiesbaden. But it is not located in any of these cities proper—hence the designation "regional." In the United States, most developers of shopping centers have chosen locations in cities in a specific suburban area, near a high-traffic freeway or street. A publicity bro-

**REGIONAL
SHOPPING CENTER**

[1] *Directory of Shopping Centers in the U.S., Canada, and Europe*, 14th ed. (Burlington, Iowa: National Research Bureau, Inc. 1973), p. 6.

FIG. 12-2. The largest regional shopping center in Germany, Main-Taunus Centre, is located near Frankfurt, Mainz, and Wiesbaden.
(Courtesy, Main-Taunus-Zentrum, West Germany.)

chure about the Main Taunus Centre calls attention to its particular location:

> This shopping paradise has now become an integrated part of economic life in the Rhine-Main areas and has also achieved fame beyond the boundaries of this trading area. It is not surrounded by housing estates, but lies in a "green park." The centre was built in the Mall style—a shopping street. All shops face onto the street, one window next to the other—a total of 74 shops including specialty stores, department stores, general stores, service agencies, cafes, restaurants, doctors, a bank and Post Office, offering a differing line of business and displaying a wide and extensive variety of goods.
>
> The continually increasing stream of visitors is not only attracted by the goods and services on offer, but by other amenities which have come to play a big part in the life of the centre. The customers can shop in peace and quiet amongst the well-cared-for plant and flower beds. The children can run around the street of shops without the danger of their being run-over, or their parents can leave them free-of-charge in the Main-Taunus Centre's kindergarten.
>
> The motto of the shopping spree is RELAX and BUY.

Do people in Germany like shopping centers?

Along with other shopping centers, Main Taunus makes use of

FIG. 12-3. The Galleria has office towers and a spacious hotel opening directly into its three-level shopping area.
(Courtesy, Gerald D. Hines Interests, Houston, Texas.)

joint advertising to achieve its objectives: "Fame in the centre has in this way been considerably enhanced in the last few years." It also maintains special events to attract people to the center, "making the shoppers' visits as pleasant as possible." For the children, well-known and well-loved annual festivals are held for eight days at a time—Punch and Judy shows, fairy stories at Christmas, and many competitive events for children with prizes of all kinds. For the adults, there are automobile shows, dog shows, and a week especially devoted to the harvest.

GALLERIA SHOPPING MALL, HOUSTON, TEXAS[1]

More than just a shopping center, the Galleria is really a beautiful city in itself. It includes office towers and a spacious hotel opening directly into the three-level shopping area. The Galleria is a sparkling version of the Old World's fabled marketplaces; its concept came from the Galleria Vittorio Emmanuele II in Milan, Italy.

The focal point of the Galleria shopping mall is the beautiful year-round public ice-skating rink in its center—this consists of three cutaway floors below a vaulted glass ceiling where the sun or stars filter through to give the mall an outdoor atmosphere. Shoppers in the mall can, and often do, stop to gaze at the skaters from any of the three levels of the mall. Private or class lessons in ice skating attract people of all ages, and during any one skating period there will be experts as well as beginners on the ice, all gliding and spinning around on the Olympic-size rink. Mothers often bring their children to the mall to learn to skate, and while they are taking their lessons, the mothers are free to shop in the beautiful specialty stores. If they wish to check on their children's progress, they can step to the edge of the balcony near where they are shopping and see their children skating below.

Perhaps the skating rink is the reason why the Galleria has a reputation among Houston residents and out-of-town visitors for being an interesting place to visit. Or perhaps it is because there is so much to do in the mall in addition to skating. There are actually over 120 shops. You can, for example, shop in any of a dozen men's specialty stores, in any of two dozen women's shops, in at least six fine jewelry stores including Tiffany's, go to any of several art galleries, decorative accessory and furniture stores, or department stores. Or if you enjoy dining, you have many choices, ranging from the sidewalk cafe overlooking the skating rink to numerous other fine restaurants offering a wide selection of foods. Or you can go to your choice of two theaters, do your banking, check on the latest stockmarket figures, or just watch the kaleidoscope of shoppers. This is a place for relaxing with soothing music for background; it is carpeted throughout, and escalators silently whisk shoppers from one level to the next. This shoppers' paradise is easily accessible from any part of Houston and parking is free inside the Galleria garage. It is truly a fun place to go in Houston.

It should be apparent that the shopping-center industry is very much the same the world over. The main purpose of these complexes is to help customers do their buying in an interesting and relaxed atmosphere. Their continued growth and expansion appears evident

[1] Information in this section was taken from brochures and fact sheets of the Gerald D. Hines Interests, Houston, Tx.

because customers do like them for their accessibility and their large free-parking areas, and most assuredly for their emphasis on interesting public events.

SHOPPING CENTERS OF THE FUTURE

When we consider how many thousands of shopping centers have been built in the last fifteen to twenty years, ranging all the way from small convenience centers to the tremendous size of the super-regional centers, we cannot overlook the future that they will have. We are well aware of how these centers have lured customers away from the downtown areas of our cities and how as much as half of the country's retail sales are now taking place in them. With their many conveniences, including accessibility and ample free parking spaces, they have been an attractive innovation in our current merchandising era.

Would it help if we lived near enough to our jobs so we could walk to work?

Some people feel that the boom in shopping centers may be over; however, many large shopping centers are planning large expansions like the Galleria in Houston, Texas. Perhaps their locations will be shifted to localities closer to the cities or in the downtown areas. Some of these have already been projected.

"Recreational retailing" appears to be a new concept for our attention. It is apparent in the malls that serve as the nucleus for planned-unit developments; these incorporate housing, offices, some light industry, and recreational opportunities besides the shopping facilities. People living in these malls will work and live and play all in the same locality, within walking distances of their homes.

RECREATIONAL RETAILING

The shopping centers of the future are not at all likely to follow a strictly suburban path. Developers are already expressing concern over the best place to locate them. If they move into downtown areas rapidly, it will be necessary for them to make better use of the more costly central-city land. As a result, they are going to become more vertical, and perhaps actually become great high-rise structures, with multi-level shopping facilities. People will be moved vertically and horizontally, rapidly and conveniently from floor to floor and from shop to shop. All forms of automated transit will be used and developed within the centers themselves, and to the centers from parking areas or urban transportation terminals. Several great transportation companies are working now on ideas to move the people and merchandise of tomorrow more efficiently.

Shopping centers in mid-city?

There is evidence that the shopping centers of the future will become cultural centers for drama, art, and music. Our conventional shopping centers as we know them today will give way in the years to come to more and more innovative complexes which will please the tastes of ecologists, developers, and the public.

FIG. 12-4. If shopping centers in the future are to be vertical, then we may be moving from floor to floor on horizontal elevators.
(Courtesy, Otis Elevator Company, New York)

Downtown Revitalizations

While there is no denying the vigorous growth of shopping centers in importance, there are many who believe that the downtown areas are also still important. That is why almost every large city is seriously planning and beginning to execute vast downtown revitalization projects.

The inland city of San Bernardino, California has been in the midst of a reconstruction development in its central city mall for several years. Interestingly, the large Harris' Department Store there has been instrumental in laying the groundwork for the revitalized and attractive civic and commercial center, and for giving assurance of stability and importance to retailing business support. The Central City Mall is unique among downtown revitalization plans because all existing urban businesses were renewed simultaneously rather than in separate stages. While the actual reconstruction caused a giant upheaval in the center of town, the finished areas are well worth the time, effort, and inconvenience that it caused.

ATLANTA, GEORGIA

The planning for the revitalization of downtown Atlanta, was also closely associated with one of its large department stores—Rich's. The words "growth," "expansion," and "profit" express this company's policies. Rich's awareness of its place in the South has always given this famous business a very special identity.

FIG. 12-5. Rich's Career Shop with African art, Oriental rugs, brass trim, and modern art provides a handsome setting for the latest in men's fashions. (Courtesy, Rich's, Atlanta, Georgia)

The recent history of Rich's is closely tied in with the decision of Atlanta's leaders to revitalize the downtown area. A concern with individual people has led this business to stock what the customers want and build new stores where customers prefer to shop. Consequently, when the idea of giving new life to the center city was conceived, Rich's was at the forefront in planning this rebirth. Mr. Harold Brockey, chairman of the board of Rich's, foresees not only the continued growth of recreation-oriented suburban residential communities, but revitalization of in-city living as well.

Notwithstanding Rich's wide success with suburban stores, the downtown store remains its base. This is significant when one considers the number of downtown stores that are moving to the suburbs. Currently, Atlanta's downtown area is undergoing a boom, and Rich's is a major part of this movement.

STORE-OWNED SUBWAYS, FORT WORTH, TEXAS

A page of history was added to retailing in the Southwest when a department store built its own subway system. The subway cars whisk customers through a vast tunnel under the city's downtown streets to and from a fairly distant free parking area accommodating 5,000 cars. Now owned by the Tandy Corporation, the subway cars carry passengers to the entrance of their huge downtown shopping complex.

The subway has proved to be a major downtown attraction and convenience. No other privately owned subways are in operation south of the Mason-Dixon line, and it may be stated with reasonable certainty that this is the only shopping complex-owned system in the world.

It was, of course, constructed as a fast, convenient method of transportation to the downtown area without worry of traffic congestion or parking problems. Customers can park in the free parking lot, walk a little way to the subway terminal near by, and be in the downtown area at the entrance of the shopping complex in 3½ minutes. This is only one of the many significant trends of the future for the retail consumer.

Development of Huge
Fashion Business Conglomerates

There is another development among retailing companies in the United States that is noteworthy in terms of future directions in fashion merchandising. Well-known companies are joining together to form huge conglomerate organizations—all profit by the arrangement, and all become greater in their merchandising power because of it.

FIG. 12-6. Fort Worth's Tandy Center has the world's only privately owned subway, which provides free transportation from a parking lot to the store in a few seconds.
(Courtesy, Tandy Corporation, Fort Worth, Texas)

GARFINCKEL, BROOKS BROTHERS, MILLER & RHOADS, INC.

Wives of presidents of the United States, Cabinet officers, members of Congress, Washington socialites, diplomats, and dignitaries shop in Garfinckel's, the first specialty store designed to offer fashion merchandise along with highly personalized customer service in Washington, D.C. There they find the finest fashions gathered from all over the world and made possible because several large businesses have pooled their resources and merchandising expertise.

To keep its established Garfinckel clientele and to simultaneously appeal to new, younger customers, the management of this conglomerate has expanded the store's offerings many times to offer youthful and contemporary fashions.

In 1946, Brooks Brothers, the oldest men's apparel retailer in the country, became a division of the corporation. Despite a reputation for conservatism, Brooks Brothers has been responsible for many style and material innovations in men's clothing. A partial list of firsts includes the introduction to this country of English foulard neckwear, the Shetland and Fair Isles sweaters, the Polo coat, cotton India

What is Garfinckel's distinction?

293

Madras for sportswear, cotton seersucker for summer clothing, wash-and-wear shirts, and perhaps the most famous of all, the shirt with the button-down collar. Much of the ability to maintain standards in clothing and furnishings, as well as freedom to experiment with new ideas, is because Brooks Brothers has had its own facilities to manufacture its apparel offerings.

Miller & Rhoads, Richmond, Virginia, operator of twelve full-line department stores in major cities through Virginia merged with the Corporation in 1967.

Miller's Incorporated, then a six-unit department store chain serving eastern Tennessee, became a division of the corporation in 1969. Beginning in 1901, Miller's has grown to become one of the leading full-lined department store groups in eastern Tennessee. It now consists of nine stores in Tennessee and one each in Virginia and Georgia.

Joseph R. Harris Co., Inc. of Washington D.C. became part of the corporation in 1971 when it was operating eleven stores selling medium quality ready-to-wear for women. Expansion since that time has increased the number of stores to twenty-seven, with units located in the District of Columbia, Georgia, Maryland, North Carolina, Pennsylvania, and Virginia. As new stores are added, the merchandise goal of this Division has been retained—to sell quality merchandise in the middle price ranges.

Entering its eighty-second year, Harzsfeld's, a greater Kansas City women's fashion specialty store retailing medium to high quality apparel and accessories, children's clothing, and specialty gifts in five stores, joined the Corporation in 1972. As one of the largest and finest women's specialty store operations in Kansas City and the Midwest, Harzfeld's provides its patrons with a comprehensive collection of leading designers.

With all these mergers, sales in the Corporation surged ahead to about three hundred million dollars in 1976. Today, the company operates over ninety department and specialty stores from coast to coast in seventeen states and the District of Columbia.

Why so many mergers?

Garfinckel's Corporation is representative of the many, many similar mergers among great retailing companies during the first half of the twentieth century. Many retain their original firm names, but all have the advantage of large corporation purchasing power. This trend is likely to continue in the future.

Conclusion

What the future for fashion merchandising will be is closely related to our changing lifestyles of today. The changes are happening so gradually that we aren't always consciously aware of them, but they are happening, nevertheless.

FIG. 12-7.   Joseph R. Harris Co., Inc. became part of Garfinckel, Brooks Brothers, Miller & Rhoads, Inc., and subsidiaries in 1971. The objective of this company is to sell selected quality merchandise in the middle price ranges.
(Courtesy, Garfinckel, Brooks Brothers, Miller Rhoads, Inc., Washington, D.C.)

The implications of what consumers will be like in the future is of vast importance to the fashion industry as a whole. The industry will be affected in the design of fashion merchandise, its production, its transportation, and its merchandising methods. One constant is the likelihood that consumers of tomorrow will be just as price–, value–, and efficiency–conscious as they are today.

So, as we move into the twenty-first century in America, fashion will be a part of that future just as it has always been a part of our past. It will surely continue to be dynamic and fascinating.

Epilogue

If you are wondering if your future in fashion merchandising is good and if you will be assured of employment, you will be interested in some facts from the *Occupational Outlook Handbook*, 1976–77 edition, published by the U.S. Department of Labor. In its projections into the year 1985, it states that persons with vocational training such as you are getting now will be in greater demand than many other college graduates. As retailing sales volumes increase, there will be many good opportunities available to you.

1. Define or identify the following:
   a. Grand Bazaar
   b. Regional shopping centers

Review Questions

c. Revitalization of downtown areas
d. Phonovision
e. International metric language
f. International standards organization
g. Mass transit
h. Recreational retailing

2. Will the needs of customers in the future affect the way of doing business, just as it has in the past? How?

3. Do you feel that electronics will be used more or less in the fashion businesses of the future? Why?

4. How might phonovision affect fashion selling in the future? What about visual merchandising as we know it today through displays?

5. What benefits do you think the introduction of the metric system worldwide have on international fashion businesses? Is it possible that a customer in the U.S. might shop with a store in London or Paris by way of phonovision?

6. How will changes in transportation in the future affect where customers live and work? Does this have an implication for where fashion businesses should locate?

7. If you were a shopping-center investor, would you be more interested in those that are located near the central part of cities, or in the central business districts? Or would you prefer the suburban locations?

8. Do you agree with those who feel that recreational retailing is a trend for the future in shopping centers?

9. How will consumers of fashion garments change in the future? What trends in our lifestyles do you foresee?

10. Evaluate what is changing in our current fashion businesses by explaining why you do or do not agree with the directions they are taking.

Suggested Student Activities

1. Evaluate what is happening in your community in the following trend areas:
   a. Moonlight sales, where stores attract customers to shop until midnight, by offering special sales items
   b. Introduction of more recreational activities in shopping malls to attract customers
   c. Sunday openings; opposition to "blue laws" that prevent stores from opening on Sunday afternoons

2. Critically analyze the locations of any new shopping centers in your area. Do you think good locations have been chosen? Why or why not?

3. Arrange to talk with a local merchandiser. Ask the merchandiser or

store manager what he or she thinks the future holds for fashion merchandising and how he or she plans to meet the new developments.

Case 12-1. Jane is about to graduate from the program of fashion merchandising. For many years it has been her desire to open a fashion store of her very own. She has worked in a small fashion store for a year and a half—has experienced market trips, knows how a small fashion store operates. Her family believes that she will be a success in her own business; it will supply the necessary capital. Jane surveys her city for the locations available and finds openings in several suburban shopping centers and one downtown location. Her first decision about opening her own business concerns where to locate.

1. What would you advise Jane to seriously consider before she opens her first store?
2. Would you advise her to open her first store in a suburban shopping center or should she select the downtown location?
3. If you were Jane, how would you plan your future in fashion merchandising? What would you consider?

Other fashion books that will interest you

ADAMS, JAMES D., *Naked We Came*. New York: Holt, Rinehart and Winston, 1967.

BENNETT–ENGLAND, RODNEY, *Dress Optional: The Revolution in Menswear*. Chester Springs, Pa.: Dufour, 1968.

BIGELOW, MARYBELLE S., *Fashion in History*. St Paul, Minn.: Business Publishing, 1970.

The Buyer's Manual. New York: The Merchandising Division of the National Retail Merchants Association, 1965.

COBRIN, HARRY, *Men's Clothing Industry: Colonial Through Modern Times*. New York: Fairchild Publications, Inc., 1970.

CORINTH, KAY, *Fashion Showmanship*. New York: John Wiley & Sons, Inc., 1970.

ERWIN, MABEL D., and LILA A. KINCHEN, *Clothing for Moderns* (4th ed.). New York: The Macmillan Company, 1970.

Esquire, Esquire Fashions for Men. New York: Harper & Row, 1966.

FAIRCHILD, JOHN, *Fashionable Savages*. New York: Doubleday & Company, Inc., 1965.

THE FASHION GROUP. INC., *Your Future in the Fashion World*, ed. Olive P. Gately. New York: Richards Rosen Press, 1960.

FRIED, ELEANOR, *Is the Fashion Business Your Business?* New York: Fairchild Publications, Inc., 1958.

HAMBURGER, ESTELLE, *Fashion Business—It's All Yours*. San Francisco: Canfield Press, 1976.

HARRIMAN, MARGARET CASE, *And the Price is Right—The R. H. Macy Story.* New York: The World Publishing Company, 1958.

HILLHOUSE, MARION S., *Dress Selection and Design.* New York: The Macmillan Company, 1968.

HORN, MARILYN J., *The Second Skin—An Interdisciplinary Study of Clothing.* Boston: Houghton Mifflin Company, 1968.

JARNOW, JEANNETTE A., and BEATRICE JUDELLE, *Inside the Fashion Business.* New York: John Wiley and Sons, Inc., 1974.

JABENIS, ELAINE, *The Fashion Director—What She Does—How to Be One.* New York: John Wiley & Sons, Inc., 1972.

KEFGEN, MARY, and PHYLLIS TOUCHIE-SPECHT, *Individuality in Clothing Selection and Personal Appearance.* New York: The Macmillan Company, 1971.

KYBALOVÁ, LUDMILA, OLGA HERBENOVÁ and MILENA LAMAROVÁ, *The Pictorial Encyclopedia of Fashion,* trans. Claudia Rosoux. New York: Crown Publishers, Inc., 1968.

LARSON, CARL M., ROBERT E. WEIGAND, and JOHN S. WRIGHT, *Basic Retailing.* Englewood Cliffs, N.J.: Prentice-Hall, Inc., 1976.

LAVER, JAMES, *The Concise History of Costume and Fashion.* New York: Harry Abrams, 1969.

LAVER, JAMES, *Costume Through the Ages.* New York: Simon and Schuster, 1968.

LEVIN, PHYLLIS L., *Wheels of Fashion.* New York: Doubleday & Company, Inc., 1965.

LYMAN, RUTH, *Couture: An Illustrated History of the Great Paris Designers and Their Creations.* New York: Doubleday & Company, Inc., 1972.

MARCUS, STANLEY, *Minding the Store.* Boston: Little, Brown and Company, 1974.

PACKARD, SIDNEY, ARTHUR A. WINTERS, and NATHAN AXELROD, *Fashion Buying and Merchandising.* New York: Fairchild Publications, Inc., 1976.

PICKEN, MARY BROOKS, *The Fashion Dictionary.* New York: Funk & Wagnalls, 1973.

PINTEL, GERALD, and JAY DIAMOND, *Retailing.* Englewood Cliffs, N.J.: Prentice-Hall, Inc., 1971.

ROACH, MARY ELLEN, and JOANNE B. EICHER, *The Visible Self: Perspectives on Dress.* Englewood Cliffs, N.J.: Prentice-Hall, Inc., 1976.

RUBIN, LEONARD G., *The World of Fashion—An Introduction.* San Francisco: Canfield Press, 1976.

SHIPP, RALPH D., JR., *Retail Merchandising—Principles and Applications.* Boston: Houghton Mifflin Company, 1976.

TATE, SHARON LEE, *Inside Fashion Design.* San Francisco: Canfield Press, 1977.

TOLMAN, RUTH, *Fashion Marketing and Merchandising,* Vol. 2. Bronx, N.Y.: Milady Publishing Corporation, 1974.

TOLMAN, RUTH, *Guide to Fashion Merchandise Knowledge,* Vol. 1. Bronx, N.Y.: Milady Publishing Corporation, 1973.

TROXELL, MARY D., *Fashion Merchandising* (2nd ed.). New York: Gregg Division McGraw-Hill Book Company, 1971.

WOLFF, JANET, *What Makes Women Buy.* New York: McGraw-Hill Book Company, Inc., 1958.

Women's Wear Daily, *Seventy-Five Years of Fashion.* New York: Textile Book Service, 1975.

Glossary

ACCOMMODATION SERVICES—Offered in a store for customer's convenience and comfort while shopping. (Rest rooms, children's strollers, mailing and wrapping services, etc.)

ACCOUNTABILITY—Taking full responsibility for the accomplishment of a task that has been assigned.

ACETATE—Man-made fiber that has high luster, softness, and drapability.

APPLICATION BLANK—Form filled by an applicant for a job that asks for specific information.

ASSISTANT BUYER—Makes sure merchandise purchased in market or on reorder is in the store, in place, and on time. Assists the buyer in all responsibilities. May place orders for assigned lines or reorders.

AUTOCRATIC FASHION MANAGEMENT—Leadership with a dictatorial, authoritarian style. So directive that it allows little or no participation by those affected by the decisions.

BASIC HUMAN NEEDS—Psychological needs often referred to as survival needs. Must be satisfied before any other need becomes important. (Needs for food, water, sleep, breathing air, and bodily comfort.)

BLENDS—When two or more different fibers are mixed together before yarn is spun. Purpose is to make the fabric better suited for a particular use.

BOUTIQUE—Small retail shop specializing in unusual apparel or gifts.

CAVEAT EMPTOR—Latin, meaning "let the customer beware." Implies that a purchase is made at the customer's risk with no guarantee.

CELLULOSIC FIBERS—Made from cellulose, a fibrous substance found in all plants. (Acetate, triacetate, and rayon are termed cellulosic.)

CHAIN STORE—Store belonging to a large group organization—usually managed by central headquarters where all buying activities are concentrated.

CLOTHING ALTERATIONS—In order to make standardized garment sizes fit the figure more precisely, changes are sometimes needed.

COLD CANVAS—Process of going from one firm to another without appointment. May be required in job applications or in a selling activity.

COLLEGE PLACEMENT SERVICES—Employment offices located on college campuses for purpose of assisting students in locating jobs.

CONSTRUCTIVE PLANNING—Setting appropriate objectives on the job and deciding how they are to be accomplished.

CONVENIENCE SERVICES—Similar to accommodation services, these services are offered in stores to make customer's shopping easier and more pleasant.

COORDINATES—Apparel separates that are manufactured to mix and match in color harmony and fabric content.

COST CODES—Word or phrase composed of ten different letters used as a code to write cost of a garment on its hangtag.

COST OF GOODS SOLD—To determine what the cost of goods sold for a period is: add opening inventory at beginning of the period plus net purchases at cost and transportation costs, and subtract inventory on hand at close of the period.

CREDIT—Means by which a customer may purchase merchandise in the present and pay for it in the future. Interest is usually charged if credit is extended beyond 30 days.

CUSTOMER APPROACH—First contact with a customer that a salesperson makes after customer enters store. Approach should be friendly and indicate a desire to help customer.

CUSTOMER SELLING BENEFITS—What the garment will do for the customer in terms of durability, becomingness, and suitability.

DAILY BEST SELLER REPORT—Contains items that sell in largest quantity each day.

"DEAD END" JOB—Seemingly offers little or no advancement potential.

DECIDED CUSTOMER—Knows exactly what he/she wants. If item is not available, salesperson should present a substitute item.

DEMOCRATIC FASHION MANAGE-MENT—Style of leadership where manager often seeks participation from employees and acts on their suggestions.

DEPARTMENT STORE BUYER—Manages one or more departments in a store—buys all merchandise at market to stock the departments.

DEPARTMENTALIZED STORES—Larger stores separate merchandise lines into individual departments—shoes, children's and infants' wear, menswear, accessories, sportswear, juniors, etc.

DESIGNER—Creates new apparel styles for each market season. Usually works at the manufacturing plants.

DIRECT MAIL ADVERTISING—Often the first form of advertising a smaller fashion store uses, because it is sent directly to a customer by mail. If the mailing list is up-to-date, this is an excellent way to reach target market.

EDP (ELECTRONIC DATA PROCESSING)—Electrical computer used to rapidly record, classify, sort, calculate, summarize, and report business information to management.

EMOTIONAL BUYING MOTIVES—Reasons for buying based on personal feeling—a desire for fashion leadership, for example. Have no rational basis for purchasing a garment.

EMPLOYMENT AGENCY—Business which specializes, for a fee, in helping people to find jobs.

EVALUATION RATING SYSTEM—Method used by modern executives to appraise their employees periodically.

FASHION—Currently accepted style adopted by a majority at any given time.

FASHION CYCLES—Recurring styles in fashions that seem to be repeating themselves through the centuries. Never *exact* repetition of a former garment, however.

FASHION MANAGEMENT—Getting things done through others, quickly and efficiently.

FASHION MANAGEMENT CONTROLLING—Measuring progress and accomplishment of employees. If deviations from standards occur, corrective action must be taken.

FASHION MANAGEMENT DIRECTION—Motivating your fashion sales people to be the best sales people they can be.

FASHION MANAGEMENT ORGANIZING—Grouping planned activities together so that the plans will materialize in an orderly manner.

FASHION MANAGEMENT PLANNING—Deciding in advance what will need to be done, how to do it, when to do it, and who will do it.

FASHION MANAGEMENT STAFFING—Hiring the most competent people to get the job done.

FASHION MANAGER—Individual who plans, organizes, staffs,

directs, and controls the business operations to achieve objectives.

FASHION MARKETS—Location where manufacturers present their new seasonal offerings to buyers four or five times a year.

FASHION MARKUP—Difference between cost price of merchandise and selling price.

FASHION MERCHANDISING—Performance of all activities to supply the apparel needs and wants of potential customers at time and place needed, in right qualities and quantities, and at prices that are satisfactory to them.

FASHION TREND—Direction in which styles seem to be moving.

FAYOL, HENRI—French management theorist who showed a clear understanding of the basic problems of business management.

FEDERATED DEPARTMENT STORES—One of the country's most profitable and largest department store operations, started in 1929 by Filene's, Abraham & Straus, and Bloomingdale's. The merger helped these companies to strengthen their buying position.

FIFTH SEASON APPAREL—Formerly known as the cruise market, this midsummer market features apparel for warmer climates. It is an added market to the usual four—spring, summer, fall, and winter.

FITTING EXPERTISE—Ability of a salesperson to recognize when a garment fits correctly or when alterations should be made.

FLAME RESISTANT—Chemical finish applied during final steps of processing that helps *slow* the rate at which a garment will catch on fire and burn. Does not make a fabric fireproof.

FRENCH CHAMBRE SYNDICALE DE LA HAUTE COUTURE—An exclusive couture trade association, formed in Paris in the late 1800s, that was restricted to fashion houses adhering to strict rules of operating their businesses. Name and activities changed in 1973—it is now Federation Française de la Couture.

G.N.P. GROSS NATIONAL PRODUCT—Total dollar value of the goods and services produced in our country.

GOLDEN RULE STORE—The first J. C. Penny store, which stood for fair treatment and honest values in merchandise.

GOAL-ORIENTED—Setting realistic, purposeful goals and working consistently toward their achievement.

GOAL SETTING—Looking into the future and determining an achievement level or an objective that you would like to reach by a certain time.

GOODS RETURNED AND MONEY REFUNDED POLICY—If customer is not completely satisfied with a purchase, it may be returned for a full refund.

GRAND BAZAAR—Large covered shopping area, thought to be over 500 years old, located in Istanbul, Turkey. Has 4,000 shops.

GRAY GOODS—Sometimes referred to as greige goods. Fabrics that are unfinished and ready to have color, design, or special finishes applied.

HARD LINES—Merchandise comprising major and minor appliances, hardware and paint.

ILLUSIONS TO DISTINGUISH FIGURE FAULTS—Wearing apparel that will disguise above or below average height and weight.

INDIVIDUALIZED SMALLER STORES —One of the most popular types of store ownership— sole proprietorship. Owners manage and operate store as a small operation. Sometimes called "mom and pop" stores.

INITIATIVE—Beginning, or originating an activity that you have the right to do without instruction or advice.

INTERNATIONAL METRIC LANGUAGE —System of measurement that will be universally used and understood.

INTERNATIONAL STANDARDS ORGANIZATION (ISO)—Organization that is working to reduce and resolve world differences through the application of the metric system.

INTERPERSONAL SKILLS—Concerns the human relations ability to perform while working with others. Requires cordiality and cooperation.

INVOICE ERRORS—Errors in billing caused by wrong counts of merchandise shipped or wrong extension calculations.

ITINERANT MERCHANTS—In the earlier days in our country, merchants went out into the lesser populated areas carrying assortments of goods that early settlers needed. These merchants stayed overnight in their customers' homes and received room and food in exchange for merchandise.

JOB INTERVIEW—Applicants talk to personnel directors about employment with a business.

JOB SECURITY—Feeling secure and safe in your job, knowing that you are doing well and that it will be yours for a long time.

JUST – ENOUGH – TO – GET – BY – Employees who are not motivated to do their very best at all times and therefore do only what has been assigned —trying to accomplish a job with the least possible effort.

"JUST LOOKING" CUSTOMERS—Customers who come into a store with no specific purchases in mind.

KNITS—Fabric produced when a loop of yarn is pulled through another loop.

LAISSEZ–FAIRE FASHION MANAGEMENT—Characterized by a management style that gives very little or no direction to employees.

"LAST–YEAR–ITIS"—The daily comparison made between last year's sales and the current year's.

LAYAWAYS—Service to customers allowing them to purchase a garment and leave it in the store until paid for. Allows customer to purchase garment early in season when selection is at its peak.

LONG–RANGE PLANS—Objectives that are to be accomplished in the future—usually planned in years. Should be as realistic and attainable as possible.

MAN–MADE FIBERS—Fibers made in a laboratory, containing no cellulose. (Nylon was the first true man–made fiber.) Rayon and acetate are synthetics, but they have forms of cellulose, and are therefore only partly man–made.

MANUFACTURER–OWNED STORES—Stores that belong to the manufacturer of a line of apparel. A store may carry only their own line exclusively or may have additional lines to assure more selection and assortments. Thom McAn Shoes is a manufacturer–owned store.

MANUFACTURER'S SALES REPRESENTATIVE—Salespersons who show and sell apparel manufacturer's lines at market or in the territory by calling on buyers in their stores.

MARKDOWNS—Reductions in retail price at end of selling seasons or for special sales promotion events.

MASLOW, DR. ABRAHAM—Noted for establishing a basic theoretical study of man's fundamental needs.

MASS PURCHASING—Stores that have access to mass purchasing have a price advantage because buying such large quantities of merchandise at one time lowers the price they can charge for individual items and still make a profit.

MASS TRANSIT—Transportation modes, such as buses, that can move large numbers of people to their destinations rapidly and economically.

MATURITY—Acting in an adult fashion. Shows an attitude of tolerance, patience, perseverance, unselfishness and dependability in everything you do.

"MEET ME AT THE EAGLE"—Famous meeting place in Philadelphia, near a large replica of an eagle, on the first floor of Wanamaker's downtown store.

MERCHANDISE ADJUSTMENTS—For whatever reason merchandise is returned to a store (faulty, employee or service errors), the policy on return merchandise must be carefully followed in making an agreeable settlement or adjustment with customers.

MERCHANDISE RETURNS—Merchandise returned to the store

from which it was purchased for a refund or exchange.

MERCHANDISE SHORTAGES AND OVERAGES—Exist when a physical count of selling floor merchandise does not agree with amount of merchandise that the record books indicate should be on the selling floor. When the physical count is less than the book figure, there is a merchandise shortage; if the physical count is more than the book figure there is a merchandise overage.

MODACRYLIC—Man-made fiber that is bulky and crush resistant. Resembles fur in appearance and warmth and is therefore used in fake furs and pile lining for coats.

MULTIPLE–UNIT BUSINESS—Large organizations having many stores throughout the country. Merchandise is almost identical and store layouts and fronts are usually similar. Controlled at headquarters location.

NATURAL FIBERS—Fibers used in clothing taken from nature— animals or plants. Cotton, flax, wool, silk, mohair.

NEEDS—The condition of lacking something necessary or desirable. Basic needs are hunger, thirst and bodily comfort.

NEWSPAPER ADVERTISING—Prevalent, popular method of letting customers know what the store has for sale. Used extensively for fashion apparel.

NONCELLULOSIC FIBERS—Fibers made from petroleum and other products in laboratories. Contain no natural fibers. Nylon was the first noncellulosic fiber produced.

NONWOVEN CLOTH—Although the majority of fabrics are manufactured by weaving and knitting, there are more and more materials being manufactured using heat, pressure, and mechanical bonding. Felt is one of the oldest examples.

NYLON—First of the noncellulosic fibers, introduced in 1939 by Du Pont. Lightweight, excellent stretch and recovery capacities, dries quickly, and is easy to care for.

ONE–PRICE SYSTEM—Offering the same type of goods for sale at the same price to all customers. Formerly, a form of bargaining existed—prices varied among customers. One –price assures fairness to all and is the practice today.

OPEN TO BUY (OTB)—The amount of money that a buyer has available to spend for new stock during any given period of time.

OPERATING EXPENSES—All expenses necessary to run a business—utilities, wages, advertising, delivery expenses, rent. Usually classified as selling expenses. Does not include cost of merchandise sold.

OUT-OF-STOCK SITUATION—Usually refers to staple stocks kept on hand at all times because of year-round customer demand. Being out of staple stock should never occur.

PATRONAGE BUYING MOTIVES—Reasons customers select one store for the major part of their purchases.

PATTERN GRADING—After a designer's new style has been put into the line, then a pattern for the garment is prepared in larger or smaller sizes than the sample garment. Standardized sizes are used.

"PENCIL SHARPENER"—Person who spends time getting ready to work but never seems to get on to the actual work. A form of procrastination.

PERCENTAGE INCREASES—Increases (or decreases) are usually expressed in percentages rather than in dollars, because percentages are a more constant basis for comparison purposes.

PERMANENT PRESS—A resin applied to polyester blends that is heat-set and improves garments' resistance to wrinkling in wearing and laundering.

PHONOVISION—Currently being studied and tested, television hookups incorporating the telephone. Viewing the merchandise on the home screen will allow customers to shop for merchandise in the future without leaving their homes.

PHYSICAL INVENTORY—Taking an actual count of merchandise on the selling floor, including understock and reserve stock. Count is taken at least once a year for comparison with book figures.

PLAIN WEAVE—Fabric construction where the same number of fibers that go crosswise also go up and down.

PLANNING A STORE FROM THE INSIDE OUT—New concept in which interior of store is considered before exterior is built. All elements such as fixtures, spacing for departments, and flow of customers from one part of store to another are planned, and then the store shell is built around the selling floor plan. Sears stores today are planned from the inside out.

POINT-OF-PURCHASE DISPLAYS—Merchandise displayed in or near the department in which it may be purchased.

POINT-OF-SALE TERMINALS—Electronic computers used like cash registers. Terminals capture all detailed information about the goods sold for central record keeping and inventory control.

POLYESTER—A noncellulosic fiber that is strong and wrinkle resistant. Washes readily, is available in all weights of fabrics, and is used in apparel for men, women, and children.

PRICE LINES—Three or more price categories are selected by a retailer for the merchandise carried. No merchandise is sold at any other price in that department. Advantageous to the customer because it eliminates confusion of many price choices.

PRICE RANGE—Refers to upper and lower prices of merchandise category. For example, blouses could have a price range of $10 (lowest priced garment in department) to $30 (highest priced garment available.)

PRIMARY BUYING MOTIVES—Reasons of first consideration in the customer's decision to buy—price, fit, comfort, need.

PROFESSIONAL APPAREL SALES ABILITY—Salesperson who becomes so knowledgeable about apparel and fitting that being a fashion consultant to a customer comes easily and naturally.

PUBLICITY—News releases in newspapers, on television, or in magazines that are an important form of advertising. A store can neither pay for publicity nor control what is said.

RADIO ADVERTISING SPOTS—Ten-, 30-second, or one-minute announcements on radio to advertise apparel or other goods. Length of spot time determines cost.

RATIONAL BUYING MOTIVES—Careful, analytical reasoning a customer has for purchasing a particular item of merchandise. Such a customer will not buy on impulse.

RAYON—First (1911) commercially produced man-made cellulosic fiber in the United States.

READY-TO-WEAR (RTW)—Garments that are manufactured in large quantities in standardized sizes. Have little or no hand sewing.

RECREATIONAL RETAILING—Entertainment and recreation offered in shopping centers to attract customers. Future may have shopping centers where people live, work, shop, and play in a planned unit. Transportation would not be needed. Everything would be within easy walking distance.

REFERENCES—Names of people who know you well and who have agreed to allow you to use their names for application purposes.

REGIONAL SHOPPING CENTERS—Shopping centers located in the vicinity of several cities, but not in any one city.

RESUME—A statement of personal information, experience, education, and other factors which is prepared and used in addition to application blanks in securing employment.

RETAIL ASSEMBLY LINES—System used in mail order companies for assembling a customer's order to be shipped or delivered. Merchandise is pulled from stock, put on conveyor belts, and when the entire order is assembled, it is mailed from a central location.

REVITALIZATION OF DOWNTOWNS—Almost every large city is planning and executing some form of downtown updating to attract customers back to the central area to shop.

SALES FLOOR ERRORS—Errors that occur because sales people are careless or inaccurate in writing sales tickets. Have caused businesses to begin using electronic data processing to avoid stock shortages and losses.

SALES PROMOTION—All activities developed by a store to attract customers and influence sales of merchandise. Includes displays, advertising, fashion shows, and other special events.

SALES PROMOTION CALENDAR—A planning calendar to space sales promotion events evenly throughout a year.

SALES PROMOTION THEME—An attention-getting title for a sales promotion. All planning for the promotion centers on this theme.

SALES RESISTANCE—Reasons customers give for not wanting to purchase a garment—may be real or contrived. Salesperson must determine which they are.

SATIN WEAVE—Least common weave for a fabric. Not a strong weave but produces a fabric with a soft, smooth surface. Either the warp or filling yarns are allowed to dominate the face of the cloth by intermeshing fewer of the threads.

SELECTIVE BUYING MOTIVES—Usually secondary buying reasons following primary buying motives. Customer considers versatility of a garment, quality, durability, and dependability.

SELF-ESTEEM—Important personal belief in one's self and abilities.

SEVENTH AVENUE—Sometimes referred to as SA, this avenue is in the center of the market district in New York City. Around it are grouped many resource outlets of manufacturers. Buyers go to Seventh Avenue to make purchases for a new season.

SHOWROOM MODEL—Men or women who wear apparel at the resource showroom of market to model it.

SHORT-RANGE PLANS—Plans that will be realized in the near future. Should be in agreement with long-range plans.

SOFT LINES—Apparel for men, women, or children, piece goods and fabrics, and domestics in linen departments.

SPANDEX—Lightweight, elastic fabric. Used in foundation garments, support hose, swimwear, and ski pants.

SPECIAL EVENTS—Activities planned during sales promotions that will bring customers to the store—fashion shows, trunk showings, flower shows, and others.

STAIN RESISTANT—Special chemical finishes applied to fabrics to make it easier to sponge away spills of food, water, or other substances. Scotchgard is a trade name for such a stain resistant finish.

STOCK SHORTAGES—Caused by losses of floor merchandise through shoplifting or errors. Are revealed when physical inventory does not agree with the book figures.

STOCKTURN—Short for stock turnover. Stockturn refers to number of times that a stock of merchandise is sold in a given amount of time. Important because it measures selling efficiency. Turning stock rapidly uses capital investment more profitably.

STORE CREDIT—Increases sales. Permits shopper to buy now and pay later.

STORE CUSTOMER SERVICES—All the activities that customers may enjoy in a store and all conveniences supplied to them without charge.

STORE DISPLAYS—Includes window and interior displays of merchandise in stores for attention-getting purposes. Seeing the merchandise inside the store may influence purchase.

STORE IMAGE—Reputation that a store holds in a community. May be for fashion leadership, good prices, fair dealing with all customers, or good salespeople. Must be carefully planned and developed.

SUGGESTION SELLING—When a customer has purchased one garment, salesperson should suggest ways in which to accessorize it. By suggesting additional merchandise, the customer has the benefit of having a well coordinated costume and the store increases sales.

SURVIVAL OF THE FITTEST—In contemporary fashion merchandising, those who survive their competition are the merchandisers who are constantly striving to be better in all areas of store operation. To survive constant moving forward is necessary.

SYSTEMS TRAINING—Training given to new employees on the use of cash registers or terminals, store procedures, and all other systems used in the store.

TAG SWITCHERS—Customers who move tags from less expensive garments to more expensive apparel and try to purchase the garment at the lower price. Alert salespeople can spot tag switchers immediately.

TARGET MARKET—The groups of customers you wish to reach through your sales promotion activities. When you analyze these groups, you can more readily choose the way in which to best reach their attention.

TELEVISION ADVERTISING—Excellent way to attract customers

but quite expensive. Advantage for apparel is showing garments in action on models, and in color. May attract large numbers of potential customers.

TRADING UP—Encouraging a customer to buy the best quality merchandise they can afford. Salespeople should point out benefits of the better merchandise in terms of durability or fashion appropriateness.

TRANSFERS OF MERCHANDISE—When merchandise is moved from one store to another. Careful records must be kept of transfers to insure accurate inventory records. Errors in transfers often cause stock shortages.

TRIACETATE—Fabric that was developed from and is similar in appearance to acetate; popular for its ease–of–care quality. Resists wrinkling, shrinking and stretching, and holds pleats well. Fast drying after washing. Better colorfastness. Whites stay exceptionally white.

TWILL WEAVE—Filling and warp yarns are intermeshed in such a manner that a raised diagonal line is left on the cloth.

UNIT SALES INFORMATION—Number of items or units which have been sold in a given time. EDP can make this information available to buyers daily or even more often. Buyer can keep stock at correct level at all times.

VENDOR RETURNS—Merchandise returned to the manufacturer.

WANT ADS—Advertising placed in daily newspapers in a special section—job opportunities, sales items, etc.

WANTS—Conscious or felt needs. May be a feeling of wishing for something that may not really be needed.

WISH BOOK—Term applied to early mail–order catalogs. In rural communities in earlier times, people looked forward to receiving their mail–order catalogs, read them and wished for many of the items they advertised.

WORK ETHIC—Value that work holds for us in our daily lives. Although work has economic value, it has many other virtues. Meaningful, challenging work gives personal satisfaction of achievement and a purpose in life.

Index